New Lives, Old Souls

Jim Alexander

PLEASE READ THIS FIRST

To really provide you with a sense of the regression experience I have
made five of the original recordings (or part of them) available for you to
listen to while you read those sections of the book. These are marked
** on the contents page. You have already paid for these in the book
price.

Hearing how people spoke and replied to my questions will significantly
add to your experience and I strongly recommend it.

Simply e-mail jimalexander.books@gmail.com **and you will be sent the
links to listen.**

I am interested to know about experiences you may have had relating to
reincarnation so you can e-mail me at the same address if you wish.

1. About the author

I have always been interested in what may be termed the 'deeper' side of life. Interested not just in what happens but *why* it happens and never keen to behave in a certain way - just because an authority figure (teachers, religious figures, experts, even parents) said that was the way things are or because it said so in a book.

I wanted *evidence* before I could believe something.

This interest in evidence and having an open mind resulted in my involvement in past life regression research and in hypnotherapy in general.

For two years I had very close contact with Joe Keeton, a recognised expert in regression, and by the end of that time I was conducting research independently. I took qualifications in Hypnotherapy because people were asking for my help and I did not take this responsibility lightly. I was able to help people with phobias, anxiety issues, weight loss, pain control (for instance in childbirth), self-confidence etc. Sometimes this involved suggestion therapy and sometimes regression and I remain absolutely convinced that the best option (though it is not always immediately possible) is to understand where our problems first arose and why so that we can change the way they affect our futures.

This book mainly focuses on past life research but I also explain why regression into this life can quickly resolve issues that current medical and psychiatric practice take far longer to help with if they help at all.

Finally I want to express my heartfelt thanks to those who volunteered to experience regression to possible past lives. I know they were interested in knowing more themselves and I hope the experience changed their lives for the better. I hope it changes yours also.

2. About the book

In this book you will learn about hypnosis and I hope I will improve your understanding of it. You will learn about regression and gain a clearer understanding both in terms of research into reincarnation and in terms of how it can and should be used to provide very effective and efficient help for anyone suffering with anxiety related problems.

In Part One you will meet several amazing characters brought back from the past under hypnosis. They all make me wonder if we have lived before but make your own mind up as you relive the experiences and review the evidence, some of the strongest evidence ever seen.

In Part Two the focus is on mental processes and how your own mind has the ability to resolve issues of mental wellbeing more quickly and more simply than you currently imagine is possible. Your mind really wants you to be the best you can be but sometimes it is over protective. The medical profession are absolutely wonderful but somehow they have become accustomed to the idea that their fairly recently introduced treatments are better than some that have worked well for thousands of years.

I am not advocating any kind of mystical or magical solutions, just a common-sense approach that seems like magic because it works so well.

In Part Three you will meet three more amazing characters. Firstly an American based in the UK in the 2nd World War and the astounding information discovered. Secondly the most famous case in recent years as you follow the sessions I had with Jenny Cockell. My original analysis differed from hers but in this updated book my research has significantly expanded. Lastly, meet a lady with such intimate knowledge of a place she had never been that reincarnation seems the only explanation.

At the end of the book I share the thoughts and conclusions I have reached so far but the research is by no means finished.

Part One - Past Lives

3. Questions, questions, questions...

Why are we here? What is it all for? Is this physical existence all there is? What happens when we die?

These questions have been asked by humankind since the first moments of intelligent thought sprang into our developing minds. In fact, since man was first able to think, he has wondered why he should be able to.

Our most primal instincts are those of self-preservation and survival of the species - we want to live for as long as possible and do not wish to contemplate that our death will be the end, wasting the progress we have made and the wisdom we have accumulated.

Is there any purpose in being alive? In many countries people have trouble simply finding enough to eat whilst in other countries 'couch-potatoes' get fat and waste their days watching others achieve. Some religious fanatics spend their time being thankful that they are alive and looking forward to the day they can die, without fully taking part in life.

Those who believe in nothing have no respect for life, neither their own nor anyone else's or the other life forms with which they share their existence.

Your particular brand of logic may lead you to conclude that we are only here once; that all living things and the nature that supports and surrounds them are the result of a series of random accidents that have occurred over enormous spans of time, beginning when a simple single cell life-form appeared from nowhere and gradually evolved into the diversity of existence we observe today. At least that, which in our infinite wisdom, we have not yet destroyed.

If that is the case you must assume that when you die you will be consumed by worms and forgotten so it does not matter whether you learn anything or make the world a better place, or even leave it the same as when you entered it. Alternatively, you could take a more open-minded position and allow for the possibility that you could be wrong.

After all, haven't you gone through life so far realising you have been wrong about an awful lot of things you were convinced of once? To me this seems the better option because if there is some part of you that is longer lasting than the body then you should consider what it needs and why it exists.

When the time comes you will either be horrified to find out that there **is** life after death, or if there isn't you will not be there to worry about it.

We have an alternative - to consider life as an energy form, a kind of electro-magnetic energy, which is in fact what powers the brain, and like all other forms of energy cannot be destroyed. It changes form or moves from one receptacle to another.

A light bulb serves as a useful example; without energy it is simply a physical form, with all the necessary components it needs to function as intended, but until the energy is passed through it there is no light.

The physical form of humans and all other inhabitants of the universe are as dead as the unlit bulb without the force which gives them life.

Is that energy transferred to another vessel when the current one is burned out?

Most of us find it more comfortable to think that there is meaning in our existence, and that what we have achieved will not be lost when we die. We cannot take wealth or possessions beyond this life but perhaps we can take what we have learned. Most of what we achieve can only be measured in terms of wisdom in the end, and it may be that this is our purpose.

The Native American culture has a philosophy that encourages them to look after their resources in a way that will benefit their descendants. Jesus advised us to do as we would be done by and that the sins of the fathers shall be visited upon the sons, and that we will reap what we sow.

Do these messages translate to tell us that we cannot disregard the nature of the planet and the destruction of society if we are to find a decent way of life in future existences? Perhaps we should not just be trying to 'clean up our act' for the sake of our children but because we too are going to have to live in what we think we have left behind. Only a complete fool leaves the mess they created today in the house they are going to live in tomorrow.

Whether the force which makes us what we are is some sort of intelligent electro-magnetic force or what could be interpreted as a "soul" is a question which will doubtless be considered for some time yet.

The key question for researchers in the field of far memory surely surrounds the reality or otherwise of the experience and recall produced.

If what is revealed by those who have previous life experiences stored in their minds is real then we can begin to search for answers to the question why.

I think that "Why?" is the most important and interesting question, and perhaps the answer is the most elusive given that scientific study has been able to get gradually closer to answering the "What", "When" and "How" questions about the universe at a physical level. "Why" it happens cannot be explained by science and has become the province of religion and philosophy, in which a wide range of opinion still exists, with many steadfastly clinging to ancient concepts and rejecting any opportunity to consider alternatives.

The process of repetition or recycling is followed in every part of nature. It is more acceptable to believe, as billions do, that life is necessary for our spiritual development. Life is frail and can be ended in the blink of an eye, so we have developed basic instincts which help us to survive and instincts which encourage us to ensure that our species is continued.

We go through life learning from mistakes, pain, hunger, responsibility, and so on, which we would not be troubled by if we consisted of pure energy or a soul which required no food, sleep, shelter, work, etc. and which could not die.

By experiencing different lives we can learn from different experiences - sickness, hunger, pain, happiness, wealth, old age, prejudice, power, slavery, contempt, respect, disability, love, being male or female, being evil or good. The list of possible learning experiences is endless but the average lifetime of around eighty years and only in one form obviously offers limited potential.

If the purpose of the material world is to develop our understanding and perhaps our spirituality until we reach a state of perfection we would surely need to have more than one chance to qualify.

The idea that we are born, live one life, are judged on our performance in that one life and either allowed into heaven or doomed to eternal damnation seems harsh, and not the sort of treatment we have been led to think a benevolent God hands out.

I prefer the idea that life is not meaningless so if it does have meaning I conclude that the purpose is to learn something from the good, bad or indifferent experiences we go through. I don't believe that we can learn enough in one lifetime to enable us to move on to whatever the result of knowing and understanding enough will be.

Seeking the evidence to strengthen or to undermine this position is what I have sought to do. I have an open mind and I know that, just as has been the case in scientific, medical, and paranormal research, we should never believe that we have the final answer. Perhaps the plan is simply to make us think.

I have focused on past life regression accessed through hypnosis. I am aware that many other types of experience have been reported, including future lives and life between lives (in spirit), both of which I have seen at first hand with some of my volunteers, but the only one that can be checked against actuality is a past life in this dimension and if none of these are real we cannot have any confidence that the others are not simply created by the imagination.

There may be a few rare individuals capable of spontaneously creating and acting out several realistic 'lives' from all the history books they have read and the documentaries they have studied, whilst also managing to keep track of each life over several sessions of hypnosis in which they could be asked to go to any one at any point in time. There are very few great actors and even they need to study their parts in depth before creating a credible performance.

Great writers, musicians, artists and poets struggle for weeks, months or years to develop their works. The vast majority of people are not blessed with such creative capability. Perhaps the mind has extra-sensory perception and can reach out to history books in libraries or even access recordings of the past that some say are captured in the raw materials around us (the 'stone tape theory') or is hypnosis opening the mind up for 'channeling' of knowledge held in the spirit world?

I am open to examining any of these things but perhaps it is more sensible to start by seeing if reincarnation is a feasible explanation as opposed to the many other suggestions which would in fact be even more incredible.

It must be said that many cases of past life regression cannot be proven correct. Some are no doubt created by imagination, others are from so long ago that historical records do not exist, and only circumstantial evidence can be gathered, such as descriptions of lifestyle, diet, work activity, prices, politics, architecture, clothes, inventions, vocabulary, etc.

If in even one case it can be shown that information given during regression can only have been accessed from the mind of the person being regressed to – such as a secret that they took to the grave with them but which is discovered to be true after the regression – then we will know that information can be passed on from one life to another.

We can only theorise on how this may be possible, but the working assumption is that through an appropriate level of relaxation we can access a 'soul memory' rather than memory stored in the brain and limited to the current life experience. Given that it is not even clear where our current memories are held it may even be the case that all memory is 'soul memory' with the brain and current life being like the surface of the ocean with all other memories being somewhere beneath the surface.

Science is continually refining the theories but there are certain areas of the brain which store visual experiences, others for sounds, others for taste, touch, smells, emotions, and knowledge. If one part is damaged it is sometimes the case that the functionality can be taken over by another area so there is some flexibility. These areas have to act together to provide a full 'memory' or 'reconstruction' of a past event so that we can describe it or use it as a reference and guide on how to react should something similar happen again. There are different places for short term memory, long term memory, muscle memory and so on and it all comes together to make us who we are. We can poke the brain and predict what the result might be.

Scientific discovery is by its nature a product of limited thinking. It has to limit itself to physical events, actions and reactions, forces, energies, solids, liquids, gases, atomic structures, subatomic structures, and it is therefore natural that the explanations it provides are only in terms of the physical world. Just because all those aspects of the brain can be assessed it cannot be assumed that there is no connection to something else, something that is not physical, and something that science will never see.

Taking this concept just a little further we should not assume that the body and mind that we are aware of is all that we consist of. We may be linked to a much grander scheme which we can't see but which stretches out and through which we can join with others (explaining intuition, psychic ability, connections to loved ones, premonitions etc), in addition to being able to see or contact the spirits of others and move in time and space without physical limitations. This is actually quite close to what the Buddhist, Hindu, Aboriginal and many other teachings have set out for hundreds or even thousands of years but I have not studied these and I don't promote any particular faith. My thoughts are my own, or I think they are but it is hard to know what may have influenced me in this lifetime.

There are many things that we currently consider paranormal because we don't understand them but if we close our minds to them we will not make progress. For a very long time it was assumed that the Earth was at the centre of the Universe, and that it was flat, so let's be willing to think about what we still do not understand.

As I said earlier, it is evidence that should be sought first, and if we can prove that something is real then the search for explanations can follow.

4. The Search for Answers

I have been involved in this search for many years and you should not be surprised that I do not have all the answers. Nobody on this planet (or anywhere in the universe) can claim such a feat. It has been a journey and along the way I have certainly learned a lot. In sharing the journey with me you may learn something too.

The experiences that I have selected to share with you are essentially the ones which I feel are most interesting or intriguing, and which illustrate some of the practical challenges faced when studying past life regression.

From a small beginning with an article in the local paper, after which I was asked to make a two hour radio programme featuring live regressions, many hundreds of volunteers have been involved to differing degrees during decades of research.

As you might expect, some were unable to relax sufficiently to be able to access their subconscious well enough to make progress in the time we had available for the radio programme. Many may have succeeded given time and we will never know what significant information could have been discovered had they been able to persevere.

There have been others who could reach their subconscious and investigate their memory banks, but they discovered that difficulties in this life had created a mental 'block' through which they were not ready to go and in these cases the 'timeline' simply stopped. All these people were living with an anxiety disorder and in many cases were able to relieve it by discovering the experience (or trauma) that lay at the heart of that problem. We'll explore more about this powerful benefit that is only possible through hypnosis later.

Some of the people that overcame such mental blocks went on to regress further.

In a small number of cases it was very obvious that the past life experience was clearly imagination and would not stand up to the detailed questioning and frequent moving around in the timeline which tested the consistency of the story. It is important that researchers in this field do not 'push' too hard for 'memories' to surface as this can lead to the imagination conjuring something up to ease the stress. Such cases are actually very easy to identify. If I ask you to see yourself in Roman Britain and to tell me about your life (work, clothes, food, money, buildings, laws, schooling, family life, government and so on) you may know a few things, but you would soon tend to generalize in ways that someone who was actually there would not.

Finally, we are left with those that had truly regressed. Some of these had very clear 'memories' but the fact is that, like most people, they did not lead very memorable lives. When trying to verify the information brought forward, the process is similar to tracing your own ancestry; you would be lucky to be able to go back more than five generations (about 120 years) before finding that verifiable detail becomes difficult.

Those presented here are a selection of the talkative, interesting, perhaps historically easier to check cases and show you that what happens during a session is not magic or strange but is really quite normal except that we seem to be talking to dead people (which never worried me).

What you will be seeing is a transcription of the actual recording or recordings. Nothing has been changed. The text in italics is the questioner (mainly me) and the text in normal font is the person being regressed. At the end of each set of recordings I have summarised the information that emerged, shown the results of fact checking, and drawn a few conclusions.

5. World famous medium recalls life as a formidable Victorian Governess

Quite soon after I had commenced my research into this phenomenon I was approached by Glyn Edwards, who was also at an early point in what was to become a very successful life as a psychic medium. He went on to travel the world and work with some of the top people in this field.

He was very open-minded and interested in regression and hoped I would be able to help him learn more. He came to one of my group sessions and this was the first time Glyn had been under hypnosis.

As was always the case, the process started with induction into hypnosis (the basic principles for which you will find in section 2 but this is not an instruction book), establishing the use of the five senses and emotions, setting up some automatic responses that meant I could end the session safely should it become advisable, followed by the exploration of memory, starting in the current life to establish that it is memory being relived before travelling further back.

I strongly recommend that you play the recording as you read the following as it will greatly add to your appreciation of the event.

Where are you?
Aldershot.
And are you at school?
Yes.
What's the name of the school?
Army school
Who's with you?
Mum
Has she taken you to school?
Yes
Is anybody you know there?

No, no.. no

You've not met any people to be friendly with yet?

No

Do you like the look of them?

I don't know

Oh, do you think you'll like school?

Not very much

Oh, why not?

I don't know anybody

You'll soon meet some people and make friends and then you'll be alright.

I can draw. (Seems very self-satisfied at this)

Can you? Do you think you could draw me...... what do you like to draw? Tell me what you like to draw.

Anything, anything.

Anything? What's your favourite thing you like to draw? Have you got a favourite thing that you like to draw?

Squiggles

Squiggles? Can you draw houses or things?

I don't know

Who taught you to draw, or do you just get a pen and do what you want to do?

Mmm.

Tell you what, I've got a piece of paper here, and a pen, and if I put it in your lap, and you open your eyes and take the pen, now you just draw on the piece of paper whatever you want to draw.

(He begins to draw)

I expect they'll let you draw at school won't they?

Don't know

Oh, I think they will. Is that a man?

No, it's a woman (as he draws a skirt on a stick figure)

Ah, it's a woman, it's very good. How old are you?

Four and a half.

Well, it's a very good drawing. Is it finished now?

No

Oh, go on then, finish it off.

(Finishes woman and starts another drawing)
Is that a squiggle?
Don't know yet. I like shapes, funny shapes, doodling - I like doodling and then colouring in ink (colours in) - not very neat, I like drawing churches
Do you, just draw a church then.
(Draws a good block church with a steeple)
Can't do any better than that.
It's very good, just drift off, drift off, give me the pen and relax. Start coming back.

Returned to the present and out of hypnosis, Glyn was shown the drawings but did not remember them. He was then placed in hypnosis again and taken back to time before his birth, and almost immediately there were physical signs (eye movements etc) that he had entered a 'memory'.

Can you see where you are?
Yes
What is your name?
Harriet
Harriet, and how old are you?
I was 32 years of age
You "were" 32 years of age?
I was 32 years of age
(The accent is very precise, good English, somewhat severe)
When were you 32 years of age?
1862
And where did you live Harriet?
I lived, for a short time before my 32nd birthday, in Northumberland
And what was the name of the town, can you tell me?
(Thinking, but no answer comes, so not wishing to force one the subject is changed)
What is your second name?
My second name is Harriet...Spencer...Rice
What do you do?

I am a Governess

You're a Governess, are you with any particular house?

I am with the Manor House

Does that mean.... go on, were you going to say something?

I have charge of the Master and the Mistress's two children

What are their names?

Peter and Joanna

And how old are they?

Peter is 12 years of age, and Joanna is 8 and some months if I remember correctly

What is the Master's name?

The Master's name is Cavendish

Is he a high-ranking Gentleman?

The Master is looked upon by the peoples of the village as being the leader of their community

The people of the village, what is the village called?

Something like Marsden, or something like that I seem to remember, I'm sorry I can't quite - my mind was centred around the things of the home

What were your particular duties?

I taught music, and I taught the children how to use their diction in a manner that was befitting their station in life, that their manners would be impeccable with their approach to those who were not of such high station as they, so that no condemnation could be brought upon the name of the family and that they could conduct themselves throughout their life with that manner and that decorum that befitted their rank and station in life

Do you think you have done a good job?

My credentials are impeccable sir! and I have never yet found any of those whose employ I have been in contradictory to that which has been stated to those whom employed me prior to my employment

I see, could you tell me what sort of earnings you have?

My earnings sir? Surely that is a matter that is kept strictly to oneself and is not divulged amongst all and sundry

Very true, I was merely interested.

Shall I say that my requirements while I lived in the home of the Cavendish family were minimal. I was given clothes enough to wear, to meet and mix in company with, I was given good staple food with which to keep body and soul together, I was furnished with a comfortable room in which there was a small library for me to read and digest the knowledge that interested me. I was able to play the musical instruments within the home. In fact I was part of the family, and was in no way made to feel as though I was a servant.

They seem to have looked after you very well.

They were indeed sir, a good Christian family

How long have you been with them?

I have been with the family Cavendish for now nigh on six years

You seem very well educated, where did you get your education?

When I started on this course - to teach - I studied in London my friend, it is from London I come, it is there I was born and there my family reside

And you went to an excellent school there or were you yourself taught by a Governess?

I was a member of a family that were able to teach me privately at home. Sir, I was what one would call a gentlewoman

Were you born in London?

Yes

And before you joined the Cavendish family, where were you then?

For some little time I taught some children that were in an orphanage, which my father was attached to.

In what capacity was your father attached there?

My father was a Minister of God sir

And where was the Orphanage where you taught?

In Clapham

In Clapham, did it have a name?

I cannot recall

What was your address in London?

12...............Grove seems to come to my mind........Grove seems to come to my mind

Was it something Grove, 12 and then a name and then Grove?

Pine...Pinewood....Pinewood, Pinewood....Pinewood....Pinewood Grove....12 Pinewood Grove...12 Pinewood Grove, yes I can see it. It was not, while I was residing in that area, very pleasant, for it is there where we had the orphanage

And you found that unpleasant?

Yes, most unpleasant

Was that because of the children?

It was an area sir, that any person with hygienic standards, good common sense and a strong religious upbringing would not wish to frequent, but because I loved my father dearly and understood his charity towards his fellow man I condescended to go

Do you know the street well?

I can remember it well

I wonder if you would describe it for me?

There are tall columns at the entrance to the door and three to four steps to the door front. I do believe that there was such a time when this particular area was quite well 'up' in society, but because of certain conditions, for some reason unknown to myself it's standing within society has greatly deteriorated. There is a space of ground towards the end of the road where there is a wall that is broken down and this land is barren and arid to look at, it is full of bricks and rubble and rubbish, it is full of things that 'these poor children' as my father calls them, play in. Full of terrible smells of excretion, vermin, quite obnoxious, but as my father would say, 'the main thing my child, that you realise when you enter such areas as this, is that here temptation is rife and the Devil is after much that is young, so remember to keep your trust in God and you need never fear no Evil. Yes I remember it well but it is a memory I do not wish to keep recalling

Can you tell me what is happening now, where are you now?

I am here, with you

Would you describe to me your surroundings?

Lightness, light, comfort, peaceful. I have no recriminations of myself sir, I am aware of all that is community, life within a home. I am at peace with myself, I am fond of the children and the Master and the Mistress. Though I do not like Lucy very much, she is a loose girl and it seems to me, and my suspicions that she has got herself pregnant

Do you know who with?

No doubt one of those farmhands that the Master employs, young Roberts no doubt - always was a bit of a spiv and a ladies' man, even, even my friend had the affrontery to try his - Machiavellian ideas upon me, me of all people, a respectable young woman such as myself! Such insinuations are beneath my dignity and I do not wish to speak about them

You used a word just now that intrigues me, the word spiv, where did you learn that word?

My friend, when you mix with the lower classes, as I did in Pinewood Grove, you get to learn such an awful lot of their slang, their mis-pronunciation of the Queen's English

What year is it?

1860, 1862 I think, somewhere in that area

And you are 32 years old?

I am 32 sir

And do you enjoy life?

You ask so many questions young man

Does it perturb you, do you mind talking to me? I have some other people here that perhaps you'd like to talk to better.

I shall decide that for myself, if they wish to address their questions and I see or feel or deem it fitting to answer then to the best of my ability I shall

I'll ask them to introduce themselves before they ask you any questions.
Hello friend, I'm Sheila, can you hear me?

Yes I can hear you but it's a very strange name for a woman

Why is that?

It just is my friend, it doesn't sound, from what I can gather about the sound of your voice it does not seem to be what I would call a fitting name for you

Oh, well I want to ask you about another name, you mentioned Lucy, who was Lucy?

Lucy was the lower chambermaid

I'm sorry, what was your name Harriet, Harriet...?

Spencer-Rice

Where did the Spencer come from, why are you named Spencer?

It has existed within our family for generations on my father's side

Thank you, perhaps one of our other friends would like to speak to you?

My name's Brian, could you tell me what young men would do, round about their 30's, you know, their habits, places they would frequent?

My friend, I never mixed in such company with men of that age, therefore my knowledge is limited. It depends upon which class of male you speak about

I would say middle class

Those that we have that come to the house are personable young men, whose manners I can only say are impeccable, but then again those that are low born, whose manners do not come up to the standard would hardly be invited to the environment in which I live

Would they not have Balls?

There is much dancing and gaiety within the Master's home, much music, much laughter, much wenching.

What does he do for a living, what is the source of his income?

The Master?

Was he in Banking?

No, the Master was a country gentleman, of means that supported his family without him having to take upon himself the menialities of work

(Jim) Harriet, may I talk to you again?

Yes

I take it that you are not married?

No sir, I am not

Do you have any desire to be?

At the moment sir - no

And have you any men friends?

No sir, I have not

Have you had in the past?

Yes sir, one or two gentleman callers
Would you say you are attractive?
I am not considered unattractive
How do you dress, do you go to the dances and balls?
Yes my friend I do
What do you wear?
I am rather partial, my friend, to brighter colours, greens, lilacs, of the
most delicate shading but then again my mistress is extremely kind to me,
and more often than not does allow me the privilege of having her
dressmaker make up the clothes I wear. Plain, nothing over-fussy or over-
fancy, and I must admit that I do have some predilection to wearing the
Bodice low
To show off your figure better?
It is not unpleasing to look at.
Hello friend, I am Kit, may I ask, how tall are you?
I am 5 foot 8 and a half
What colour is your hair?
My hair is of a goldenish brown
And your eyes?
They are of a more almondy colour, if I can describe it to you, that
almondy brown, it's the only way I can describe them, lightish sort of
brown, rich warm brown
And you live in Northumberland?
At the moment I reside there, yes
Do you live near the sea?
No my friend, not near the sea
*Do you know which part of Northumberland you are in, where it is close
to?*
(thinking but no answer, so Jim returns)
Do you know who is on the throne?
Victoria
And is she married?
(no answer)
Do you not hear very much about the Queen?
No

I thought perhaps you would have to teach the children in your charge about the Royal family.
They have another tutor, I am only their Governess my friend and I teach them the rudiments of good manners, music, deportment etc. and I do instruct them in the Bible.
(Kit) What instruments do you play?
I play the pianola - the piano

(Glyn is asked to relax and come forward ten years at this point, and seems to go through some brief stress and then relax again)

Where are you Harriet, can you see where you are?
I am nowhere
Is everything black?
Grey
Is that all you can see around you, just grey?
Just grey
Drift back then, drift back to the last memories of Harriet, drift to the last things that Harriet can remember, can you see where you are?

She coughs several times and begins breathing in a distressed fashion, as though suffering a fever. Further questioning reveals that Harriet is ill with chest pains and is weak and hot, and a little delirious. On moving forward a little further she is gone and Glyn is then returned to the present and normal wakefulness.

Glyn enjoyed the relaxation and at first had little recollection of what had happened but as the group commented on events he began to remember and was quite surprised at what he had talked about. He could not see any links with his present life and agreed that it would be good to explore things further in future. I moved on to the next volunteer.

Sadly for me Glyn went to America soon after so those further visits never took place. It would have been wonderful to have gathered more information to check into.

It takes considerable time and effort to follow up and research what is said in regressions and the table that follows was actually created some years later.

Checking the story

Harriet said	Research found
Her name is Harriet Spencer-Rice She is 32 in 1862, so born in 1830 She dies between 1862 and 1872.	I was able to find the birth record of a Harriet Rice who was born in 1830 and a death record of a Harriet Rice who died in 1863 but whilst this would fit very well I believe them to be different people.
She is employed as a Governess by the high ranking Cavendish family and works at the Manor House, which is also a farm. This is near Marsden (or similar) in Northumberland, not near the sea.	I could find no Marsden or similar in Northumberland until I found that I was looking at today's Northumberland. In 1860 it actually came down as far as the Tyne (covering an area now in North Yorkshire) and there is a Marden in that area, though it is not very far from the sea but not by the sea so perhaps this is relative.
She has been there six years (since 1856) and cares for twelve year old Peter and eight year old Joanna. Their father is a country gentleman.	Peter was 12 and Joanna 8 so it would be normal for Peter to have gone to a prep school at 8 and for Joanna to work with the Governess (available in the latter part of the 19th century to wealthy families as opposed to only aristocracy) to become a well brought up, marriageable woman.
Her father was a Minister and ran an orphanage in Clapham, at 12 Pinewood Grove which was not a pleasant area, though it used to be better.	In 1827 the British Orphan Asylum was founded in Clapham Rise (this later moved to Slough) which was intended to care for destitute children descended from middle class families. There was a Carter Boys Home in High Street, Clapham in 1870 and Stockwell Orphanage, Clapham Road, Stockwell. There were also C.H. Spurgeon's Homes which started in 1866 after a clergyman's widow (Mrs Hillyard) gave Spurgeon £20,000 for the foundation of a home for fatherless boys. Substantial building was done to house 500 six to ten year olds.\n\nFrom the 1850's Orphanages begin to take children out of workhouses as they were no longer seen as

	suitable for them and there was a large and famous one built in Clapham in the 1870's but the names don't link. Clapham was upmarket in the late 1600's, Samuel Pepys moved there in 1700 (died in 1703). In the late 18th Century a number of mansions were built around the common and residents included a Henry Cavendish who was related to the Duke of Devonshire, and there is a Cavendish Road on an 1877 map of Clapham. In the 1850's more grand houses were built for top people but as transport became easier more affordable houses were built, including terraces and the area lost its prestige.
In the 1860's Harriett mentions wearing her bodice low.	The bodice was a garment that formed the upper part of a dress (waist up) and in the 1860s they would wear one that approached neck height for day wear and one that was lower cut for evening wear.
She knows that Victoria is on the throne but is reluctant to discuss her.	Victoria was the British Queen from 1837 to 1901 and married Albert in 1840. They had 9 children, 5 by 1845. Albert died in 1861. Perhaps Harriet thought it wrong to talk of it so soon?
Use of 'spiv'	'Spiv' apparently has been in use since around 1890 so 1862 is early but history is not always right.
The phrase "The Queen's (or King's) English"	This has been in use since before Shakespeare so is valid.

Thoughts and conclusions:

As impressive as the dramatic and descriptive presentation of this 'life' is it may be merely the creative construction of a reasonably educated mind and I cannot count it as proof of reincarnation, especially after just one session. When the detail is checked there are a number of good contextual matches but also significant errors or omissions. Is it possible that the memories are real but the personal details have been changed, a possible motive for this being that if we were able to confirm the spiritual dimension there would be no need for the 'University of the Universe' to exist?

Some people suggest that the regression experience is one of mediumship or channeling and that a spirit can speak through the person in hypnosis whilst their mind is relaxed. This was naturally an interesting opportunity given that Glyn was a medium and since I too have an open mind it would be just as significant to prove this as to prove any other theory, but the starting point must be to verify the information that is produced. One argument (and there will be more later) against this is that there have been no cases where the 'spirit' has spoken through different people (as long as we are happy to accept that the claims to be Mary Queen of Scots or Cleopatra's handmaiden are the fruits of imagination).

It seems that the 'lives' are only accessible to one individual and that they do not overlap through time, so that looks like a continuity of experience – or reincarnation. Glyn's experience of hypnosis and regression was very similar to that of others and did not seem to be mediumship.

As part of the research basis I have always sought to gather information before carrying out any checking activity. To have a bank of reference books available to check information would be wrong as it involves the risk that this could inadvertently be used to 'lead' the regression and corrupt the research. If I had looked up the date of Prince Albert's death it may have led me to take 'Harriet' to 1861 and ask if anything significant had happened to the royal family, which in turn might have triggered the recall of such information from the subjects memory and we would not know the true source.

Sadly, as I mentioned earlier, I only saw Glyn once and whilst preparing this book I discovered that he had passed over in 2015 so there was no chance of finding additional information or checking for other 'lives'

The next story (actually several years earlier than Harriet) provides more explanation about the research process.

6. The regression process and Margaret Jones - housemaid

I became involved in this research in 1976 when my wife spotted a small item in the local paper and contacted Joe Keeton to ask if we could attend one of his meetings. Joe had been researching hypnotic regressions for over thirty years and was very well known in Liverpool. We informed my parents and sister about it and went as a family with open minds but keen to understand more about the nature of regression.

Several people volunteered as 'guinea pigs' to help Joe's research and it was a fascinating experience resulting in a range of responses to the hypnosis and the regression process.

At the end of the meeting we approached Joe to ask how we might be able to try again. He invited us to attend one of the sessions he held regularly at his home in Hoylake and we were delighted to accept. This was the beginning of a long and very interesting relationship where we became involved in his television appearances and research for his books.

At the next session my wife was hypnotised, and after some preliminary steps to show her that our experiences are stored in the mind using all the senses and that when recalling them in hypnosis we use the same senses so we can see clearly, hear what is going on, taste, smell and feel the whole experience. After also ensuring that she would respond well to instructions to leave a memory and return to the present Joe asked her to go back to the memories of her third birthday, where she saw a doll…..

(Joe) Is the doll dressed?
Yes
What kind of dress has it got on, what colour?
It's a velvet dress.
You can see it quite clearly?

Yes.
Is anyone in the room with you?
Yes
Who?
My Granddad
Can you see him quite clearly?
Yes.
Anyone else in the room with you?
No
No-one else at all, where's your Mummy?
Gone out
Where's she gone, do you know?
No
Are you having a party?
No

No party? Drift off to sleep, now go back one more year, you are now two years old, it is your second birthday, you have total recall, you know exactly where you are, you know exactly what you are doing. Where are you?

I'm at home
What are you doing?
I'm playing
What are you playing with?
I've got some bricks
Oh, what colour are they? Can you see all the colours?
Yes, they're yellow and they're blue
Yes, good. Anyone in the room with you?
My Granddad
Oh, your Granddad, you seem to spend a lot of time with your Granddad.

Drift off to sleep, drift off to sleep and go back in time, you're one year old, you're 6 months old, you're now in times before you were born, now keep going back through time and remember, it is your memories we want, it is your memories we want, we do not want you to use your imagination. Can you see anything at all?

A house

You can see a house? What's your name? My name is Joe, what's yours?

Pause, Um

Doesn't matter if you can't remember, it'll come. How old are you, do you know how old you are?

Twenty

You're twenty, are you married?

No

Where do you live?

(pause)

Never mind, how do you look, what colour hair have you got?

Dark

And your eyes?

Blue

Are you good looking?

No

Why not?

Plain

Plain? That's unusual. Are you tall?

No

Do you know your name?

Margaret

Margaret what? My name is Joe Keeton, I live in Hoylake. What's your name, Margaret...

Pause

Never mind, you'll remember later. Do you work Margaret?

Yes

What do you do?

I work in a house

Whose house, yours? Your parent's house?

No

Whose house?

Someone else's house

A big house is it?

Yes

Do you know their names, can you remember their names?

(Thinking)

What kind of work do you do?

I'm a maid

You're a maid are you? What, upstairs maid or downstairs?

Upstairs

Upstairs?

Yes

How many are in the family you work for?

Six

And are they important people?

Pause

What does the master do for a living, how does he make his money?

He's a Businessman

A businessman. In London, do you live in London?

Yes

Where, do you know the address?

No

Never mind, it will come to you. Do you wear a uniform Margaret?

Yes

What kind?

Black

Black. Do you know the date, do you know what year it is?

1922

1922 is it? Are you courting, have you got a boyfriend?

No

No, don't you see.. don't you get much time off?

No

How much do they pay you a year, or do they pay you weekly?

Week

Pay you a week, how much a week do they pay you?

Two shillings

Two shillings a week, and your keep?

Yes

Are your parents alive?

No

I've got a young man here, he'll introduce himself. You'll answer his questions won't you?

(Jim) Good afternoon, my name is Jim Alexander, can I see the master of the house?

No response

(Joe) Do you know that voice?

No

(Joe) You've never heard that voice before?

(Jim) I'd like to see the master of the house please

No response

(Joe) What is the master's name, so that we can introduce him to the gentleman?

Barrington

Barrington? And what's his first name?

Pause

Bring out all the memories of Margaret, bring out all the memories of Margaret, you have a full set of memories of the whole life of Margaret, now bring out all the memories of Margaret. What is your second name Margaret?

Jones

Margaret Jones, is your mother and father, are they still alive?

No

They're both dead are they?

Yes

What a pity, never mind. How long have you worked for Barrington's, a long time?

About six years

About six years, have you any ambition at all, is there anything you
particularly want to do?
I'd like to be a lady's maid
Is there any chance do you think?
No, not at the moment
How did your father die, do you remember him at all?
Yes
What happened to him?
In the war
Oh, he was in the army was he?
No
No, what was he in, the Navy?
No, he was at home
Yes, what happened?
A fire
Oh I see, a fire. And your mother, how did she die?
She died with him

Oh. Drift off to sleep Margaret, a deep sleep. Now come forward 12 years,
you have the full memories of Margaret but you are 12 years older, you
are now 32 years old. Where are you Margaret?

At the house
Your house?
No
Are you married yet?
No
Are you a ladies maid yet?
No
What are you then?
Upstairs maid
You're still with the same people are you?
Yes
But they pay you much better now though don't they?
Yes

What year is it Margaret?
30... 34
Can you tell me who is on the throne?
Mary
Mary, what Mary?
Queen Mary
Queen Mary, but who is the King?
Pause
Can you remember?
No
Doesn't matter if you can't. Who's the Prime Minister, you must know who the Prime Minister is?
(She can't remember)
Doesn't matter at all if you can't remember.

Drift off. Come forward. The year is now 1950, you still have all the memories of Margaret but the year is 1950, where are you Margaret, can you see anything?

(Blank)
Is everything black?
Go back to the last memories of Margaret, straight back to the last memories of Margaret. Where are you Margaret?
In the street
Where, in London?
Yes
And where are you going Margaret?
Across the road
What year is it Margaret?
1949
1949 and what is happening?
There's a lot of traffic
Yes, and what are you doing, crossing the road?
Yes

Alright, you'd better hurry up and cross the road. What's happening now, come forward a few minutes, to the last memories of Margaret, where are you, what is happening?

I'm lying on the road

Lying on the road, and what's happening

I don't know, there are people

And what are they doing?

Looking at me

What has happened?

I think a car hit me

You think, you should know, go back a few seconds to the time you were hit, I know you're afraid but go back and see exactly what has happened, what kind of a car is it?

Big, black.

How do you feel?

Pain in my side and my arm

Come forward a few moments, feel anything now?

No

Everything black?

Yes

That's it, drift off to sleep, drift off

She was then brought to the present day and out of the hypnotic state.

It is clear that this initial experience was hardly spectacular, and that there was a vagueness about the whole thing. This is not what would be expected if the subject simply used imagination to piece together a story. My wife said that she did see more than she described but was not very interested in answering the questions.

It is worth noting that Joe did not suggest any avenue of thought or try to weave a story, but simply asked what was happening. Many 'regressionists' do not follow this approach but actually tell people where or even who they are or follow a pattern that they believe to be meaningful. If anything is to be of value it must come from the person under hypnosis and not be led in any way. If there is nothing there then that is a finding, and if there is something there then it should be impartially investigated.

There was not enough information at this stage to make research worthwhile. Future sessions could have been used to gather more detail but there were much more interesting 'memories' to explore as it turned out.

7. Out on my own – and finding Katherine Stanley - who knew Sir Christopher Wren

During the time we had with Joe we took part in his sessions at least fortnightly and there were usually eight or so others there too. I did put myself forward to be regressed but I did not manage to relax enough on the first occasion and with so many others available the opportunity did not readily arise again. This meant that I became a keen observer and I learned a lot about the subject. I reached the point where I felt I could and should contribute in my own way and adopt the role of hypnotist.

I began carefully but the activity quickly grew and the local paper ran a two week spread about my work and then Manchester based Radio Piccadilly asked me to work with them on a programme, initially doing a phone-in about therapy and regression, in which a call for regression volunteers was put out so that three weeks later we would broadcast live regressions in a late night show. This led to me meeting about 1,500 volunteers and selecting four to be on the programme. The programme was well received and even more people offered to help so over the following years I was able to do a lot more research.

I have seen other practitioners simply ask groups of volunteers to relax and go back to a time earlier than their current life and either relate what happens or just experience it inwardly and report anything interesting when the experience is over.

This I believe to be irresponsible and potentially dangerous for the volunteers. It is estimated that around 1 in 5 people suffer from anxiety that is serious enough to result in phobias (fear of going out is frequent), obsessive compulsive behaviour (repeated hand washing, checking lights etc), eating disorders, self-harm, distorted views of one-self (fat, thin, ugly e.g.).

These can be related to recent traumatic events such as war or terrorism but are most likely to relate to events from childhood and these will be discussed further in part two. The point for now is that taking a subject on a random journey through memory without taking proper precautions runs the risk that they spontaneously revisit the traumatic event (which has probably been hidden from them since it happened) and suffer an 'abreaction' or severe emotional distress. This experience may worsen their condition unless they can be guided through the experience with the result that it is rationalised and the associated anxiety removed.

I believe that all regressions should be conducted in person, not in large groups or over the internet, or using recordings or self-instruction texts. It may be that most people are safe enough in such situations but if even 10% of volunteers are harmed because there is no-one present to safely end an undesirable situation then that is too many. This group or remote activity is only conducted for sensationalist motives and little, if any, checking of the information produced is done to see if more than imagination is used. It may be fun for some people but in my view there is serious risk of harm for others.

In my sessions every new volunteer will be taken to various times in their current life to establish that they are using memory and not imagination, to enhance their ability to access those memories and to check that there are no traumatic events that create 'mental blocks'. If such blocks are discovered then if it is appropriate they should be dealt with separately before considering further regression.

In this case Helen was initially taken back to her 12th birthday.

What can you see?
A room.
Which room is it?
Living room
Who's with you?
Mummy
Anybody else?
No, Daddy's coming home.
Where's he coming from?
From Camp, Little Rissington, in Gloucestershire
Have you had any presents today?
Not yet
Is it morning?
Yes
Are you having a party?
No, got a cake for tea
Is it a special cake?
Mmm, a round cake with icing on the top
Has it got any writing on it?
Mmm
What does it say?
Happy Birthday
Drift off to sleep and come forward one day. What can you see now?
The bedroom
You're not still in bed are you?
No
What are you doing?
Talking to my Dad
Oh, has he brought you a present from camp?
Yes
What did he bring you?
Chocolates
Have you eaten any?

No

What did Mummy give you?

Some money to buy something

Do you know what you're going to buy yet?

No

Did your Auntie give you anything?

It was meant to be a dolls pram but I was too old

What did she buy you instead?

Clothes

What is your Daddy talking about?

About school

Is he telling you to work harder?

No

Just asking you how you are doing?

Yes, he's talking about the new school

Are you going to go to a new school?

No, I go to a new School

Oh, have you been going there very long?

About a year

Have you got any friends?

Di, Susan, all sorts of friends, Barbara

Popular are you?

Well, sort of

Drift off to sleep, go deeper and drift backwards through time, 9 years old, 7 years old, 5 years old, 3 years old, you're now one year old, stop at your first birthday, what can you see?

(Unable to answer but looking at something)

Drift on backwards through time now, 6 months old, 3 months old and now into time before you were born and you have all the memories of times before you were born, drift back and keep going back until you reach the year 1600 and give us any memories of the year 1600, can you see where you are?

(Nothing)

Keep going back until you reach 1600, can you see anything?

Yes, light
Go towards it and see what is there, what can you see?
Fields
What is your name?
Katherine
Katherine what?
Stanley
How old are you Katherine?
14
Where are you?
Near the barn
Where are you living?
Petersham
Petersham?
I'm playing with Henry and Elizabeth, playing Kings and Queens
Playing Kings and Queens?
We're named after Kings and Queens
You're named after Kings and Queens as well. Do you remember talking to me before about this?
(Blank)
Are you playing at Kings and Queens?
Yes
Is it a good game?
I like it, it's my favourite game.
Would you like to tell me about where you live?
It's a farm, near the river
Which river?
The Thames, it's a very lovely place
You like it there?
Yes, it's lovely, lots of trees
Any animals?
There are cows, pigs, all sorts, chickens, ducks
Lots of things.

How old is Henry?

16

And Elizabeth?

About 11

What do you look like?

Dark hair

What colour are your eyes?

Blue

Are you pretty?

I don't know

Do people think you're pretty?

Oh, I think so

What sort of clothes are you wearing?

Frock, pinafore

What about your shoes?

Don't wear any shoes

You don't wear shoes?

I have boots

Boots, Sometimes?

Yes

You wear boots when you go out? Where do you go?

To market sometimes, to Ham and Richmond, to London

You go to London?

Been to London

How many times have you been to London?

Only once, when the war was on. They brought some ships up the Thames and the Queen was there.

They brought some ships up the Thames?

Captured some ships, brought them back

And you saw that?

Yes, the Queen was there

Which Queen was that?

Anne, big fat lady

Big fat lady. Whose ships were they?

French

Did they have funnels on?

No, funnels on??

Big chimneys with smoke coming out, no, what did they have?

Just normal ships

Can you describe a normal ship to me? I'm blind you see

Big wooden thing, lots of sails, lots of ropes

Did they have many people on; did they capture prisoners as well?

Mmm

How many ships were there?

Three ships I think

You don't know any of their names do you

No

Were you a long way off

Yes

And that's the only time you've been to London

Yes

What year was that, how old were you then?

As old as Elizabeth, three years ago

What year was that?

Oh I don't know, its 1715 so 1712 it must have been

Oh, so it's 1715 now?

Yes. Grandmother came from London

Does she live with you now?

Yes, she left when there was a big fire, a long time ago, people became very sick, she left

How old was she when she left London, do you know?

A child, she came to the farm, a lot of people died, the house was burnt in London

And people became sick as well, was that before the fire or after the fire?

Fire

The fire made people sick?

No, the fire got rid of the sickness. People died, a lot of people came out here

Did they? Did they work on the farm?

Yes, as labourers, there aren't many now

Why aren't there many now?

Well, Sir Christopher is going to build a new palace

Sir Christopher, is that Sir Christopher Wren?

Yes

He's going to build a new palace?

Yes, father knows Sir Christopher

Does he, your father must be quite an important man

I don't think so

But he knows Sir Christopher?

Yes, Sir Christopher has been building more onto Hampton Court

Oh I see

And he's finished now

So he built a wing onto Hampton Court or something, built an extra bit?

I haven't seen it but he built more onto Hampton Court and he might be building a new palace at Kew for the King

A palace at Kew, for which King

George, German George

Did you say Joe?

German George

Oh German George

He's a fool

Is he, how do you know? Who said he's a fool?

He can't speak a word of English

Oh, can you speak German?

I don't have to speak German

Well he's German and can't speak English, you're English and can't speak German

But he's our King!

You've got a point there. Are they going to teach him to speak English?

Who knows?

Is he married?

I don't know, I don't think so

And he's going to build a palace at Kew

Sir Christopher

Sir Christopher is, but he's building it for the King?

Oh he might, he's been building a lot of things in London
I see, do you know what else he built?
A church, a big church in London, it was burnt down
He built it again?
A big church, I don't know what it's called, Saint something, they're all called Saint something
So when you went to London you had a good look around did you?
No, mother doesn't like it, it's a horrible place, it smells, she took a pomander in the carriage
She took a pomander and yet she lives on a farm?
Old London!
Smells worse than a farm?
Yes it does, it smells horrible
How long did it take you to get to London?
Oh, half a day's ride
And how did you go, on bicycles?
By carriage, no other way, we could walk but it would take me a week
(Katherine has been coughing at intervals throughout so...)
You seem to be coughing a little bit, is there anything the matter?
A cough
You've just got a cough. Have you been doing that for a long time?
Mmm
Has a Doctor seen you?
Yes
Does he say anything?
No, not to me
Have you ever heard what he's said to your mother or father?
No
Never mind. What kind of food do you eat?
All sorts of things, meat and fish, vegetables.
Do you get fish from the Thames?
I don't know where they get it from
Have you ever eaten a curry?
No
What about a beefburger?

Beef

Not a beefburger? Chips?

Stones?

Stones no, what about hotdogs?

(Laughs) Dogs??)

It's not really a dog, it's a big sausage that you heat up and put it in a bread roll and eat it like that, with tomato ketchup on, do you think you'd like that? They call them hot dogs.

Mmm

Have you ever had any ice cream?

No

Do you drink, what do you drink at table when you have a meal?

Wine

Any ale?

No

Doesn't daddy drink ale?

No

Oh, father drinks wine

Men drink ale, workers.

Do you like music?

No

Do you like reading?

Mother plays music

Does she, what does she play?

Harpsichord

Do you like reading?

No

What do you like to do?

Play in the meadows, the barn

And you say the men have gone off to build things?

They might

And where were they before?

They've been in the war. A lot of them didn't come back

Which war was that?

I don't know what it's called

Where was it?
France
Who was the King of France at the time?
With the Spanish
With the Spanish you say?
We were fighting with the Spanish, against the French
And who was the King of France?
Oh, I don't know
Do you know who the King of Spain was?
No
Drift off and go deeper. (Session ends)

It is important to bear in mind that over the course of several months Helen managed to recall twelve individual 'lives' and in any particular session she never knew which one we would visit or to what point in that life we would go . It would also be a few weeks before we met Katherine again. The idea that she could have prepared or researched anything is just not realistic.

Katherine Stanley – Session 2

Can you see where you are?

Yes

Where are you?

I'm in the kitchen

In the kitchen, what are you doing?

Oh, I'm just watching

What are you watching?

Cook

Oh, what is Cook doing?

She's making a pudding

Are you going to help?

No, I just watch

How old are you?

I think I'm about 9

Oh, what is your name?

Katherine

And what is your second name Katherine?

Stanley

Katherine Stanley, that's a nice name, my name is Jim, is it just Cook in the Kitchen with you?

No

Who else is with you?

There's a maid

Tell me, what is Cook wearing?

Oh, Cook wears an apron, she's got a bonnet

She's got a bonnet has she, is she a nice lady?

Yes, she's a fat lady

Is she, most Cooks are I think, where do you live Katherine?

On the Farm

Where is the Farm?

It is on the meadows, Petersham

Do you know what County that is in?

No

Is it near any big cities or towns?

London is not far

Have you ever been to London?

Not as far as I know

Would you like to go to London?

No

Do you know who is on the throne?

I think it's a Lady

Is it, do you know what her name is?

I think its Anne

Oh, Queen Anne is it, what is she like, how long has she been Queen?

Quite a while

Have you got any brothers or sisters?

Yes

What are their names?

Henry and Elizabeth, Henry is six

Do you like it where you live?

Yes

What are you wearing Katherine?

A good frock

What colour is it?

It's blue

What else are you wearing?

A Bonnet

What is that like?

It's got a ribbon

Do you tie it under your chin?

Yes

What have you got on your feet?

Nothing

Nothing at all, don't you wear shoes?

I do sometimes, I don't like them, they pinch

You'll have to get bigger ones, what is the Kitchen like, can you describe it to me?

Yes, it's got a stone floor and a big table. The maid scrubs the top to keep it clean. It's got stone walls, beams.
What do they cook on?
She's got a fire.
What does she do with the fire?
She just keeps it going and puts pots on the fire
What sort of things do you like to eat best?
I like bread
You make your own bread do you?
Cook makes bread, it's nice
What colour is it, is it white?
It's brown
Does she make cakes?
Yes, puddings, she's going to make a pudding
What goes in it?
I don't know
What is usually in it when you eat it?
Plums, from the trees, from the orchard, and apples

Relax now, and come forward to the time you are in London and down at the docks, what can you see Katherine.

Can't see anything very much, there's a big crowd.
Lots of people are there?
Oh, Yes
What's going on?
They've got the ships, came to see the ships.
Did you?
But I can't see
What ships are these?
They're French ships
Are they, how did you hear about this?
Father brought me, and Henry and Elizabeth
Oh, Henry and Elizabeth are there as well, how old are you now?

I think I'm about eleven, quite big, and Henry's quite big. I'm going into the coach

Into the coach, where are you going to now then?

To see.

Going to see the ships?

I'm going to see better from there

Oh, I see, you're going to get up higher!

Mmm

Oh, that's good

Henry's there, he said to come up on the top of the coach

Oh yes, is it your coach?

Yes

So you're going up there with him now are you?

Yes, there's a big platform, and the Queen

The Queen? The Queen's there is she?

Yes (smiling)

Are you happy to see her?

Mmm, I waved

You waved, did she wave back?

No

What does she look like?

She's got a great big head

Has she (laughing)

She's got more hair on her head than I've ever seen before

Is she wearing a crown?

No but she's got beads and jewels

What colour dress has she got on?

Oh, it's all sorts of colours, all sorts of jewels

She must be a rich lady

Yes, she is (chuckles)

What's she doing?

She's very fat

Is she? And what is she doing, why is she there, do you know?

She's... I don't know, she's got a sword and some men are kneeling by her

Men are kneeling by her, what's she doing?

They're taking it in turns
What, to kneel down?
Mmm
And what's the Queen doing?
She touches them on the shoulder
Oh, do you know what she is doing?
No
Have you ever heard of the phrase "being knighted"?
No
You've heard the name Sir though haven't you?
Yes
In front of men's names
Yes
*That's what she's doing, she's making them so that they can be Sir
something*
There's a very grand man
Is there, what's he like
He's got a big beard
Has he, is he tall?
Yes, he's very big
Is he, what's he wearing?
He's got a dark blue jacket, and breeches, lots of buttons
Has anybody said his name?
He has a wig too
A wig?
They wear wigs here
Oh do they, why do they wear wigs?
I think they want to keep their heads warm. They carry canes, some of
them do, and they've got white faces, I think they put something on their
faces
Goodness me! The men?
Not the sailing men, some of the men watching. Father doesn't.
Has anybody said the name of that grand man that you saw?
No, I don't think so
Do you know any of the names of the people up there?

I don't know the names of the men, they've all been fighting
Have they, where have they been fighting?
They have been fighting out on the sea
Who have they been fighting?
The French
What for?
I don't know, it's something about Spain, I don't know what it is for
because the Spanish were helping us.
And what were we trying to do, do you know?
No, I don't know.
*And these men that are going to see the Queen, they've brought some
ships back have they?*
Mmm, three beautiful ships
What are the ships like, can you tell me about the ships?
High, very high, they're stood out by the quay
Which quay is it?
It's Southwark
Can you see the names of any of the ships?
They have names but I can't read. There is one, but I can't read
You can't read?
No, not very well yet, I'm trying
Do you go to school, do you have a teacher?
No
You don't, who's teaching you?
Mother's going to but she teaches Henry because it's more important
*I see. What can you see of the names on the ships? You can see one of the
names can you?*
Yes, I know letters
Oh, what are the letters?
There's an L and A
What comes next?
There's a B, I don't know if it's right
That's alright, just tell me what you can see, it's probably a long way away
No, it's quite near
Quite near is it, can you see the next letters?

It's B, E, L, and another one, and another E and
There's another word is there?
Yes
What's the last one?
D, A, M, E,
Is there any more?
No
That's it is it, oh very good, that's clever
The others are called... I can't see. The other one is an L and A, and then it's a long word
Is it, do you think you could go one letter at a time you could tell me?
I can't see it.. it begins with an F, an O, I can't read it, the ship..
Another ship in the way is there?
Mmm
Never mind, if you can't see it all it doesn't matter
The other ship is by the side of it
Well I think you are very clever to have read what you read
I don't read very well
You will, you'll learn. Now, where's your father?
He's here, outside the coach. Mother is still inside the coach, she doesn't like it.
Doesn't like it?
No, she says it smells
Oh, does it?
She has a pomander, on her wrist
I see
She doesn't like London
Doesn't she?
No, she says it's worse than the farm
Worse than the farm, doesn't she like the farm?
I don't know, she's a lady
Oh is she?
We haven't got so much money now
Oh, what happened?

Well the men went off to war, and there wasn't anybody left to look after the animals and the land, and father had to do a lot
He wasn't able to do very much I suppose really, not as much as he should have done?
I think he tries to do too much. And the men didn't come back
Didn't they, where did they go to?
They went to fight the French
And they haven't come back?
No, not many. They're the ones who were going to build
What are they going to build?
Well they were going to build a new palace, for the King
What were they going to call it?
I don't know
Do you know where it was going to be?
At Kew
They were going to build that were they?
Yes
Oh, have they not built it yet then?
No, I heard about it, I don't know
So they've put it off a bit, because of the war. For the King, which King?
I think it must be Anne
Oh, Anne's King
I think it must be
What's the name of Anne's King, do you know?
No
Who was going to build it?
I don't know, I don't think I know
Well you probably don't.

Relax and come forward two years, its two years later, where are you Katherine?

I'm out by the barn
Are you, what are you doing there?
Just playing

Playing

Mmm

On your own?

No, I'm with Elizabeth

What are you playing?

Just playing, we've got stones

You've got stones?

Mmm

What do you do with the stones?

Throw them

What, throw them at the barn?

Mmm

I see, what's the countryside like?

Oh it's very nice, its summer time

Any rivers nearby?

Yes, there's a river

Which river is that?

It's the Thames

*I heard somewhere there was an island in the river Thames, somewhere,
do you know of one?*

An island?

*Yes, a little island, a piece of land in the middle of the water, not sure how
big it is, do you know of it?*

I don't think it's here

It might be a bit down the river from London, from where you are

Is it at Richmond?

Might be

It isn't here

No? I just wondered if you knew what the name of it was

No

No, never mind, it was just a thought, How's the farm doing now?

It's a bit better now

Bit better is it, that's good, some of the men come back?

Some of them did

Did they build the Palace?

They're still going to build the Palace I think, for the new King
The new King?
There's a new King
What's his name?
I think its George
Which one?
I don't know, I think there's only been one
Where's he from?
Oh he's foreign
Foreign, what's he like?
He's German
Is he, what do they say about him?
I don't know anything about him
Don't you?
I think the Queen's just died
Oh ---- Session ended here.

I usually limited the time in regression to 45 minutes, even if the memories were very interesting. This gave other people attending that wanted to help with my research a chance to participate.

The principle was also adopted that none of the information recalled would be investigated until it had been decided not to go to the same life in future.

Katherine Stanley – Session 3

Can you see where you are?
Yes
Where are you?
I'm in the meadow
Where is the meadow?
Near my house
What is your name?
Katherine
Is anybody with you?
Yes, Henry and Elizabeth
Who are Henry and Elizabeth?
My brother and sister
And how old are you Katherine?
Oh, I don't know, I think I'm about nine. I'm playing, it's been snowing.
Oh, do you get much snow where you are?
I don't know
Was there much snow about lately?
Oh yes, there's been a lot of snow.
What do you do in the snow?
Stay by the fire, or play, I can go out to play
Can you? What sort of clothes do you wear when you play in the snow?
Oh, I have to wear warm ones. (She shivers)
Cold is it?
It's cold, my hands are cold, I made a man out of snow
Tell me what you did.
I collected it and put it in a heap and made it into a man
What do you wear on your feet when it's snowing?
They're like boots, they're quite warm
What are they made of?
I don't know, I think they must be made of cows
Not made of rubber?
I don't know, I think they're cows

Are you still outside?

Yes, cold. It's very deep

I was going to say, how deep is the snow?

It's very deep

Where does it come up to on your leg?

Well it's been cleared away a bit here but it would be up to my knees or more in the field

What do the animals do when it snows?

They've brought them in, the sheep are out, I don't think they're very warm. The cows are in, in the shed and all the other ones are in, goats

Goats?

There are goats, they're in the shed, the chickens are in, but the sheep are out

Where are your mother and father?

I think they must be inside, I know mother is inside

What does your father do for a living?

He farms, he owns land, he owns a lot of farms

A lot of farms?

There are little farms on the land, some poor people have got cottages on they live on his land. I think he's kind to them

He's kind to them?

I think so, he lets them stay there, that is kind

Does he pay them?

I don't know about that

Do they all work the same land or has he split the farm up into a lot of little farms

I don't know, I think they are little farms, they each have a little bit to work

And its winter now

Yes, I go in soon

You go in soon, all right, can you remember anybody talking about other winters

Oh yes

What have they said about other winters?

It's like this, it snows

You've been around for a lot of winters now haven't you?

Yes a few.

Have there ever been any really bad ones?

Oh this one is bad, they say this is bad because the animals are in, because the cows are in and it's hard to feed them, father says it is. Last year's wasn't as bad I don't think. We get a lot of snow in the winter.

Are all the men on the farm, I mean is the farm fully stocked with people to work it?

I think the men are on the farm, yes I think so.

What's going on in the world, do you know about anything going on in the world?

No, I don't really see anything here. Sir Christopher comes sometimes.

Sir Christopher?

He's an important man

Is he?

But I don't really see anyone else

You only see him?

Yes

Does he bring you presents?

No, but he has a kind word

Oh, what's his last name?

Wren

Sir Christopher Wren. What does he do?

Oh I think he builds things, builds big things

What does he look like?

Oh he's an old man, he's very wrinkled and he's very thin

Very thin. What sort of clothes does he wear?

I think they're very nice. He wears a fine jacket and silk stockings and a wig.

He wears a wig does he, do you like wigs?

I think they're funny.

What's funny about then?

We don't wear them in the country

But he wears one when he comes to visit does he?

Yes, you do see.. grand men wear them, I see them going by sometimes, in the coach

Where are they going to when they are going by, do you know?

I think they must be going to Ham or Richmond, one of the palaces probably

What do these wigs look like, do they just sit on top of their head?

They pull them down over their heads otherwise they'd fall off, they're different, they're not all the same

What does Sir Christopher's look like?

It's got curls at the side and it's tied at the back

Tied at the back?

Yes

And what colour is it?

I think its grey

Are they all grey?

Some of them are white

They don't have any black ones?

I've never seen a black one, grey, they like grey

Do you think they wear them because they haven't got any hair?

Yes I think so.

They don't wear them just because it's fashionable, like a hat?

I don't know, I think to keep their heads warm, ladies do as well

What kind of wigs do ladies wear?

Perhaps they haven't got any hair

Perhaps they haven't got any hair either. Have you seen any ladies with a wig on?

I've seen ladies in the coach.

What sort of wigs do they wear?

They're very high with lots of curls, they're white.

They're white as well, what sort of dresses do the ladies wear?

Oh beautiful dresses, silk dresses, lovely, and velvet dresses. I'd like one like that, they're very big and wide

Do you think you'll ever have a chance to wear one of those?

I will when I get bigger

Have you seen any in the market towns?

No, not grand

Where would you have to go to buy one of those?

London

Have you ever been to London?

Where the Queen gets her dresses from

Which Queen is that?

It's Queen Anne

Have you ever seen her?

No, she's never been here

Does she travel, does she go around the country?

I don't think so, I think she stays in her palace, but I don't know where it is, maybe it's at Richmond, they live there, some of them.

Some of who?

Some of the court

Do they, live at Richmond? Do you know which ones?

It's a very nice place.

Do you know any of the famous people of the court?

No

Don't you hear people talking about them?

No

Just Sir Christopher?

Sir Christopher talks about them but I can't remember their names – Lord Randall

Lord Randall?

Lord Randall is one of them, because he talked about him. I think he said he didn't pay him the money that he should

Oh Lord Randall didn't pay Sir Christopher?

No, Sir Christopher was annoyed

I expect he was if he didn't get his money

But I don't know any others

Drift off to sleep and come forward to the time when you are in London – where are you Katherine?

I'm on top of the coach (she seems excited)

On top of the coach? What are you doing there?

I'm watching the Queen

Are you? Can you tell me about what you can see, can you describe what you can see all around you?

Well, there are so many people but I can see the Queen, she's on a platform and there are men and she's got a sword and she's touching them on the shoulders, there's a big man, a big man with a beard, he's there now.

She's touching him on the shoulder is she? Do you know any of these people's names?

No, they come from the ships, they must be seamen

What ships are these?

Well they're the French ones they brought in

Where did they bring those from?

I don't think they're all Englishmen, I think they are Spanish as well

Spanish?

I think so

What makes you think they are Spanish?

Because they've got dark skin

Oh, and what are they doing, the Spanish ones?

They're stood there

What, on the platform with the Queen?

No, they're stood back from the Queen but I think they are part of it

Do you know why it's all going on?

I think they brought the ships back from the war, I think they're being rewarded

I see. What was this war all about?

Well they were fighting, they always seem to be fighting

Who was fighting who?

We were fighting with the Spanish

Fighting with the Spanish, why?

I don't know

How old are you Katherine?

Against the French

Against the French?

I think so. I'm eleven.

You're eleven? So this war, we were fighting with the Spanish against the French?

I think so. I've got to go down

You've got to go down have you?

Mother says to go down

Why? Does she think it's not very safe?

Yes

Oh. I expect you could see a lot from where you were?

It's very warm

Is it? Do you know what month it is?

August

You don't know what day of August do you?

Thirteenth I think…. I think

It's roundabout then. Have you been in London very long?

Oh no.

When did you arrive?

Today

And this is the first place you came is it?

Yes

And are you going back tonight?

No

What are you doing tonight?

We'll stay at the inn

Where is the inn?

Southwark

It is in Southwark is it, is that where you are now?

Yes

What's the name of the inn?

I think it's called the Griffin

Is that what your father told you?

Yes, it's very, very grand, it's lovely. It's only there.

It's close by is it?

Yes it's back there

Near the waterfront?

There's a lot of people. It's near the water

Can you see any buildings around that you can describe to me?

I can't see anything now, there are too many men in the way

Oh dear, you're down on the ground and now you can't see a thing

But there are buildings, all around

Are there any funny looking ones, or special ones, that they do special things in?

No, they look alright, it's a row of buildings there, the top parts come out.

What colour are they?

Well they're black with white on them

And have they got windows in?

Oh yes

What do they put in the windows, what are the windows like?

They've got glass in the windows

Big bits of glass or little bits?

Oh no, little bits.

How long has this war been going on for?

Oh I don't know I think its years, perhaps it isn't, I don't remember, I don't know, I think it's quite a while because the men went away.

Did they, the men went away?

The men, the farm men went away, and didn't come back

They didn't come back, what happened to them?

I think they must have got killed, or captured perhaps

Who's winning the war?

We are winning the war, we always win them

Oh I see.

England always wins

Have you heard any news of major events or political events going on in London? What's in the news at the moment?

I don't know

Can't you think of anything?

I don't really hear, because I'm only little, they don't tell me

I just wondered if you may have heard your father talking about anything?

Father talks, but I don't listen

Oh, because he's not talking to you?

No, he talks to mother. What sort of things? (She seems frustrated at not knowing anything)

Oh it doesn't matter, if you haven't heard anything it doesn't matter. It's just something...

I might have heard him say something about it. I think there's always a lot going on in London

Yes, I'm sure there is, it's probably a very busy place. What kind of people are there around? Are they all people with money or are they just..

Yes, I think there are ordinary people, and there are people with money, there are coaches, there's a row of coaches

Are there any grand ones there?

There are some that are better than ours, much better, there's a nice one there

What does is look like?

It's beautifully polished, its dark wood with flowers in it and it's beautifully polished and it's got beautiful horses

How many horses does it have?

That one has four, beautiful grey horses, and a very grand man sitting on the top

Sitting on the top, is he the driver?

I think so

He's not up there to get a better view?

No, he's the driver, there's no-one else on the top. It's not dignified to climb to the top

Perhaps that's why your mother didn't want you to go up there?

No, if you're a lady, you don't. That's what she said

And what is this grand man wearing, the one that's driving the coach?

He's got a wig

He's got a wig as well?

A silver wig, and he has a jacket with gold on it and (pointing) gold there, and there

What colour is his jacket apart from the gold?

It's red

And what else has he got on?

He has breeches and silk stockings and buckled shoes – shiny

Has he got a whip?

No, he might have one but he hasn't got it, he's just watching

Can you see who owns that coach?

No, they're inside. They might be from the court

They could be. Do you know where the Queen lives?

No. Perhaps she lives at Richmond, a lot of them do, I don't know

Don't you think she has a special place in London where she lives?

I don't know, she probably does, I haven't heard

Are you very rich Katherine?

No, not any more, because of the war when all the men went away and it's hard now but father has the land, that's all.

There must be poorer people than you around?

Oh yes, some very poor people

Do you think the Queen cares about them?

No, no I don't think so. They say she doesn't help anyone.

Why do they say that?

I think she's a proud Queen

Does anybody care about the poor people?

Not really no. Father does, he gave a beggar some money

What does father think is going to happen to the poor people … why are we poor if we're winning the war?

I don't know

Oh, bit difficult that question!

I suppose.. I think the men go and don't come back so there's nobody to farm the land

I suppose they bring treasure back do they? Or is it just a war where they fight people?

I don't think they bring anything back, only these ships

Relax, drift away. Come forward three years. Where are you Katherine?

I'm in the meadow

What are you doing there?

Just strolling, looking at the river

Is anybody with you?

Yes, Henry

How old is Henry now?

Oh I think he's perhaps sixteen, or more. He's quite big. It's a lovely day
Is it, how are things going with the war?
I don't know, I think it's almost over... I think it is over
It is over is it?
I think it was over...a month ago.
A month ago, oh, what month is it now?
I think it's about July, maybe August, it's warm.
And what year is it?
I think it's 1714
And it's August, I get a bit lost with dates as well
It is 1714
When is your birthday Katherine?
My birthday... I can't remember I think it's.. I can't remember, I can't
think. I think I'm about 13
When do you think you might be 14?
Next year I think
Do you celebrate birthdays?
No
Did you ever?
I think once we did but we don't now
Times are hard are they?
Might have a cake perhaps
When did you have your last birthday cake, do you remember that?
I think it might have been winter, I don't remember the month
Never mind, I suppose if they don't give you presents it ..
It doesn't really matter any more

Drift off to sleep and come forward one year, where are you?

I'm outside, I'm by the barn
What are you doing there?
Oh I'm just playing
What do you play?
Well we're playing a game called Kings and Queens
How do you play that?

Oh, it's silly

No, I expect it's a nice game

Well, it's because of what we're called, Henry and Elizabeth, and me, it's because we're named after them so we just play a game about them, we pretend that we're Kings and Queens

None of you are called Anne are you?

No

Anne is the Queen isn't she?

No, there's a new King

Is there, who's he?

It's George, German George

German George?

Mmmm, I'm not supposed to say that

Why, is that not very respectful?

Mother says it's not polite, but he is.

He is German is he?

Yes, he doesn't speak English

He doesn't speak English? Why did he come to take the throne of England?

I don't think there was anybody here to take it

Are the people happy about that?

I don't think Anne left anybody to take it

Didn't she have any children?

I don't know

Do you know if she was married, did she have a husband?

She had a King. They don't call them Kings though, when they're married to Queens do they?

No, otherwise he'd be in charge of the country wouldn't he?

Mmm

Do you know what they did call him?

No, I don't think we heard about him

How long has George been there?

I think he's only just come. I think he should try to learn to speak English, don't you?

I suppose he should but he's probably got people at court who can speak German and translate for him

That's silly

It is a bit I suppose

He comes from a different house, they call it something different

Can you remember what they call it?

They call it Hanover. Anne wasn't Hanover, she was ... she was Tudor

Have there been any other Hanovers?

No

He's the first one is he?

Yes, I think so, I can never remember another one, I think they've just come

Is there anything you can think of that's happened lately in the last few years in the world or in London or anywhere, any other wars going on?

No, well I hope not

Any major criminals around? Have you heard anything about a major criminal or trials or that sort of thing?

It's all quiet here, maybe in London

Don't they have newspapers?

We have news

How does news travel around the country?

People come and tell you

They don't have it on a piece of paper that comes around and you can buy or listen to people read it or anything like that?

I think in London they have a piece of paper and somebody goes round reading it – I've heard..I think, mmm, I think they send news out from London to different places, like a letter they send out, to York

A letter to York, is York quite a big centre then?

Yes I think so, it's a long way in the north. And Southampton.

And Southampton?

That's a big place, I've heard of that

Oh, do they send letters there as well?

I think so, a coach goes there but I've only heard, I've never been

Relax, relax, drift off to sleep, come forward one year, it's one year later, can you see where you are? Where are you Katherine?

(She is breathing heavily and seems distressed)
I'm sitting up.
Sitting up, where?
By my bed
By your bed, what are you doing?
I've been allowed out of bed
Why are you in bed?
I'm not very well
Not very well, what's wrong with you, do you know?
I can't breathe very well
Oh, anything else?
(She coughs)
You've got a cough have you?
Yes
Has anybody been to see you?
Doctor John came
And did he give you something?
No
No, he just came to see you?
I don't think there's anything they can give you
Oh, you just have to get better on your own do you?
My Aunt had the same
Did she, and what happened to her?
She didn't get better
Didn't she, never mind, I expect she was a lot older than you are?
Yes
What does Doctor John look like, can you tell me about Doctor John and what he wears and things like that?
He wears a dark jacket that goes up here and goes down there, and breeches and silk stockings.
What does he wear on his feet?
Oh buckled shoes I think, and a wig.

And a wig, does he wear anything else, does he have a hat as well?
Sometimes
And what does he bring with him when he comes, does he bring a bag?
He has a bag, a big bag
Did you see what he kept in there?
No, he wouldn't show me, he kept it out of the way
And what did he do?
He listened to my chest with his ear down there and then he said "Tut
tut"
Did he, and then did he go away?
He went to speak to mother
Do you know what he said to mother?
No
And has he been since?
No
And you're sitting up outside bed now are you?
I'm very tired
Very tired, are you looking out of the window?
No
What are you doing?
I'm just sitting
Just sitting?
I have some embroidery but I can't do it
How long have you been in bed for?
Oh weeks, some weeks
*Do they give you anything to make the pain a bit better, is there anything
you can take?*
No, mother makes some herbs into a drink, I don't think it does any good
What does she put in it?
Just some herbs she got from a woman
From a woman?
At the market I think
Oh I see
She said it would make me better
And what does she put the herbs into?

She either puts it into water or into milk
And that's supposed to make you better?
Yes
Come forward one week, it's one week later, can you see where you are?
No
What can you see?
It's all black
Relax, relax, start coming forward etc.

End of session.

Note:

You may have noted that sometimes the word 'sleep' is mentioned as part of the relaxation process. We should always try not to confuse hypnosis with sleep, which it is not, but it can help the subject to feel limp and heavy to 'think' of sleep.

Checking the story.

Katherine said	Research found
Christopher Wren was a "Wizened old man with stick legs"	Christopher Wren lived from 1632 to 1723 so in 1715 would have been 83 years old
He was going to build things in London	He was the chief architect involved in the design and rebuilding after the great fire of 1666, including 52 churches in the city, the greatest of which was St Paul's, which took 35 years to build and was finished in 1710.
He had built at Hampton Court and was going to do more	In 1689 he had been commissioned to design additions to Hampton Court for King William and Queen Mary. The very substantial South Front and Fountain Court are his designs. The Old Court House on the Hampton Court estate became one of Wren's homes in 1708 when Queen Anne granted him a 50-year-lease of the property to settle his salary arrears for building St Paul's Cathedral. I recently read that in 1706 he was significantly remodeling this house. In fact, Wren's position as Appointed Royal Surveyor meant he was entitled to a home in the grounds of each palace in Britain. Wren, having helped restore some of the capital's most famous landmarks to their former glory after the Great Fire of London, held on to his post for 49 years.
Queen Anne was on the throne in the 1700's	Queen Anne was on the throne from 1702 to early 1714
England was at war helping the Spanish against France	The war of the Spanish Succession was waged between 1701 and 1714 with England and other allies seeking to ensure that France would not rule Spain. After the battle of Malaga the French fleet had left a squadron of 13 ships of the line and two frigates near Gibraltar in order to assist in the siege. On 21 March 1705 this French squadron commanded by De Pointis was on a mission near Marbella when it met an English squadron commanded by Admiral Sir John Leake (knighted in February 1704). Near Cabrita point a battle was fought in which Leake captured 3 ships of the line and destroyed two others.
Queen Anne was by the Thames to see three captured ships brought	In July 1702 a big Anglo-Dutch fleet was sent south to capture Cadiz, and thus gain a naval base near the Mediterranean. It reached Cadiz on August the 23rd 1702

back to England in 1712	and besieged it for about a month before retreating. On the way home they heard that the Spanish treasure fleet from America was in the bay of Vigo escorted by a French fleet. The allies after landing a force to capture the fortifications sent in their small ships to take the fleet. The French admiral then ordered all ships to be sunk to avoid capture of the fleet and its treasure. 15 French and 3 Spanish ships of the line were lost by the two crowns, of which 6 would be carried home by the allies. Of the 13 treasure galleons 3-5 would be taken home and the rest destroyed. Sadly most of the treasure had already been unloaded, and a lot of it had sunk, but the allies were still able to lay their hands on treasure worth £1,000,000. This illustrates the type of activity that went on. By 1711 the fighting was virtually over but it took the next four years to settle the peace. Small battles did happen and victories were probably celebrated but I have not been able to find reference to the specific event in Queen Anne's reign where she may have been at the dockside to welcome the naval return from battle. I did approach the Naval History Museum but was informed that the archives relating to that particular period had been recently destroyed in a fire (if only they had been stored digitally).
Queen Anne was fat and wore large wigs. Men in the crowd in London wore wigs.	Queen Anne was painted several times and was definitely overweight. Louis XIV made the full bottomed wig fashionable in the late 17th and early 18th centuries. At the beginning of the 18th Century this was the most popular dress wig. It became less fashionable by the 1720's when it was only worn by professional men such as lawyers and doctors. Wigs were very expensive. A man could outfit himself with a hat, coat, breeches, shirt, hose, and shoes for about what a wig would cost. A wig also required constant care from a hairdresser for cleaning, curling, and powdering. How likely is it that the subject knew that this was the peak period for wigs and that in the early 1700's they were dwindling in popularity except among the professions such as Doctor John, and that they were often tied at the back, and that she deliberately made it part of her story?

They stayed at an inn called the Griffin and she mentions a Lord Randall	I have not been able find the Griffin and the only Lord Randall I can find is the subject of a folk song written in the 17th century (perhaps a reader knows more?)
She mentioned fashions and farming methods	The description of clothing was also good, mentioning jackets, breeches, stockings and shoes with buckles. This was typical fashion of the time. The enclosure style of farming in which plots of land were rented and farmed by tenants of the land owners was also usual.
News is spread through 'letters' read out by travelling people	The first 15 years of the 18th century saw the beginnings of journals and newspapers so they would have been known about but not yet readily available outside large centres.
Queen Anne might live at Richmond as some of the royal court do.	Richmond Palace was a favourite home of Queen Elizabeth, who died there in 1603. It remained a residence of the Kings and Queens of England until the death of Charles I in 1649. Within months of his execution, the Palace was surveyed by order of Parliament and was sold for £13,000. Over the following ten years it was largely demolished, the stones and timbers being re-used as building materials elsewhere. Ham is between Richmond and Hampton Court Palace (which was Henry VIII's residence. It is safe to assume that the area was home to much of the court. Queen Anne lived at Kensington Palace, a few miles closer to London along the Thames.
King George was on the throne in 1714, was German and didn't speak English He was from the House of Hanover, whilst Anne was Tudor.	Queen Anne's husband was Prince George of Denmark. Anne's seventeen pregnancies by George resulted in twelve miscarriages or stillbirths, four infant deaths, and a chronically sick son, William, who died at the age of eleven. Thus she left no heirs to the throne and on August 1st 1714 the house of Hanover took over in the form of the first of four Georges, who was ridiculed by his British subjects, due to his inability to speak English, though he corrected that later in his reign. She was right about Hanover but Anne was actually Stuart though Katherine enjoyed playing Tudors in her games.
General note	I have not been able to find a Stanley family living in the Petersham area but there was a famous Katherine born in 1701 – Katherine Hyde, who became the Duchess of Queensbury on marrying the 3rd Duke of Queensbury and they lived at Douglas House, Petersham from 1725 to 1778.

This portrait of Wren in 1711 shows his age as well as the fashion in wigs and clothes.

It should be understood that Helen knew very little about London and the south east, and had not studied this period of history to any extent.

Again, some remarkable evidence but not final proof.

What do we learn from living many lives?

In some of the published material about regression it is claimed that each life should result in some learning points for the individual or wider audience. These first three cases do not seem to offer any significant wisdom but seem to be lives without any great success or tragedy.

I did not ask what lessons may have been learned from these lives because this is a leading question. By asking the question the hypnotist is assuming that the subject has an answer and the subject will feel embarrassed if they cannot provide one. Usually a simple answer such as "I should be more understanding of other people" or "I should be more generous to others because wealth means nothing in the end" or "I need to live this life more fully because I missed opportunities in that life".

Such questions also encourage the subject to focus on this aspect of their memories and come up with something rather than simply relating what is happening or what they recall.

The first objective should be to see if the memories are real. Once this is established we can pursue many other thoughts. I tend to think we are unlikely to understand lessons for the soul through a mind suffering 'limited thinking' due to being largely concerned with our present existence.

By 'limited thinking' I mean that we generally base our beliefs on what is most obvious. In this view the body is seen as the top priority and everything else serves it. Raise your view to a higher level and consider that the body is just a tool. If it was a drill and could think it would conclude that its purpose was to make holes. If it could see the bigger picture it would realise that the hole was just a means of achieving a more useful objective.

8. Jane Moore – Plague victim?

The session starts in the usual way, traveling back in time with me asking 'Where are you, what can you see?'

I can't see anything, I can't see
You can't see, what can you... do you know where you are?
Yes
Where are you?
I am in London.
You're in London. Do you know what year it is?
I know not.
How long have you been blind?
I cannot remember.
What's your name?
My name?
My name is Jim.
Jane
Would you tell me your second name Jane, your last name?
I cannot remember
Where do you live, you live in London but whereabouts in London do you live Jane?
I cannot see.
No, but you must know your address, you must know which part of the town you live in?
Near the Smoothfield.
The Smoothfield, Smithfield, near the Smithfield!
Smoothfield
The Smoothfield, I thought you said Smoothfield.
Chancery Lane.
Chancery Lane, do you know what number, which number house?
I have no number.
Does the house have a name?

It has no name.
Do you live alone?
No
Who lives with you?
My father.
Just your father?
And my mother.
And your mother, are there any servants?
We keep servants.
So are you a wealthy family?
We prosper.
What does your father do to earn his money?
Wool
He's a wool merchant?
He sells the wool
Where does he sell the wool?
In the Smoothfield
Whereabouts is the Smoothfield, is it close by?
It is close
Who's on the throne?
Charles
Do you know which Charles, does he have a number?
The second
Charles the second. And do you know what year it is?
Sixteen hundred, sixteen hundred and sixty.
1660, how old are you?
My age, I'm not yet 20
Are you nearly 20?
I am nearly 20.
(She is quite breathless and seems nervous)
Are you happy?
I know not.
Why are you breathing so heavily, is there something wrong with your breathing?
I fear

What do you fear, do you fear me?

Yes

Well don't worry, I am a friend, I will not harm you. Why do you think you fear me?

I know not.

Don't worry about me, I mean you no harm, I mean you only good

Have you any memories of seeing?

I have seen

What did you see?

I have seen the street

You've seen the street that you live in?

I remember the street

How long ago was it when you saw?

Many years

Can you tell me why you don't see now, what happened to take your eyesight away?

I do not recall

You don't remember. Do you have any friends?

I have a friend

You have a friend, is it a lady friend?

Mary

Mary, your friend Mary, and does she help you to go out, do you go out?

I do

You do, you go for walks?

I do

With Mary?

Yes

(Still nervous)

Don't be frightened Jane.

I go to the Lincolns Inn.

The Lincolns Inn, and what do you do there?

I stroll

Do you meet any boys?

No

Have you brothers and sisters?

I have none

Is it a big house where you live?

It is

Are there many houses in the street, in the lane?

There are

Is there anything distinctive about yours that you can remember?

There is a balcony

Is there a park nearby?

There is the Lincolns Inn

Has anything happened in that part of the town, has there been any trouble there?

I know not

Do you know what happened to Charles the first?

I cannot remember, I do not know.

Is Charles the second old now or is he young?

He is not old

Is he married?

Yes

Do you know what his wife's name is, do you know who he is married to, who is the Queen?

No I cannot remember

Don't worry, do you know if he has any children?

I know not

Have you been to school Jane?

No, I can't go

Is that because you cannot see?

Yes

Have you ever been to school?

No

You must have been very young when you lost your sight then?

Yes

Does anybody teach you?

Yes

Who teaches you?

(Becoming quite laboured now)

Mistress Riley

Is she a nice woman?

She is kind

And what sort of things does she teach you, does she teach you about America?

I know not

Does she teach you geography, about other parts of the world?

She tells me tales

Nice tales?

Yes

Does she tell you Bible tales?

She does

Do you know if you are a particular faith?

I am of the one true faith

Are you a Catholic?

I am not

Which is the one true faith, Church of England, Judaism?

The faith of the King

What sort of food do you like to eat most?

Fowl

Do you get that very often?

I do

And does your father buy this from the market?

No

No, where do you get this meat?

The servant buys the meat

Oh I see, father doesn't buy the meat, how many servants are there?

We have many

Can you remember your last name, how is your father known?

I cannot remember

Is he a Lord, does he have a title?

He has no title, he is a merchant

Does he have premises in the town, does he have a place where he works from?

He stores the wool

You're getting cooler, are there any other signs of the death than the swelling under your arms and the feeling of heat, how else do you know you have the death?

They say I have the rings

The rings, where are these rings?

I know not

You know not, but they say you have the rings, do they mean on your face?

Yes

Drift off to sleep, come forward to the last memories of Jane...

Where are you Jane?

I'm running

You're running, where are you running, why are you running Jane? Where are you Jane?

I am in the street

Why are you running?

There's fire

There is fire, and what is happening?

I cannot...

You can't see?

I cannot see, I have fallen

You've fallen, and what is happening Jane, are you burning, are people walking over you

(Very breathless and panicky)

Just relax, relax and come forward.

Session ends

One session with this memory seemed to cover a lot of ground and provide as much information as we were likely to obtain, so the checking process began.

The map below shows how the fire progressed and the subsequent map shows modern London and the oval shows where Jane lived in 1666.

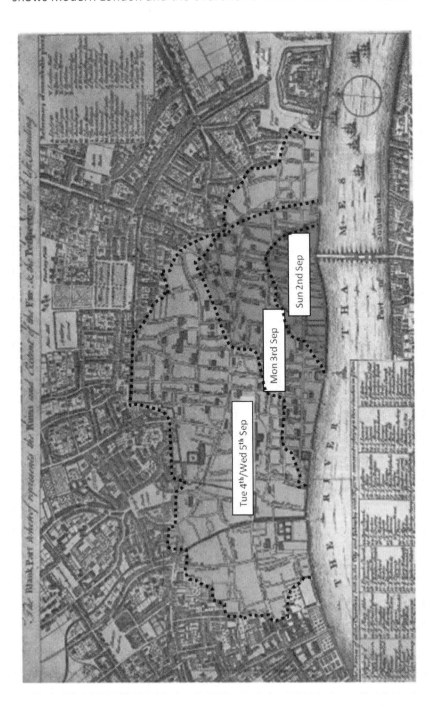

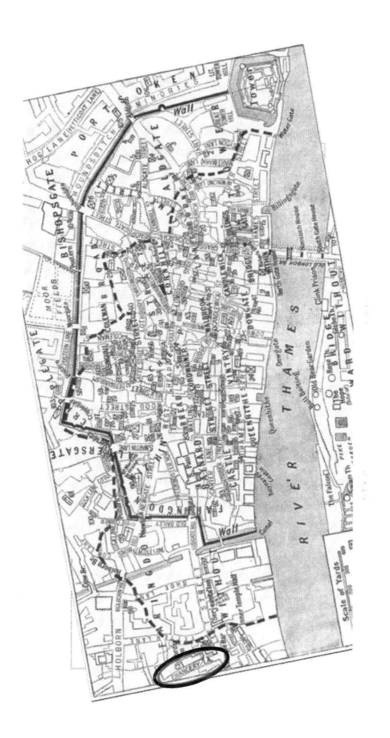

Checking the story.

Jane said	Research found
She lived in Chancery Lane, near the Smoothfield	From the 12th century Smoothfield was known as an area where markets or fairs were regularly held and it was near Chancery Lane, to the east. Maps from the late 16th century show it as Smythefelde and Smethfield (Smeth was Saxon for Smooth) so the name was changing. In 1660 it is feasible that people still called it Smoothfield.
Her house did not have a number or a name	The royal postal service was just about operational but only for the very top people so house numbers or names would not be needed for some time yet.
Her father sells wool at the Smoothfield	Smoothfield had been a market for various things for several hundred years (horse, cattle, sheep, and other items). Eventually it has become known for meat.
Charles 2nd is King in 1660	Charles 2nd was reinstated as King in 1660 and reigned until 1685
She walks in Lincolns Inn	Lincolns Inn Fields is next to Chancery Lane, to the west.
Charles 2nd is not old	He was 30.
Charles 2nd is married	He was not married until 1662.
In 1665 she is hiding from 'the Death' She has a fever and swellings	People were dying in an outbreak of Bubonic Plague (or Black Death). It was a ghastly disease. The victim's skin turned black in patches and inflamed glands or 'buboes' in the groin (Jane said she had swellings under her arms but might simply have not seen it proper to talk about more personal areas) combined with compulsive vomiting, swollen tongue and splitting headaches made it a horrible, agonizing killer. In London it started slowly at first but by May of 1665, 43 had died. In June 6,137 people were recorded as having died, in July 17,036 and at its peak in August, 31,159 people died. It is believed that at least the same number died but were not recorded and in all, 20% of the population perished during that summer.
Her servant has told her she has 'the rings'	A song about the plague is still sung by children today. 'Ring-a-ring of roses' describes the symptoms of the plague, one of the first signs being a ring of rose-coloured spots.
In 1666 she is killed whilst running from the Fire of London	Starting on September 2nd and lasting five days the fire destroyed most of the medieval City of London. Around 13,200 houses, 87 parish churches, St Paul's Cathedral burned. It is estimated to have destroyed the homes of 70,000 of the city's

80,000 inhabitants.

The famous diarist Samuel Pepys witnessed the fire and wrote of people running about in panic and carrying belongings and sick people from their homes by hand and in carts to escape the approaching fire.

Chancery Lane was not quite reached by the fire but the occupants would certainly have fled as it approached. Only 6 deaths were officially recorded but many more were probably cremated in the intense heat.

It seems that Jane may have survived the Plague and the Fire but been trampled in the panic because she could not see.

Possibly of even more interest than these references in my view is the way that Jane behaved. Given that she was blind it appears that she was very concerned at this new voice (mine) being different from any that she knew. She would not have known that I was not a physical presence and therefore felt threatened. If we are to consider that she may have made this up I find this quite a complex set of thoughts to generate and keep consistent to without any chance to plan ahead.

9. Tom Hope – Poacher and Boer War Soldier

During the time spent with Joe Keeton one of the more interesting characters encountered was Tom Hope. He was a bit of a 'wide-boy' but unfortunately I don't have recordings of the first sessions so we begin with the third time that we visited Tom's memories.

In the earlier sessions it was established that Tom was born around 1860 in Devon. He enjoyed drinking (a lot more than the person actually in the regression chair) and poaching until he joined the army and went to fight in the second Boer War - but he didn't last long.

Listening to the recording of this session will give a good idea of how things were. I have tried to capture his accent in the text and hope it does not annoy.

Tom Hope – Session 3

Can you see where you are Tom?
Aye
Where are you?
I'm where I always be (implying the pub)
Oh, do you know me?
Nah, are you from up house?
No, I'm just a traveler, just come in for a drink. What's the beer like then?
Oh, it be good stuff
Good stuff is it?
I be 'avin one with you
Eh?
I be 'avin one with you, if you like

Oh, I see, you want me to buy you a drink do you?

Aye

Oh I don't know, I'm not all that well off you know

Aye, like me

Oh, anyway, you've got a drink haven't you?

Aye, be here, I had one or two

Have you?

Aye, but I won't be ere long

Oh, where are you going

Oh I'm off out

Off out?

Off out

Oh, where are you going then?

Oh I got a bit of business like

Have you, what business are you in then?

Oh I buy's a few things now

You buy a few things do you, but you want me to buy you a drink, I should think you'd be buying me drinks

Well...

Where do you get your money from?

Well I, I sells them

What do you sell? Reckon I'd want any?

No, if you're just passin' by you don't want it

What is it, what do you sell, what do you deal in?

Oh, I don't reckon I wanna say like

No, why, is it good stuff?

Aye

Oh, where are you going tonight

Oh, I just be goin' out, on the moors

What, looking for game?

No, I just be 'avin a walk like

Oh, you've got a glint in your eye when you say that

Well, be 'ard times ain't they

Yes. What's it like for work round here?

Oooh

Is there any work?

Well, not for the likes o' me there int

What about me, what kind of things I'd be able to do round here if I were to stop?

Well, you could keep a store, or you could go out and fish if you like that sort o' thing

Where would I fish, out at sea do you mean?

Aye, go to sea

Does it pay well?

Nah, nothing pays well

So you, uh, are you a gamekeeper then?

Oh in a way I am, aye

Are there any other gamekeepers round here?

Only Charlie

Which one's Charlie?

Be Charlie 'Arris

Oh, is he here as well?

Aye (nods to the right)

Oh he's sitting next to you is he?

Aye

How do you do Charlie?

'e be alright

And he's a gamekeeper is he?

Aye, of a sort

Oh, same as you is he?

Aye

If I wanted a... , supposing I wanted a Pheasant, do you think you could get me a Pheasant?

Well, depends who you are like, if you be the law?

Oh no, I'm not the law, you don't have to worry about that, I'm as bad off as you are, I takes my chances

Well, in that case I'd try to get you one

How much do you reckon I'd have to give you for one then, a few bob?

Well, I could let you 'ave it for ten bob

Could you, ten bob eh, that sounds a bit much

Well, say five bob
Five bob, that sounds a bit more like it
Aye, .. I be off
You're off now are you? Oh well, see you again then. On second thoughts
I'll come with you
Well you'll be 'avin a long walk

(Moved forward a little way, 'Tom' shivers)
Cold is it
Be a cold night, be a good night
Is it good when it's cold
It's good when it's cold, it's clear, the frost and the Moon, it be a good
night, they're good the winter nights, they be long
Yes I suppose they are, a lot of night yes. The more it's dark the more you
can get eh?
Be right. I got a few .. traps to put down.
What kind of traps are you using?
They be .. like they is, bits of iron with a spring and I puts 'em down with
the spring open
Where do you put them?
Oh, I puts 'em where I know the rabbits be, by the warrens
By the warrens
Aye but I not be tellin' you where, you'll be after me rabbits
I don't think so, you're a bit bigger than I am
Aye, I look after meself
What do you put in the traps to get the rabbits to come and step in them?
Oh, I ain't puttin' anything, I just covers 'em up, and I know they come
out, they come out to play and they runs around and then they get
caught, they just yumps in
Does it hurt them?
Oh arr, kills the poor little things
Still, you've got to eat haven't you
Aye
Are they big springs, I mean are they big traps or small ones?
They be what I can get

Oh, where do you get them from?
I get's them around
You don't go to a shop and get them?
No, I got a man
He makes them does he
Aye, he comes in The Fox, he, he sells them
Oh I see. How much would I have to pay if I wanted a reasonable trap from this fellow then?
Ooooh!
I wouldn't trap round here, I'd go somewhere else, I wouldn't take your territory.
Aye.
Always looking for a good trap
Well I gets it as cheap as I can – about two shillin', and I gives im a bit of what I get.
Yeah, well you've got to keep in with him haven't you?
Oh I have, he's a good un.
How do you catch Pheasants, what do you use to catch a Pheasant?
Well, I can shoot em, I a good shot, but they be difficult to …
You've got a good gun have you?
Well, it be a bit old, belonged to me Dad
Oh did it
Aye, bit out of date like
Yeah, how do you look after it, do you oil it and things?
I oil it, I cleans it inside
What kind of.. how does it work?
Well, like they all works, you get your cartridge, you put it in, you cock it back and off you go like, its, its like – a gun! I haven't seen no others, except Charlie's.
Oh Charlie's got a gun?
Oh aye Charlie's got a gun
How many barrels has it got?
Well two!
Are there any one barrelled ones?
Oh aye there be one barrel guns

You prefer twin barrels though

Well you got more shot haven't you. I buys the cartridge if I can get em

There's a shop in the village is there?

No! I got this man like, same one who does traps, he makes them

Or does he buy them?

Oh I think he makes 'em, it takes a bit of skill, gotta pack 'em right.

They're good are they?

Oh aye, stout paper, I stick em in and off I go

They go off every time do they?

Aye

They do, you've never had one fail?

Oh, I don't think so, I think they can be relied on. I'm a good shot

Are you

Oh hell aye, I've had a few years experience like

How many years have you been doing this?

I dunno, I think I always done it

Did your Dad do it before you?

Aye, Aye, he 'ad 'is lot a long time ago

Did he, what happened there then?

Oh, what happened to 'im, it's so long ago…. I think 'e fell in the river, he drowned

How old was he when he drowned?

Oh he was a young man, it was a waste

He could have taught you a lot I suppose

Oh he did, 'e taught me quite a bit, and I picked it up as I go along

Are you married?

Aye, I be married

Got any kids?

Aye, I 'ave

How many have you got?

Oh, maybe three

Three?

Aye, it be three. Aye, they be way

They what?

They be way, down the road, they be at 'ome, they don't come 'ere.

Are you going to teach them to do what you do? Have you got any boys?

Aye, Billy, he be me oldest. I dunno, it's an 'ard life but they be 'ard times

What else do you reckon he could do?

He could go for a soldier

Is there something for soldiers to do then?

Aye, there be a war on, been on a long time

Is there, where's the war, I haven't heard about that?

Well it's over, over, sea

Is it, what in France?

No, No, over sea, Africa

Is it?

Aye, been on a long time

It's a long way away isn't it?

Oh aye,

Do you know what it's about, what they are fighting about?

Nah, don't know nothin' about it, nothing about it

Not interested in going off to fight?

Phew! Me, I'm alright where I am

Are they looking for volunteers, do you know

Aye, they always be looking

Does that pay well?

No

No?

You get by

They give you your keep I suppose

They do

And something to wear

Aye

Still, you're alright where you are for the time being aren't you?

Aye

Is Charlie with you now?

Aye

He's very quiet isn't he?

Well he be talkin' to me, he be speaking about ..

Oh he must be standing too far away, what's he saying

I reckon he just thought he saw summat
Ooh, what did he see?
Oh, it was an animal, I think it was a Beaver, nah! What they call it –
Badger, the one with the stripe on, I think he thought he saw a Badger
and I said "Tuh, Charlie, you don't see no Badgers round 'ere" but 'e said
it was so.. but I think he's 'ad a few too many tonight, I don't reckon he
can get along like. "Come on Charlie"
Slow is he?
Caw, 'e's slow on 'is feet
Is he older than you?
Aye, e's gettin' on a bit now like
He's your old pal is he?
Aye, been me pal many a year
Bet he knows a bit about trapping does he?
Aye, he taught me a lot
How old are you now?
Oh I reckon I be about thirty
Thirty?
About thirty. We'll put them down 'ere
You putting the traps down are you? Is that a good place then?
I reckon it might catch a few
When are you going to go back and see if you've caught anything?
Well, it's wise to wait 'til its dark, I come when its dark tomorrow
So you leave them here all day then
Aye, be alright, they 'ang 'em anyway
Eh?
They 'ang 'em up for a few days anyway so it don't matter, they don't 'ave
to be like just dead. They be alright, they takes the skins and make 'em
into things

At this point we moved forward in time, to the time when he had just
joined the army

How are you doing Tom?
Oh I be alright, I be off like, soon

Off are you?

Aye, be goin'

You're going off to the war after all?

Well, I got nothin' to do and like, well, I gotta get outta the way

You've got to get out of the way have you?

Well, I reckon I'd best be outta the way

Who said you've got to get out of the way?

Well I 'eard that, up at the house like, they hear about me up on the moor, and I be gettin' a bit..

You reckon they'll be chasing you soon?

I reckon they might be out after me, they got a new man up there and 'e gets around a bit more than the other old bugger! 'e don't get very far at all

What will he do to you if he catches you?

I dunno, they used to string 'em up but I don't think they do that any more. Put me inside.

He'd probably have a few shots at you would he?

He would, he would. Aye, put me inside I think

Oh well you wouldn't want that, you're an outdoor man aren't you?

Oh I couldn't stand that

Better off going off to war

So I'm off, I'm off. I'm going to pack a few things

You've joined up have you now?

I 'ave

Did they give you a number?

They give me... they give me a bit of paper

Did you look at it?

Nah

Didn't you, don't you know what it says on it?

Don't mean nothin', I can't read it like

Oh, do you know numbers?

I don't know, I can see 'em but.. I know a 2 and my number starts with a 2

Try and remember it for me, I'd be interested because I could probably follow your progress in the war if I knew what your number was, they know you by your number don't they?

Aye, they say they do, I can't remember it, I can't

Haven't you looked at it at all?

Nah I don't reckon I did, it didn't mean nothin' to me

You probably had a quick look before you put it in your pocket when they gave it you?

I don't think I did, I just went like that and I stuck it in me pocket.

Not to worry. They probably know you if I wrote to you as Tom wouldn't they?

Well they know me round 'ere as Tom, be no different out there

Tom Hope isn't it, your name

Aye, be 'ope.

Just to make sure we knew

'ope by name an' 'ope by nature

Always looking for the best are you?

I be 'oping for the best. I be 'oping for the best for Bess and them young uns, well they're not so young now but they're still around 'er.

How old are they now, how old is Billy?

Ooh, lor, he be twenty, he must be.

Oh well he can look after the family can't he?

Aye, I be 'opin', I be relyin' on 'im

How old are the others, do you know?

Oh they not far behind

How many are there, two?

No, there be four

How old is the youngest one?

Oh I dunno, thirteen I think, that sort of age

Oh well they're all..

A damn nuisance

They all are at those ages

Aye, they are at any age I think

How old are you now?

Oh I dunno, I be, I be getting on I suppose

Are you over fifty do you reckon?

Nah, I ain't fifty, I don't look fifty do I??

No, no my eyes aren't very good these days, I'm getting on as well

I don't reckon your eyes be too good no, I should get some of them ...
them things they wear
Oh glasses, spectacles
Spectacles. Nah I'm fortyish, it don't mean nothin' to me like, a man is as
young as he feels I always say, I feel ..
You've always felt young anyway
Oh I've always been in good health, well the drink keeps you young
Doesn't it do something to your brain though?
Ain't done nothin' to my brain
I suppose its Gin that does that
I guess it 'as to Charlie's but I don't know about mine
Is Charlie still around?
Poor old Charlie, e's still on his legs, just
Bit too old for the Army though wasn't he?
They wouldn't 'ave 'im no, lucky they 'ad me, don't usually 'ave you but
they be desperate. I'm away
*Oh well, I expect you'll shoot a few of them out there won't you? Are you
still a good shot*
Aye, I'll be useful, aye
*I should say that's why they've taken you because you're a big strapping
man and you're a good shot*
I be on foot an' I'll shoot 'em
Yeah, you're in the footsoldiers are you?
Aye

At this point we move forward to the final memories

What's happening Tom?
We be goin' over top
What are you doing?
We bein' off to try and get 'em
Tell me what's going on
(Gasp) I got 'im
Who did you get?
One of 'em

How did you get him?

I got 'im wi' me bayonet

Where are you going now?

(Seems to collapse)

Can you still hear me Tom?

(Shallow breathing)

Can you hear me?

I reckon they've got me

They got you? What with, a bayonet or a bullet?

There not be much left

Do you reckon it was.. oh, not much left?

Where are you, are you outside?

(No answer but grimaces)

Is it painful?

Aye

Relax, just drift away now. Session ended.

Tom Hope - Session 4

Joe Keeton asking most questions with a few from others present.

Taken back to the memories of Tom at the age of 21...

Where are you?

(Tom is laughing)

What's the matter, what are you laughing about?

Fox

What Fox?

I'm in the Fox

You boozing again, how long have you been in there?

A while

How much have you had Tom?

One or two
What's your second name Tom?
'ope
Hope, Tom Hope?
Aye
What do you do for a living? How do you make your money?
Trade
What do you trade in?
Rabbits
Rabbits, and where do you get the Rabbits?
One or two Deer
One or two what?
Deer
Are you a poacher?
Well..
How do you catch the Deer, how do you kill them?
Shoot 'em
What about the gamekeeper, don't they hear you?
No
Oh, where do you live
Barnstaple
Barnstaple, on whose grounds do you poach for Deer?
Moorland
Oh, I didn't know there were any Deer round there actually but.. What are
you drinking?
Ale
Do you like the girls?
Aye
Are you married?
Aye
Any children?
Aye
How many
Two young un's
What are their names?

Billy, Jane
What ages are they?
I dunno
Have they been born long?
Ah, young un's
Have they learned to walk yet?
Oh aye, oh aye
Are they a nuisance, sounds as if you don't get on too well with them?
What's your wife's name?
Bess
Is she nice?
Well, bit fat
Well why did you marry her if she's a bit fat?
She weren't fat when I married 'er
Oh.. What year is it Tom? Who's on the throne?
Victoria
How old is she, is she an old woman?
Aye
Getting on a bit is she?
Aye
What sort of gun do you use?
Two barrels
Do you load your own shot?
Shot and powder
What?
I carry powder
You carry powder, do you make your own cartridges
No, I buy 'em
You buy the cartridges, and why do you carry the shot and powder then?
Powder
What do you use the powder for then?
Put down the gun
But I thought you said you bought cartridges?
I buy 'em sometimes
And you make them sometimes?

(Takes a drink of beer)

You like your beer, you like your ale don't you, how much is it these days?

Copper or two

Well what is a copper or two, what do they charge you?

Tuppence

A pint, is it good stuff

Aye, quite strong, and there's Cider

Cider as well, where does the cider come from?

It's always there, I don't know

You don't care where it comes from, as long as it's there. Any war on at the moment?

No

No? Have you ever been in a car?

No

Do you know what a car is?

No

How do people travel around?

Well, by horse, or maybe train

How much would it cost to go to the nearest city from where you are?

I don't know, I just walk

Do you walk because you haven't got any money?

Aye

Haven't you got a horse?

No

How old are you Tom

Ooh, twentyish

Do you do any other thieving apart from poaching?

Well, not really, no

Have you never taken anything?

Well....

Don't worry, we aren't the Police, we're only interested. Have you got anything with you now that I might want to buy off you?

Rabbit?

No, I'm more interested in something more valuable, have you got any silver?

No, only this necklace
Where did you find that?
Round where I live
Was it lying in the road? Did it drop off the back of a lorry?
Didn't drop off Nellie
That's her name
On the estate
On the estate was it, which part of the estate?
The house
In the house, what were you doing there?
Having a look round
Who lives there?
The Moorville estate
Moorville, Morvel... are you having another pint?
I'll have another
Have you been to school?
Not much
Did anybody teach you anything?
Nah
Can you write?
Nah. I sees em write, I aint any good but I tried
Can you sign your name, what do you put for your name?
Tom
Put Tom do you? Let's see if you can. I'll give you a piece of paper, will you write Tom Hope for me?
Aye
Here it is on your lap, here's a pen, open your eyes and write Tom Hope for me

(Trying to write, scribbles)
Blooming thing won't work

(Joe clicks the pen to make it work)
There you are, try it now, that better, haven't you ever seen one of those before?

(Tom is in awe)
Come on, write your name
Tom writes
Where did you learn it? That's it..

Relaxed again, taken forward 5 years

Where are you Tom?
Moans
What's up?
Leave it
Why, what's the matter, got a hangover?
(Moans)
What's the matter? Don't you feel well?
Had one or two last night
Got a headache have you?
Aye
Where's Bess?
At home in bed
Do you think you'll drink any more?
Lord no, never touch another drop, long as I live, swear that!
Where did you get your money from, for all this ale last night?
It was only a copper or two
*You need more than a copper or two to get a head like that. What about
your friends, did they buy you some.*
Aye, he does
What's your friend's name?
Charlie
Charlie what?
Charlie 'Arris
Have you got any other friends? Does he live near you?
Yeah
*What's your address Tom, if we wanted to send something by post to you,
where would we send it?*
Cottage

What cottage, what's the name of it?

(Blank)

Well is it in the town or outside?

Outside

What's the name of the lane it's in, or is it in a road or what?

No lane

Well what's it in?

A track, oh I dunno, what's it called, maybe it hasn't got a name

It's got a name, since you're a poacher you should know the name of everywhere

Bess

Pardon

I think Bess likes to call it something else, Rose Cottage

That's a nice enough name. What about Charlie, where does he live? Does he live in a farm or what?

A cottage

Is he married?

Aye

Any kids?

A few

Where does he get his money?

Same with me

Do you go together?

Aye

Where do you sell the things you poach?

Here and there

Have you got people who buy them? What about the Police, is there a village copper, what do you call the Police, have you ever met them?

(No replies)

Haven't you got a Policeman there at all, you've heard of the Police Force though haven't you?

Aye

What year is it?

(Little response, headache related probably)

Taken forward 12 hours

Where are you Tom?
(Holds his head again)
I thought you said you wouldn't any more, What's the landlord's name at the Fox?
Bert
Bert what? And what beer does he use, does he make his own?
No
Where does it come from, what's the brew?
It's there
I know it's there but uh, is it Trophy then?
Trophy?
Yeah, Trophy beer
(No response)
Do you like Guinness?
Yes
You do, do you like Mackesons?
Can I drink 'em
Yes, you can drink them
Aye
Do you like whisky?
Oooh
What's the matter, too expensive?
Aye
How much a bottle is it?
Can't buy a bottle, a glass
How much is it a glass?
A bob or more
Is it?
I've had it a few times
Is it as good as ale?
Oh aye
Are you faithful to your wife Tom?
Oh aye, oh aye

Why, why Tom?
Well, you gotta be
What about the barmaid here?
Aye, she's alright, Moll
What's her second name, do you know?
No

Taken forward ten years

Where are you?
Home
What are you doing at home?
Everything's out
Why, are you going away?
I be going off
Off where?
War
What war?
Boers
Joined up have you?
Going to
You're going to, what does Bess say about that?
It's my last night
Well, what's making you want to go and fight the Boers, I wouldn't have thought you'd like the army?
It's better than nothing
Why, aren't you working, are the pickings not so good?
No
Have you got your uniform?
No
Not joined up yet, oh, what's the ritual, do you know what they do, how do you join up?
Have to go to Barnstaple
Where do you go in Barnstaple?
Town Hall I think.

(Still quite vague)

Relax, taken to the time when he is joining the army

Where are you Tom? What are you doing, have you joined up?
Aye
Did they give you anything when you joined up?
No, well a uniform
What colour is it?
Green
Pure green or...
Mucky green
And they didn't give you anything else?
No

Taken forward one year
Dark, not Tom any more, nobody

Taken back six months
Still nobody, Joe says that having been through the death before she (the volunteer) didn't want to go back to that, so the session was ended.

Joe says he was trying to see if Tom had been given the Queens or Kings shilling straight after joining up as he thought they still got that.

The King's shilling (or Queen's shilling when the Sovereign is female) referred to the payment given to recruits to the Armed forces of the UK in the 18th and 19th centuries. To "take the King's shilling" was to agree to serve as a sailor or soldier in the Royal Navy or the British Army. The practice officially stopped in 1879 so Tom would not have been paid one.

The Devonshire regiment was based in Barnstaple and had a Khaki coloured uniform as most soldiers did.

Tom Hope - Session 5

Taken back to the memories of Tom at the age of 25...

Where are you?
I be leaving the cottage
Where are you going?
Going to do a bit tonight
Do a bit of what?
Well I'm going down the Fox, wet me whistle
Oh yeah
Then I'm going out for a bit with Charlie
Where are you going to go with Charlie?
Well, I don't reckon like I should say
Oh I see, private is it?
Well, I, I don't want them up at house to hear about it see, they might be after me
Alright then, you go on down to the Fox then. Can you see anybody on your way?
It be dark
Is it
Aye
What kind of night is it tonight?
It be dry
Is it summer or winter?
Oh, I reckon it be spring like
Spring is it?
I reckon, aye
What time of day is it?
Oh, it be early evenin', I see a light
You see a light, where's that?
It be Fox, in the window
(Other questioner) Do you know where Minehead is?

Minehead, oh, I've 'eard of it, it not be 'ere, it be a few miles off, I aven't been there.

You haven't been there?

Wife's been

(Jim) How long would it take you to get there?

You'd need a good 'orse I think

Would you?

Couple of days I should think, I think it be a long way

That light getting closer?

I be at the door

Oh right, where is the Fox, is it on a main road?

Oooh, it be a track

On a track, and you haven't got a road near it?

There be a road near, go along to Barnstaple

Yeah, where does it go to the other way?

Oh I reckon it go up to a few villages like,

Can you think of the names of the villages

Don't know, there's a lot of them, just little places, I don't know what they're called

Do you ever go to them?

No, I stay round here, got me work to do like

Do you know a place called Creech St Michael?

No, don't reckon I do

(Someone whispers "She's nodding")

I be gettin' down a drop of ale (explaining the head movement)

They be goin' down quick tonight

How much do you usually drink?

Well it all depends what I've got like, if I've got a shillin' or two, then I do alright

Is the pub very full?

Nah, nah it be too early for 'em yet. Charlie's 'ere

Charlie's there is he?

Aye, he been waitin' for me

Do you always go out together?

Aye, we're together a lot. Ah, I finished that drop of beer now

Are they getting you another one?

Aye, they're getting one

What kind of beer is it? What does it look like?

Ah it be good stuff.

Is it Tetleys

It be Bert's, don't know Tetley

Who's Bert

He's behind the bar

How many do you drink before you're flat on your back?

Oh, it'd take a few

Would it

Oh aye, 'Bout a dozen I reckon

A dozen!

He gets it in from somewhere I think

Does he, he doesn't make it himself then?

No, he don't make it himself, it comes on the cart, I dunno where it comes from. I think it comes from Taunton way

Taunton way?

Aye, somewhere out there, they makes it and brings it down.

We 'ave it regular

Is it always the same?

Aye, it be the same, nearly the same, sometimes it's got a few more clouds in it

What colour is it?

It be like brown

Light brown or dark brown?

Oh it be a rich colour

Has it got a lot of froth on?

Froth, oh no, no. Right, I got that lot down now, and we gotta be off

When are you going?

We're going in a minute

In a minute, you won't have had much time at the Fox then will you?

I can't tonight

Why, what's the rush?

Charlie, he said he thinks he wants to get a few fish like, tonight

Does he, where do you get the fish from?

It be down the , well quite a walk

What river is it?

It be.. Taun

Is it

Taur, maybe Tor I.. Taw!

Or Ton, not so sure

Something like that is it?

Aye, not so sure

What kind of fish do you get there?

Oh be anything, be rough old things really, I dunno

How do you catch them?

Charlie's got this net, like he's just got it and he wants to try it out, see if it be any good

Not used it before then?

Only just got this net

What's he going to do if he can't see any fish because it's dark?

Usually has a few rods. Oh I think he said he'd string it out

Oh, it's a .. it's not a net you hold in your hand then?

Oh I think he said he's gonna, there's a part where the river's narrow see and I think he said he's gonna string it across, 'cos it be quite low. I said he'd get just old weed with stones on it but he said he's gonna try. I got to go along see, if he tells me like

To make sure he doesn't fall in?

Who Charlie?

Yeah

Aye

You have much more to drink you might be falling in

Oh no, I'm off now

You're off now are you? What are you going to do besides going fishing?

Oh just the fish tonight

Just the fish?

Aye

Isn't it the season for anything else then?

Well, we do the fish like and then we'll do summat else another night. You from up 'ouse?

No I'm not from the house. I'm just wandering about the countryside, trying to write a book about local customs

Oh, I see

Do you know any?

Customs, nah I don't be bothered with customs

What about dances and parties and songs and things like that?

Oh we don't 'ave none o'them

Oh you must have when it's harvest time or something?

It's just quiet folk round 'ere

Or are you just trying to fob me off?

No, it's quiet folk round 'ere

I'll give you a shilling if you know a song

I don't think I know one, I don't spend my time singin'

No, alright, go fishing, have you left the pub now?

Aye, be walking out now, in the cold

What have you got on the keep the cold out?

I got this jacket thing, be warm enough, Charlie got 'is net there

How far is the river from where you are?

Well be a good walk

Go on then, hurry along

Well, you 'ave a long walk if you stay with me

Just relax, and come forward ten minutes

Where are you now?

I be walking

Are you there yet

No

Blimey it's a long way isn't it?

Aye, be a good walk

How many more minutes will it take you to get there

Oh, I expect I'm 'alf way

What's Charlie doing

He's behind there, he's got 'is net
He's behind
Aye, doesn't walk so fast
Why don't you wait for him?
I think he should walk a bit faster
Trying to make him catch up with you are you?
Aye

Relax, come forward ten minutes more

Where are you?
I can see river now
How's Charlie doing now?
Oh, poor old fellow, I think he's tired out. Don't think he's so keen now
He's got to walk all the back though hasn't he? Hope he's fit enough to do something
We'll be here all night though
Well he'll recover, now what's he doing?
Oh, the man'll drown himself
What's he doing?
Oh he's got his trousers rolled up, he's in the water, he's trying to set up his nets
Doesn't he look very steady?
I'll go and 'elp 'im out I think
What's the water like?
Oh, cold. He's got it tied up like
What's it tied to?
Well, one side it's tied to a tree that's leaning over, then there be a rock on the other side, be narrow 'ere. I think that'll do now
What are you going to do now then?
Oh, just sit back
Pity you didn't bring something to drink
Aye
Didn't you think of that?
No, I didn't think of it, I could do with some now

Are there any other pubs around?

Oh, I don't know of any. I expect there be some in Barnstaple

It's the only one out where you live is it?

Aye

How's Bess?

Bess? Oh she alright

What's she doing tonight?

Oh I reckon she in the cottage, dunno

Oh, you are married though aren't you?

Aye

How long have you been married?

Oh good few years, she looking after young 'uns

How many are there?

Be three

What are their names?

There's Billy and Jane, then there just be the little un, Lizzie

How old is Lizzie?

Oh she just crawling around, I dunno

How do you manage to keep them in food?

Well, like I does a bit of work here and there

Really, what kind of work do you do?

I dunno I should... You're not from up 'ouse!

No, I won't tell anybody

Well, like I get a few rabbits, maybe a deer

Deer?

Aye, sometimes, if we're careful

How do you catch a deer?

We shoot 'em. We trap the rabbits, and a bit of fishing

What kind of traps do you use?

Well, just little things, they got teeth on 'em, we sets 'em open, and they run in. We sets 'em where we know they're gonna be

How do you know where they're going to be?

Well, like I know the places. They got their little 'oles they live down

And they come out do they?

Aye, they come out and they play around, they jumps in

And snap!

Aye, that's the end of 'em. They makes a good meal

Do they?

Aye

But only in the spring?

Oh, they makes a good meal anytime

I thought they might be small in spring

Nah, you can always get a big 'un

Can you?

Aye

What sort of gun have you got Tom?

Oooh, it be an old thing, been around a long time, it belonged to me Dad

What size is it?

Ooh, be a good size, got two barrels

Two barrels, what do you fill it with?

Oh, I get cartridges, I'm 'avin a man who comes in Fox, 'e makes 'em up for me, and then off I go

Cartridges must be expensive are they?

Nah, they're not much – copper or two, a few coppers, nah, I gives 'im a bit what I get's see

Where does he live?

He lives around like, he's got a cottage

Anywhere near yours?

Oh I don't think it be far

And does he sell to anybody else around?

I dunno, perhaps he does, I wouldn't like to say

Is that all he does for a living?

Oh I don't know

Because there can't be very many people like you that go around getting rabbits and things for him to sell cartridges to can there?

Oh there be a few round 'ere

Are there

I'm sure there'll be a few aye, they keeps 'emselves low though. Charlie

What's he doing?

Got blinking smoke

Smoke?

Aye

What's he done, lit a fire?

Hah, his pipe

What does he put in his pipe?

Oh I dunno I think it be 'orse dung

(laughter from others)

Do you not smoke Tom?

Naah, not me

Why not?

I don't like it, I never have

Have you tried it?

Aye, I tried it

Or has the smell of Charlie's put you off?

Aye, aye that's right

What does he light the pipe with Tom?

Oh he got some matches, got some old box he keeps round with him, where he gets 'em from

Have you seen his box?

Aye, think so, be a dirty old box

Does it say who makes the matches on it?

I dunno, I think it got a picture on it, a picture of a ship or something

Has it?

I can't see no name, expect it's been worn off

Uh huh, picture of a ship?

I think so

Have you caught any fish yet?

He reckons he might have just got one

Oh, so what's he doing, is he just going to have a look or is he going to get the net in?

Oh he'll be out in a minute

Are you not frightened of being caught Tom

Well I always gotta watch out, but I got away with it so far

What will happen if you do get caught?

Oooh I dunno, perhaps they string me up

You'd better watch out for yourself
Ah I don't think they do that no more, they used to though mind you
How long ago was this?
Oh, in me dad's time I think or maybe before 'im
What year is it Tom?
Oh Lor, it be about 1870 summat I think
Who's on the throne?
Oh Victoria
Is she married
Aye, think so
Has she got any children?
Aye, she got young uns
How many?
Oh I dunno, I think she got a few
Do you know anything about the Prime Minister?
Nah
Don't you ever hear about the Prime Minister?
Don't hear about nothin' round 'ere
If somebody did catch you, who would it be?
Oh it be 'im from up 'ouse I expect, the gamekeeper
Oh
They don't get round much
Don't they?
Nah
Is there anybody else that might catch you?
Nah, only gamekeeper, in the city there be people but they don't get out 'ere

Relax, and come forward to the time when you're in the army. You're in the army.

Can you see where you are?
Aye
Where are you?
I be down in a ditch

What doing

I be watching for 'em, coming over top

Oh yeah, who's coming over the top?

Them we fighting, Boers. I been 'ere a day or two now

Have you?

In this ditch

Oh in the ditch, how long have you been.. wherever you are?

Oh, I've only been 'ere about, ooh, you lose track of time I think it's about a week

You're away from England aren't you?

Aye, oh aye

You've only been away from England about a week?

Oh no, no

How long have you been away from England then?

Been 'ere about a week, got off boat. Oh, from England, be a long time now

Is it?

Aye, takes a long time

How did you come?

Weeks

Weeks?

On a boat

Just on a boat

Aye

Where did it land?

Durban

And where did it go from?

It come from Plymouth

From Plymouth to Durban, do you know what the name of the ship was?

Arr, I reckon it was called.. think it was called Vulcan or summat like that, it was a steamer

A steamship?

Aye, I don't know nuthin' about 'em really but...

Did you know what the captain's name was?

Oooh no

You don't know that?
No, he be on there see, we don't...
You don't mix?
No
I just thought somebody might have told you

At this point there is a problem with the recording so we don't have a
record of what followed. There is enough material to justify a review.

Checking the story

Distilling the conversations revealed a substantial amount of circumstantial evidence that could be checked, including national and local history, geography, language and lifestyle.

Tom said	Research found
He sometimes poached Deer	Deer have been kept and hunted on Exmoor (near Barnstaple) for thousands of years
Minehead is a couple of days away by horse	Minehead is 35 miles away. Horses walk at 4mph so it would take 9 hours, best done over two days with rest and food breaks
Beer comes from Taunton which is quite a way off. It cost 2d for a pint	Taunton is 50 miles east of Barnstaple In 1880 it was 2d so probably similar in 1900
The River Taur or Taw goes through Barnstaple	The River Taw is the main one flowing through Barnstaple
He had his father's twin barrelled gun	12 bore single and double barrelled shotguns began to replace Blunderbus guns from about 1800 so he could have a decent gun
Gun cartridges cost a few coppers	I estimate he would have paid around 3d per cartridge
When examining his matchbox he thought it had a picture of a ship on it	England's Glory matches had a picture of a Victorian ship on but I am not sure they were around before 1900
Around 1875 he knew Victoria was Queen and thought Prince Albert was alive.	Victoria was Queen (not a hard question) but Prince Albert died in 1861 so he was out of touch here, perhaps not a priority for him?
He thought Victoria had "a few" children	She had nine children and in 1875 they would have been aged from eighteen to thirty five
He travelled by steamship ("Vulcan") to Durban and it took weeks	Vulcan could not be found but steamships did go to Durban and it would probably have taken about three weeks
A week after landing he was in a trench.	Durban is the closest port to the location of Boer War activity, being about 200km from Colenso and Ladysmith – four to five days marching

The following historical information (with grateful acknowledgement to Google) gives a contextual view and understanding of the events that would fit with Tom's death in the Boer War.

The Battle of Colenso was the third and final battle fought during the 'Black Week' of the Second Boer War. It was fought between British and Boer forces from the independent South African Republic and Orange Free State in and around Colenso, Natal, South Africa on 15 December 1899.

Inadequate preparation and reconnaissance and uninspired leadership led to a British defeat.

General Sir Redvers Buller was appointed Commander-in-Chief of all British forces in South Africa.

One of his Brigades, under Major-General Henry J. T. Hildyard consisted of the 2nd Devonshire Regiment, the 2nd Queen's Royal Regiment, the 2nd West Yorkshire Regiment and the 2nd East Surrey Regiment. The plan was that this group would capture Colenso while other regiments would take a bridge across a major river. This attack was to be supported by artillery and battery of six naval 12-pounder guns.

Early on the morning of 15 December, the attempt to take the bridge went badly wrong due to a misunderstanding about the target and this resulted in a large number of troops being exposed repeatedly to heavy fire from the Boers.

As Hildyard moved towards Colenso, the two batteries of field guns under Colonel Charles James Long went ahead and deployed in the open well within rifle range of the nearest Boers. Once again the Boers opened fire. The British gunners fought on, even though suffering heavy casualties, but ammunition could not be brought to them and they were eventually forced to take shelter in a donga (dry stream bed) behind the guns.

During the afternoon, the British fell back to their camp, leaving ten guns, many wounded gunners and some of Hildyard's men behind to be captured during the night. Buller also failed in the rescue attempt, particularly when Major General Barton refused to support Dundonald's or Hildyard's hard-pressed troops.

This map shows the layout of the battle and that the Devons were right on the front line and very vulnerable.

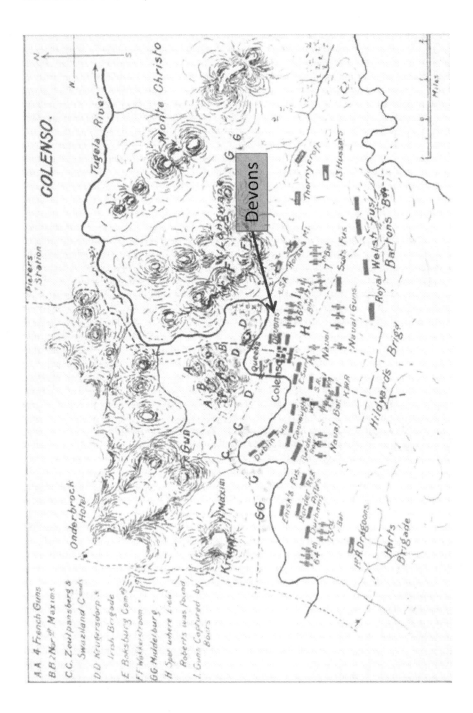

Buller's army lost 143 killed, 756 wounded and 220 captured. Boer casualties were 8 killed and 30 wounded.

Information recently available on Google reveals that The Devonshires were a formidable fighting force and provides even better detail, as follows.

The 2nd Devonshires sailed on the Manilla about 20th October 1899, and arrived at the Cape on 15th November. They were at once sent to Durban, and, along with the 2nd Queen's, 2nd West Yorkshire, and 2nd East Surrey, formed the 2nd Brigade under Major General Hildyard.

At Colenso the Devons losses were serious enough, 9 men being killed, 5 officers and 60 men wounded, 3 officers and about 33 men missing. When the guns got into trouble the 2nd Queen's and Devons went straight for Colenso village, which they actually entered, driving out the enemy. When the order to retire came the Devons were so far forward that they did not all get the command timeously, and Colonel Bullock, 2 officers, and about half a company could not get back. The story is told that the colonel, refusing to surrender, had to be knocked on the head by a Boer as the kindest and firmest method of bringing him to accept the odious facts. The loss of such a splendid fighting soldier was a most serious one for the battalion. In his despatch of 17th December General Buller says: "Colonel Bullock, 2nd Devons, behaved with great gallantry. He did not receive the orders to retire, and his party defended themselves and the wounded of the two batteries till nightfall, inflicting considerable loss on the enemy, and it was only when surrounded that he consented to surrender, because the enemy said they would shoot the wounded if he did not".

In the fighting between 16th and 24th January at Venter's Spruit and Spion Kop the Devons were not very heavily engaged. On the 24th they were not far from the fated kop, and all day had to lie longing for a chance of helping their hard-pressed brothers. At Vaal Krantz they had to endure their shelling like the rest of the brigade, and lost 2 men killed and 32 wounded.

In the fighting between 13th and 27th February they again had their share. Their casualties were approximately 6 men killed, 2 officers and 77 men wounded.

From the Devon Times 29 December 1899

THE LOSSES OF THE ENEMY - TRENCHES FULL OF DEAD

Chieveley Camp December 16th
(The day following the battle)

The Field Artillery were, in proportion, the heaviest sufferers in yesterday's battle. The whole of the 66th battery and four guns of the 14th were captured. The 7th Battery had all its men wounded and all its horses killed. In the course of a gallant attempt to save their guns from falling into the hands of the enemy, Captain Schreiber was killed and Lieutenant Grolls wounded.

The whole misfortune was due to the mistaken, but heroic, action of Colonel Long, R. A. in taking his batteries into action within 800 yards of the river to the left of the railway, and 1,250 yards from his objective - a ridge situated beyond Fort Wylie.

The guns were exposed to a perfect inferno of rifle and shell fire. Officers, men and horses fell in rapid succession but, nevertheless, the guns went on unlimbered and opened a steady fire, causing that of the enemy to abate to an appreciable degree.

In this position, the batteries remained for an hour and a half - as long, indeed, as their ammunition held out, and until the casualties had become so numerous as seriously to interfere with the efficient re-using of the guns.

In recent years the list of those serving with the Devonshire Regiment in the 2nd Boer War has been developed against difficult odds.

Information about some of the men who served in the 2nd Boer War (1899 to 1902) can be found in the National Archives. These records were retained because they related to the award of a pension but pensions were only awarded to men who held Long Service and Good Conduct medals - the files of men who died in the 2nd Boer War, for instance, were later destroyed because these men were never eligible for a pension. Of the remaining records, what did or did not survive seems to have been the result of a completely hit-or-miss process, making searching very difficult and often fruitless.

I have looked at the information gathered and there is no mention of anyone called Hope but this does not mean he wasn't there. He might well have been in the Devonshire Regiment that suffered that day, and perished soon after arriving in Africa, in line with his description.

Troops did travel from Plymouth, they did arrive at Durban a month later, and at Colenso a month after that, so the timing fits. The ship was a steamer but not called Vulcan, so not all the details fit.

Continuity of life experience

A question often asked is whether we just keep going from life to life. The answer is we don't know but it is worth noting that in sixteen sessions spread over a period of nine months this volunteer was taken to ten 'characters'. Two of these she visited four times, at different points in their history, not in chronological sequence and never knowing where she would end up.

Examining the dates associated with the 'lives' shows that apart from two time periods which were not visited they fill the period from about 1520 to 1949 and that the end of each 'life' fits with the start of another (with a gap for pregnancy).

The 'lives' that were visited several times involved going to different points in time at random but there was consistency in the information recalled. This is also generally the case with other volunteers I have seen and the enormity of the task of holding the necessary information in the imagination and being able to weave such plausible stories would surely be worth several Oscars.

The findings are suggestive of there being an 'essence' that inhabits physical forms in order to learn something and that it moves on to another form at an appropriate point. If this is so it does not preclude the possibility that this 'essence' is not limited to the physical body but can at the same time be part of a non-physical existence where time and space are not limiting factors so the time between physical lives could accommodate all non-physical experience. In fact the non-physical existence could be doing many things at once, one of which is living here.

All the theories about spirit existence, reviews of life, travels between lives, ethereal beings etc. can still be part of the overall truth. This world may just be the 'school' we need as part of it in order to gain the knowledge our 'essence' needs. There is an illustration in Part two.

10. Further thoughts and questions about regression

When discussing where the information revealed in regressions may come from, various theories have been proposed to me, ranging from actual reincarnation to genetic memory (if it was genetic how do we get memories from the period of life after having children, or of those who had no children?), the Akashic record (claimed to be a library of everything that has happened in the universe, accessible through meditation), spiritualism, telepathy, parallel universes etc. Many of these seem to be far more complex and less likely than the idea that if life is a learning opportunity then we need to take many and varied courses so the soul will occupy many bodies over the course of time. Many of the alternatives would also mean that the same memories should be available to every psychic, meditator or telepathist yet the existing research normally shows that the memory is unique to the individual regressing.

The possibility of 'carrying over' skills like musicianship, artistic ability and so on is often mentioned. There have been a small number of claims made and it would be nice to quantify this but it is probably more likely that there is simply a range of aptitudes, whereby most people are close to average but some people are considerably better and some considerably worse and this is as natural as the fact that some are taller and some are shorter than the average. In most aspects of life there is a range rather than everyone being the same.

Another frequent question concerns language. If the remembered 'life' is of someone of a different nationality (say French) to the volunteer and the hypnotist (say English), should they only be able to speak or understand their own language?

I have had cases where the time visited was so long ago that there was no recognisable language, and cases where I was talking to a Viking or a French person. Initially some of these did not speak English but they did understand my instructions. Others spoke English.

Two explanations can be useful here, firstly some people can be experiencing the regression as one of reliving it but others can be viewing it as if it were a film. This can change as hypnosis gets deeper but it is also true that regression is not time travel and we are always talking to the volunteer, and they are translating from the memory. The hypnotist is talking to the volunteer's subconscious so they are able to respond in their natural language but they can also try to use the language of the memory. This connection route is not always perfect so we should perhaps forgive some amount of inaccuracy and confusion, as is the case even with memories of this life.

Another question that often arises concerns the population explosion. The maths are a little tricky, but if you assume that a finite number of 'souls' (for want of a better word) exist, then the fact that over the course of time, due to advances in health care, the average lifespan has increased means that the countable population has grown, but the number of lives started may be constant. Infant mortality was far greater in the past, especially in poorer parts of the world, and for a woman to have a dozen or so babies, of whom perhaps only two or three survived to the age when they would be counted as part of the population, was not unusual.

In other words, most of the 'souls' spent their time recirculating, rather than living as long as we do now.

In addition, there have been many more plagues, famines, and wars to reduce the population count, and it is unlikely that very many areas of the world actually bothered to count anyway. The numbers are largely conjecture, but do we know how many people lived in America, China, Africa and so on in the past?

We could also consider life elsewhere in the Universe and that our soul need not be limited to experiencing existence from only inhabiting the human form on Earth.

Naturally we must also appreciate and consider the point made by most scientists and physicists, that our lives and thoughts are the result of evolutionary processes over millions of years which saw microscopic particles of gas or electricity or nothing turn into the universe we now accept, with rocks, water, trees, flowers, animals, dinosaurs, insects, germs, and humans. Some of these became clever in order to survive longer than others, and some became more creative and inspirational rather than just being driven by instinct.

We still don't know how this happened. We don't know where the matter came from to make the universe and we don't know what happened to make some parts of the universe appear creative and intelligent.

I am not sure I like the idea that just by putting a load of parts together to make my physical form and then starting the heart, lungs, kidneys, microbes etc working it will be able to think. We have learned how to put a car together from a bunch of parts but it won't go anywhere without a driver (or a set of instructions created by a driver).

I think I do like the idea that I am my driver and in the same way that I will get another car when my current one dies I will eventually do the same with my current body.

Part Two - Dealing with Anxiety

11. Regression used for therapeutic benefit

As my research progressed people began to ask me if hypnosis could help with problems that seem focused in the mind and not the body. I had been studying this aspect whilst with Joe and read widely on the subject and reached a point when I felt compelled to help if I could. Some of the volunteers I had already seen had found that the regression process had revealed the source of current difficulties and in so doing found that this had removed them and I had never had any difficulty in managing the process to produce a positive (often life-changing) outcome.

Whilst parts one and three of this book are focused on research into past life regression my experiences have also been very educational and I am strongly convinced of and committed to the significant benefits that hypnosis is able to bring to people suffering a wide range of anxiety related 'disorders'. I believe it is my duty to encourage anyone to make use of the technique to achieve the improvements in mental well-being that are possible.

I am going to hope that you are not reading this book just because past-life regression is amazingly intriguing but because you are interested to investigate what life is about and how it might work if it is not just an accident. Therefore at this point I am going to set out my thoughts relating to the mind-body-other relationships and this automatically includes exploring how our minds control our mental well-being.

I think it is good that you understand this aspect of hypnosis as it may be of use for you or someone you know and these notes are intended to introduce the basic concepts and to de-mystify the subject. I like to think logically and often come up with small stories that I hope make things easy to understand.

It is only 26 pages but feel free to skip to Part Three if you wish.

12. The Job of the Brain, the Mind and the Body

Protection, Development and Healing

During our formative years the primary objective of the brain is self-preservation. Other needs develop as we mature. Start at the bottom of this pyramid and work upwards.

HUMAN NEEDS

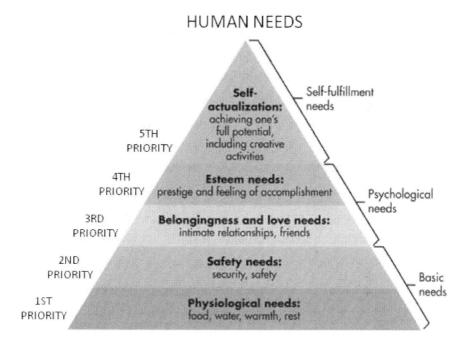

If we consider the mind as part of our being, whether it is situated in the brain or the brain is simply a conduit through which our sensory experience is interpreted (sight, hearing, taste, smell, touch all needing to be fed into our experience bank so that we can recognise what is good, dangerous or any level in between when we encounter it again), then it could be that there is yet another part of us which stores experiences in a similar way but on a grander scale. First let us look at the known parts.

The mind essentially operates at three main levels –

UNCONSCIOUS activity - Heartbeat, breathing, cell production, digestion, physical healing, fighting infection, growth, neural activity, the five senses. These are not controlled by your conscious mind (though you can hold your breath for a while – not enough to harm yourself).

UNCONSCIOUS

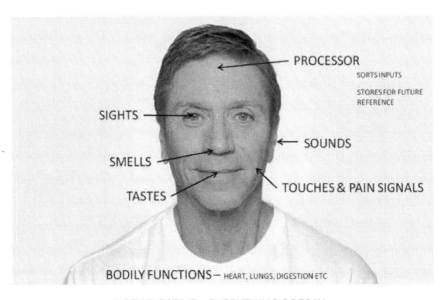

NOT SELECTIVE – EVERYTHING GOES IN

This level is accessible through serious medical intervention to remove or repair. This is what we might call the 'hard-wired' section as it is built in whilst in the womb and we cannot change it. Also note that our eyes, ears and the other senses do not decide what to sense, they have no censors.

SUBCONSCIOUS activity - acting on decisions, checking the uncensored sensory inputs for safety, managing response to danger, hunger, desire, illness. Filtering sensory input for conscious awareness.

SUBCONSCIOUS

DECIDES WHAT TO SEND TO THE CONSCIOUS AND HOW TO RESPOND

E.G. SOUNDS, SMELLS, SIGHTS OUT OF THE ORDINARY – COULD SIGNAL A FIRE

ANY COULD REVEAL –
> THREATS – FIGHT OR FLIGHT
> OPPORTUNITIES – FOOD, FRIEND, PARTNERSHIP
> INJURY/ILLNESS – PAIN, DISCOMFORT, TIREDNESS

This level is accessible through Hypnosis, dreams and drug or alcohol induced altered states. This is not 'hard-wired' but is developed by experience to manage our life. Here we can be selective about the sensory inputs we take notice of (e.g. which sounds we listen to (pass from subconscious to conscious) and which we ignore even though we hear them) and how we behave accordingly.

Many people say "I'm just made that way, I can't change" – that is not true, you are changing all the time because as experience grows the associated decisions are changing. In other words, we learn from our mistakes and so try not to repeat them. Sadly we rarely learn from the mistakes made by others.

In our early years the subconscious picks up clues from those around us about how to behave and how to achieve our goals and sometimes those around us are not as perfect as we think they are. This can lead to confusion and problems as you will see in a minute.

CONSCIOUS activity - considering alternative strategies, making decisions. Mindfulness, meditation, yoga.

CONSCIOUS

TAKES NOTE OF SIGNALS FROM THE SUBCONSCIOUS

OBEYS THE SUBCONSCIOUS

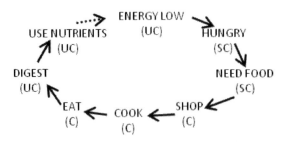

ISSUES INSTRUCTIONS WHICH THE SUBCONSCIOUS CARRIES OUT

MOVE, TALK, WRITE ETC (CONSCIOUS ORDERS)

MUSCLE CONTROL, THINKING, MEMORY (SUBCONSCIOUS DELIVERS)

Consciousness is a tiny part of our mental activity, you might decide 'I will go for a bike ride to x' but all the mechanics that follow are handled without conscious control so the heartbeat increases, the ears deal with balance, the muscles take care of the movement. Your conscious can ride along and mainly look at the scenery. If you tried to control all of the processes consciously you would fall off. A modern example is the uncanny way we can walk down a busy street whilst focused on a mobile phone screen and not bump into too many other people.

The graphic on the next page illustrates how these levels work together and adds a fourth level (UNKNOWN) that may or may not exist – look carefully, think it over and decide.

The conscious and subconscious do not feed into the unconscious but might have links to and from the unknown.

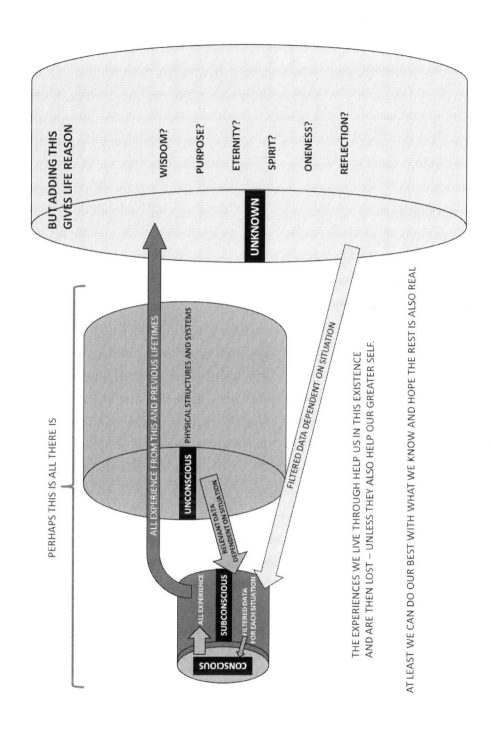

BUT ADDING THIS
GIVES LIFE REASON

WISDOM?

PURPOSE?

ETERNITY?

SPIRIT?

ONENESS?

REFLECTION?

UNKNOWN

ALL EXPERIENCE FROM THIS AND PREVIOUS LIFETIMES

PHYSICAL STRUCTURES AND SYSTEMS

FILTERED DATA DEPENDENT ON SITUATION

UNCONSCIOUS

RELEVANT DATA
DEPENDENT ON SITUATION

PERHAPS THIS IS ALL THERE IS

ALL EXPERIENCE

SUBCONSCIOUS

FILTERED DATA
FOR EACH SITUATION

CONSCIOUS

THE EXPERIENCES WE LIVE THROUGH HELP US IN THIS EXISTENCE
AND ARE THEN LOST – UNLESS THEY ALSO HELP OUR GREATER SELF.

AT LEAST WE CAN DO OUR BEST WITH WHAT WE KNOW AND HOPE THE REST IS ALSO REAL

13. Using the subconscious more effectively

The subconscious can be thought of as a SatNav for the brain - and "YOU"!

When setting out on a journey, once you have firmly decided where and when you want to end up, and perhaps some 'staging posts' on the way your SatNav will keep you going in the right direction, even if you take a detour or there is a temporary blockage it will issue new directions to get you back on course. If your target is to achieve inner peace, master the piano, lose weight or become independently wealthy your subconscious will (subtly) remind you of your goal and of the next steps you defined and the timeframe you envisaged so that you remain focused and determined to get there. You cannot stop this happening unless you decide (again definitely) that a new goal is a better one.

If you are not <u>definitely</u> decided then you will be going nowhere because your SatNav will be in idle mode.

As an example, if your goal is to try and cut down your smoking you will fail. Only when you properly decide to be a non-smoker will you succeed, and you won't need patches, substitutes or even hypnosis to do it.

The mind that we are aware of requires information so that we can cope with future experiences but we all know that there are some things we can consciously control (speaking, writing, playing games, moving around, using tools, eating) and some that we cannot (going pink when embarrassed, sweating when nervous, shivering when cold or scared, heart rate, the five senses just mentioned, and bodily functions).

Just realizing these things will make you more aware of the impact your subconscious has on your life but you can also ask more of it.

The developing mind in one person will be affected by any event in a different way than another mind experiencing the same event. One will be able to place it in a proper perspective and not be too concerned about it whilst the other will become distressed, fearful and may even see it as life-threatening, giving it a level of importance that is not rational. Being wisely wary of something is not the same as having a panic attack.

HOW COME PEOPLE DON'T REACT THE SAME WAY?

 IT IS NOT THE SNAKE'S FAULT IS IT

SOMETHING HAPPENED TO MAKE YOU THAT WAY
YOU ARE THE ONLY PERSON WHO HAS EXPERIENCED EVERYTHING THAT YOU HAVE EXPERIENCED

The difference between these two reactions has nothing to do with the actual event. It is most likely to be related to the earlier upbringing and the observed reactions of parents and other influencers to all sorts of events. The first child has become predisposed to a 'fight or flight' reaction and wants to get away whilst the other has been encouraged to be curious and interested. Parents that are scared of snakes or spiders will probably influence their children to hold a similar fear, just because of the way they react and not through what they tell their children (telling a child not to be frightened of spiders will immediately cause them to suspect they should be frightened). There will always be an emotional element (embarrassment, fear, shame etc.) attached to these associations. Those that adopt the 'flight' response when it is not rational are the ones that end up needing therapy.

My experience as a therapist has demonstrated to my satisfaction that it is essential to identify the underlying causal factor that created a psychological problem in order to have a real chance of permanently overcoming the problem and eliminating the symptoms.   This allows the sufferer to rebalance their life and achieve more of their potential.

A lady I saw was suffering with severe agoraphobia and we discovered that it was caused by embarrassment when she had her first menstrual period in a shop and had no idea what was happening to her so she was afraid she was dying. Her subconscious had locked this away so that she forgot (repressed) it but on recovering it and now understanding, she quickly realised that there was no need to be fearful of being outside and her phobia was gone.

Another lady came to me with a fear of flying, sudden noises and bright lights. She regressed to the age of about four and a wartime memory of an air raid. Her father was not at home and her mother was extremely scared that he would be killed. This in turn scared the child and created the associations. Again it was clear that the situation was unlikely to be repeated, and in fact her father was OK, so the irrational reaction was not justified and her subconscious removed it. Two weeks later she sent me a letter from Sardinia, where she was having dinner whilst a thunderstorm (previously the cause of panic attacks) was in progress outside.

I did not need to suggest that the future would be better or that the problem could be 'coped with'. I carefully helped them find the moment in their experience which had created their problem and helped them to understand that their (then immature) mind had been over-protective so it was now able to change the decision it had made and take a more sensible approach. When such repressed emotions are released there are often a few tears but there is great relief that this burden has been finally lifted.

It continually upsets me to hear about people (including a rush of celebrities with books to sell) suffering from anxiety that I can easily recognize as similar to the above situations. They are usually encouraged to try all sorts of 'treatments' that do not work and waste a lot of time and money, rather than use this method to see why their young mind made a decision that can now be changed quickly and permanently.

Understanding our learning power

There are two ways to learn - Instant learning and gradual learning.

Instant learning occurs when we are exposed to imminent danger, like fire or something that hurts us (nettles, needles, knives, wasps, snakes, deep water, high exposed places, sour food which may be poisonous, etc). The subconscious generates a strong reaction to get us away from the danger and stores this response so that when in potential danger again we react instantly without thinking about it. If we relied on the conscious mind to take our hand away from fire we would get seriously burned.

Gradual learning happens when we seek to acquire new skills or improve existing ones (languages, trivia knowledge, times tables, names, places, driving, music, sport etc). Nobody learned to speak French in a second! It is necessary to 'chip away' repeatedly at our memory stores using our slower conscious mind in order to install new knowledge. It is even difficult to recall the name of someone you just met until you have heard it (or repeated it to yourself) several times. After enough repetition these skills become automatic and, in fact, subconscious. Driving is a good example.

Mental health treatment should make the most of the mind's power

Virtually all current treatment for mental health problems is based on training the conscious mind, which is why treatment plans are so lengthy and often fail. Anxiety in various forms affects the lives of millions and as long as the treatments adopt the wrong approach this will only increase.

In my opinion Mindfulness represents the latest nonsense fad, and it and many other so called remedies are only attempts to encourage the sufferer to 'get used' to their problem and 'manage' it better. Being more aware of a problem for which you have no solution is likely to make things worse, increasing the anxiety level. I prefer the idea of removing it rather than 'managing' it and the only way to achieve lasting change is to correct the imbalance that the mind has created due to a misunderstanding or a failure to benefit from more mature experience.

If you imagine for a moment that the mind is a jigsaw then what trauma does is to hide a part of it and until you can find the hidden piece you will not see the full picture, and will therefore not be able to understand it and learn from it. Using regression to revisit the experience and understand it better helps you to complete the picture and use your whole experience for your future benefit.

The success provided by any treatment should be properly assessed but the criteria for success must be carefully considered. Those who support CBT (Cognitive Behavioural Therapy), Mindfulness, and many psychological treatments consider success in terms of how a problem can be managed or coped with but I contend that merely managing a problem represents failure. My measure of success is the removal of the problem and on that basis the treatments mentioned above regularly fail, leaving patients having to work hard (and even become addicted to drugs with side-effects) to get by when they could, and should, be enjoying a **normal** life.

I am not suggesting that hypnotic regression is a panacea for mental wellbeing but it could certainly help a vast number of people more quickly and using fewer resources than these other offerings.

So, you ask, why is it not being used? Why are increasing numbers of people admitting that they have problems such as those I described earlier and yet most of them are not getting the help they could have?

Part of the answer is that the medical profession is strongly controlled by treatment guidelines created by NICE (National Institute for Clinical Excellence) in the U.K. and similar bodies elsewhere. The problem is that they are generally driven by clinical evidence and treatment trial results. They are mainly focused on drugs and physical treatments and in such things it is possible to conduct tests and measure results much more easily than is the case in mental health, particularly where trauma related anxiety is concerned. Such bodies are likely to promote the idea that 'managing' the continuing problem is a success.

To back up my statements here is a very brief summary of the guidance and what in my view are serious faults.

The guide says	My view of it
The first thing it says is that it aims to help people achieve complete relief from symptoms (remission), which is associated with better functioning and a lower likelihood of relapse.	This is the right objective. Unfortunately the treatment is not aimed at achieving it.
The second thing it raises covers antidepressants suitable for longer-term management of panic disorder.	There is that "management" word straight away, plus an assumption that "longer-term" maintenance with drugs is required.
Next it mentions laws relating to specific drugs because of a risk of abuse and dependence under the Misuse of Drugs Act.	They know the drugs are dangerous.
1st stage treatment is reading of therapy material and self-help plus perhaps an occasional five minute telephone update with a doctor.	Largely ignoring the initial cry for help and investing very little time in the patient. This could lead to them giving up on treatment.
If stage 1 does not help the 2nd stage treatment is self-managed CBT or therapist guided CBT as an individual or part of a group.	There is almost no research on the efficacy of CBT and what exists is inconclusive. It may help for military/terrorist based PTSD because it is hard to find a rational interpretation for the violence involved.

If stage 2 does not help the 3rd stage treatment is a "high-intensity psychological intervention". This can be CBT based or "applied relaxation". Applied relaxation should be based on treatment manuals used in 1987 and "Intervention is restricted to progressive muscular relaxation training and application of relaxation at onset of anxiety". The alternative is drugs. Drugs may involve many and varied side-effects including anxiety attacks, sexual problems and addiction.	Still CBT focused. Relaxation only comes up once and then it is highly restricted and based on very outdated ideas. Hypnosis is not even mentioned. The idea seems to be that if you suffer a serious anxiety attack someone should tell you to breathe deeply and calm down – or more likely to take some drugs. The intention is purely to temporarily cope with symptoms (a panic attack) rather than to provide any kind of permanent solution. Patients might feel better or worse, lose or gain weight, feel tired or excited or suicidal, etc. Clearly it is very "hit and miss".
If stage 3 does not work the 4th stage treatment is a combination of Psychotherapy and drugs or a period in a Psychiatric Hospital.	If earlier treatment is not effective more people will reach this stage. Some clearly need to be managed this way but better early intervention would reduce the numbers.
Progress at any stage should be assessed using routine outcome measures and the patient should be involved in reviewing the efficacy of the treatment.	The "outcome measures" used are vague and ambiguous. The scales used are not specific enough. The questionnaire designs are based on the therapist's need rather than the patient's so can confuse. (I have over 30 years experience in questionnaire design). Measures should not rely on patient's judgement of how they feel but on factual events (did they sweat, faint, become dizzy, escape etc.)

This situation is seriously inadequate and denies patients the help they deserve but at present if a doctor suggested using regression therapy they would risk being criticized by NICE (even though it is only guidance) and would be unlikely to do so even if they thought it could help their patient.

This is somewhat understandable because there has been a major growth in therapists offering 'regression' to 'past life' events that may have caused current life problems (phobias, attitudes, disorders etc). Very few seek to prove the authenticity of the past life and seem quite happy to allow clients to use their imagination to conjure up a suitable life that contains a trauma that can be blamed for the problem.

I believe that most relief provided this way will be temporary because it is imaginary. This could in fact be dangerous because all that has happened is that the subconscious has been provided with a way of concealing the real cause of the problem and it will continue to 'protect' itself by creating symptoms to prevent the real issue being dealt with.

At best these 'remedial interventions' are similar to the previously mentioned offerings in that they just might allow sufferers to 'manage' their problems better. At worst they may be responsible for worsening the situation because the sufferer will be disappointed when their hopes of relief are dashed, and because in this situation it is possible (even likely) that they will substitute one problem for another, for example if fear of flying is removed but replaced by agoraphobia (fear of open spaces and crowds) then they are clearly no better off.

Here I make a plea for the medical profession to take note of the next four paragraphs and give a significant proportion of their patients a better chance.

It is absolutely necessary to discover the real source and the emotional reaction associated with it, and for there to be enough time between the event and the current moment in order for the subconscious mind to accept that the original response was protective but not rational and not appropriate for the patient's current and future benefit.

When that is achieved a true change instantly occurs in both the conscious and subconscious mind and the difficulties are resolved.

Of course, in some cases a mental difficulty is the result of a physical abnormality in the brain and in such cases it may be that the best we can do is to medicate and control. I believe that the vast majority of mental difficulties people experience are not due to any physical cause and therefore they do not need physical or permanent medical control. Most were acquired as a result of a life experience, at which point the mind made a decision and that decision can be changed.

It must also be accepted that not everyone that suffers from anxiety or depression or dysmorphia or OCD etc. will be able to resolve the problem through the technique I have described. Revisiting the trauma would not improve matters unless there has been enough opportunity for the subconscious decisions that were made at the time to be regarded as no longer appropriate or helpful.

Another lady came to me wishing to put her life back on track two years after her husband had left her to partner with a man. This had left her with damaged self-confidence and a lack of trust in relationships. After careful consideration we agreed that not enough had changed in her life to lead to a radical change in her view of the events so instead of regression I showed her how to make each day more positive and focused on the future so that the past would become a distant, less important memory but one that she would learn from and become stronger.

So in cases where regression is not the best solution there are still techniques which can help in a very wide range of problems, most of which I assert that the medical profession have been shown to be unable to really help.

I am saddened by the attitude of most of the medical profession, and even the psychiatric profession and if it comes to it also by many of the hypnotherapy practitioners.

Doctors are trained to reach for physical treatments ranging from plasters to pills to operations and most are not properly prepared to deal with patients that need other support. Recently I have seen some enlightened Doctors admit that in many cases they are only able to 'patch up' the patient and alternative solutions would be welcomed for exactly the reasons I have outlined. Sadly they still promote ideas which are based on managing rather than resolving the issue (such as joining a sports club to take your mind off the problem for a while).

Those in Psychiatry and Psychotherapy seem mainly to want to retrain the conscious mind or again reach for pills to suppress it. Most Hypnotherapists limit themselves to the use of suggestion, which can be effective in relation to minor problems such as low self-confidence or mild pain control, but they are reluctant to take the analytical approach including regression to achieve a real solution to the more deeply seated issues that result in many mental health problems.

The 'talking therapy' treatment offered by the psychiatric profession may at some point reveal the source of a problem but it will be by accident and it could take many months/years of precious time from all parties. Studies show that the majority of patients do not achieve real benefits, many give up and just hope that they will get better one day. They often even pretend that the extended therapy has helped just so that they can stop it without making the therapist feel bad.

When hypnosis is used properly (and this must be in person rather than on-line or using self-hypnosis because the patient needs to have confidence that they are safe in order to fully engage with the process and 'let go' and the therapist needs to be able to properly judge how the patient is responding) it should take between four and ten sessions to understand why the subconscious decided to 'install' a protective behaviour, and to see that it is no longer appropriate.

There are numerous different 'behaviours' that can be created in this way so I am not going to list them. Anything that you do that seems to be outside your control can qualify so panic, stress, problem eating, running away, compulsions, headaches/migraines, stuttering, relationship problems, and so on are all included, unless you were actually born with the problem.

The problem or the effects may be unique but in fact the cause is very much the same, so the method of treatment (seeking the source of the emotional reaction) looks the same but in fact will be very personal and individual.

It may be that the therapists have been frightened by the emergence of 'False Memory Syndrome' a few years ago. Briefly this involved patients describing being sexually abused as children on the assumption that this was often the cause of anxiety issues. It led to major problems when these patients confronted and accused their parents and others. Most, if not all, of these cases proved to be imaginary and brought about as a result of therapists actually asking subjects to search for such memories rather than simply examining actual memories to discover the cause of the anxiety. If I ask you to describe a two foot high red elephant you will be able to, and under hypnosis you might even think it is real, but this is because I have suggested so and not because you discovered it. The medical professionals decided that this discredited hypnotic regression and instead of stipulating that patients must not be led by therapists they have discouraged the use of an excellent remedy.

Pills are not personal and the only way they can be said to work is by delivering a drug that does the same thing to all users, which is to dumb them down, which may be exactly what is needed for initial relief but in most cases it should not become a long-term treatment or be regarded as successful.

I know this may seem controversial but I want everyone to have the full, productive and natural life they should have. Being captives of the Pharmaceutical manufacturers (who do deserve great credit for the good they do) is not part of that life.

14. The current Medical/scientific approach is flawed -

Whilst I am truly in awe of the compassion and dedication of those in the health service there are very unfortunate and well known consequences of their policy of seeking to be the only source of help.

- Pills for pain, depression, etc prescribed too frequently.

- Antibiotics overused so much we are becoming immune to them, too many erroneous prescriptions handed out.

- Increasing pressure on Doctors, Nurses and Surgeons due to people reporting for non-medical reasons. The profession automatically tries to help rather than referring people to more appropriate treatments, which would reduce their workload to more manageable levels.

- Increasing cost on the economy from people being off work and unproductive but not physically ill.

- Social cost - people having difficulty fitting in due to agoraphobia, claustrophobia, OCD, eating disorders, etc causing others to avoid them.

- Time lost on talking therapies like CBT or Mindfulness that don't work (and can't work) or that take too long.

- The supposed current focus on mental well-being is sadly missing out on potentially very significant solutions.

To get a better result requires changing to a better solution. Part of the Hippocratic oath that Doctors take states that they should accept that sometimes they don't know enough and should be prepared to refer patients to colleagues that have more specialist knowledge in order that the patient is helped. I believe that Professional Hypnotherapists should be included in the definition of colleagues.

I heard that Rembrandt made two gifts for a friend. The painting was fabulous but he would have preferred it if Stradivarius had made the violin. The phrase "different horses for different courses" comes to mind.

I like analogies so - if my leg was broken I believe the treatment would involve a temporary restriction of movement to allow the bone to heal and that I would be provided with a crutch to support mobility. The restriction and the crutch would be removed once the bone was healed and the medical objective of getting the leg back to as near normal as possible was achieved.

To consider that a better solution might be to prescribe painkillers and permanently restrict movement and screw the crutch to my body is insane and would leave me actually disabled.

So why, when your mind gets misaligned, do you seek antidepressants or reminders that you have a problem (CBT is a crutch, not a solution) when the answer is to sort out the cause of the problem and get back to normal.

This would take people out of the cycle of visits to the doctor and costly treatments whilst at the same time improving the life and health of the sufferer.

The cynic in me wonders if the intention of CBT is to keep people in this loop so that the health service is under enough strain to justify tax increases to pay for it and keep staff employed needlessly. Cynicism is not always the wrong approach, it is wise to think about the motivation behind some decisions before you just comply with them.

In terms of the medical claims of success I don't think it takes a genius to realise that most drugs do <u>something</u> to our bodies or minds, the question is whether that effect is useful or not. Anti-depressants are intended to calm things down temporarily and the fact that they do this reliably may be mistaken for a successful outcome.

Before you dismiss these concerns just consider for a moment whether a well person or an ill person is worth more to the health industry. Billions are spent and fortunes made supplying drugs and treatments that well people don't use.

Why not think of depression and all sorts of other mental conditions as being in need of temporary support until it has been possible to deal with the cause of the problem (something has broken but it can be mended) and once achieved the supports are no longer needed.

15. The alternative approach

Use the natural abilities we all have (and use daily) in a more focused and effective way.

Just as any skill we have can be made more effective by training and practice (sport, music, art, writing, debating, generating ideas) and following the principle that anything you do a lot you get better at, so the functions and abilities we have in our minds (and this is of course everything that we do) can be enhanced.

Consider something most people do - driving - the difference between a learner driver and Lewis Hamilton is essentially practice. Of course he has a faster car but without the training and practice he would simply crash out of every race. With practice people can take charge of their own ability to sleep better, eat better, think better, and live better.

Hypnosis lets you have access to your own 'control systems' and is the best and most effective tool that you can use on yourself to achieve many powerful and permanent changes and to remove negative effects and create the best you that you can be. Learn how to use your own mind to drive yourself better.

Your mental set up is unique to you because only you have lived your life and you have reacted to your experiences in ways that are different from others reactions to similar experiences. Pills cannot offer a flexible treatment, for example anti-depressants can only subdue activity and cannot be prescribed to deal with individual needs. In most cases there needs to be some experimentation in drug and dosage before a reasonable 'fit' is achieved for the patient and on top of that there are side-effects as your body tries to reject the chemicals.

Only your own mind can know what lies behind your reaction to difficult situations and only your own mind can find the specific solution. By gaining access to the subconscious, hypnosis can be used to discover what lies behind your reactions, and allow the swift adjustment in thinking that would change your future. It is a bit like having an exploratory operation where it is necessary to go beneath the skin to understand and repair what is going wrong inside. We don't normally see what is inside our bodies but it is certainly there - and so is the subconscious.

Many people need help to resolve problems that Doctors don't generally deal with, perhaps mainly because they don't have the time needed or because they are not trained to help with things that don't require medical intervention.

These people need help from therapists with time to listen and that have experience and skills that focus on non-medical solutions - in other words – mind based solutions.

The mind is extremely powerful and usually acts in our favour, protecting us and directing healing activity as well as running the normal day to day business of living (moving, breathing, heartbeat, digestion, sleeping etc).

Sometimes the mind makes 'emergency' decisions that protect us but when a short term solution is allowed to remain in force for too long it can do more harm than good (a temporary tooth filling is only meant to protect you until a proper repair is possible).

Encouraging the mind to review the decision it has made and change it to a more appropriate one is not 'brain washing' but simply allows you to see that the path originally taken is no longer the best one and in doing that you will simply take a different path, leaving behind the problems associated with the old path.

It is vital that this review takes place in the subconscious, where the original decision was made. Any other approach would be like trying to fix a leaky roof by repainting your living room. Fixing the leak is the obvious and instant solution.

CBT and similar 'therapies' cannot work for real anxiety problems or phobias because the principle is based on the repeat learning process (Cognitive Behaviour). It will be necessary to spend a long time repeatedly pretending to be better before your brain starts to accept this as normal behaviour. By using the subconscious memory through the hypnotic process the old behaviour can be seen as wrong and harmful and the desired behaviour is accepted instantly as right and beneficial.

Put very simply, sticking to CBT, mindfulness etc instead of going into the subconscious is like going to the hairdresser if you have earache – you are in the wrong place. Problems are mainly solved where they were created.

If you still need proof that the subconscious is more powerful than the conscious, and you'd like to improve the use of your memory, try this.

Next time you are having difficulty recalling someone's name or the name of a book or film or anything you think you know but no matter how hard you try to remember it you just can't get it back, just stop trying and become quiet. Think about something else, for example have a cup of tea, or sing a song, or read a poem, or just take a few deep breaths. You have asked your mind a question and all you have to do is give it chance to respond. Within a very short time, as soon as you have stopped causing confusion and even panic by consciously trying, the answer will simply arrive, brought to you courtesy of your eager to serve subconscious.

The more you use this method the better you will become at it and you will even notice that when you need to solve more complex situations your mind will start to present ideas and inspiration to move things forward.

Another story to help explain

Imagine you have a bicycle. The front tyre is regularly going soft and you need to pump it up again, which makes you tired. One day you decide to look into the problem and find that you have a small puncture in the inner tube, so you mend it and the problem goes away. A while later the tyre starts going soft again and you pump it up for a while but decide to examine it again. There is a puncture again and this time you look further and see that one of the wheel spokes is too long and this has been causing the punctures. When that is fixed there is no recurrence, no pumping, and no tiredness.

The point is that conventional wisdom dealt with the symptom (by replacing the air regularly) but really the cause needed to be addressed as well. The additional point is that sometimes the first explanation is not the real cause so it pays to look deeper.

Everything you experience contributes to the person you are and the person you become. Everything you do makes you different from the moment before (even reading this has changed you) and you should know that you can choose how much you will be affected by your experiences, so you can be a different person tomorrow from the one you are today.

16. You do not have to suffer for life because of one event

One mistake and you're out happens in cricket but not in life. How often do you only get one chance to be perfect?

When making a cake if you have too much of any ingredient (or too little) the result will be less pleasing and if an incorrect ingredient gets in (salt instead of sugar for example) then you need to accept that it was a one-off mistake that does not need to affect your future cooking.

It isn't what happens to you that matters, it is how you respond. Make the correction and move forward.

You don't have to be the product of your history. You can re-create yourself every day if you need to.

They didn't give up on heart transplants, antibiotics, blood transfusions, etc. when they didn't succeed, they sought to define the best way to make them work. It was not the concept that was wrong, just the execution and the same is true for hypnosis - it works when the right techniques are applied.

It really puzzles me that people seem prepared to try hypnosis once and if they don't get instant results they give up and decide that it doesn't work! If their doctor or dentist or solicitor or teacher or gardener or car mechanic etc. etc. did not come up to their expectations they would not give up but would seek out one that suited them better.

Let's clarify a few things.

Hypnosis can be used by most people, it is not just (or even) for people of low intelligence, it is not brain-washing, you cannot be made to do things you believe are wrong, you cannot get 'stuck', and most people remember what they experience in hypnosis.

You do not go to sleep, which would not be good for communication purposes, but people have described the experience as "like being asleep but aware of it at the same time".

In addition, it does not hurt, or involve drugs or operations so it cannot do the harm that they potentially can.

Some people will be able to use it well from the start and others may need some time and practice to achieve results but the majority will be very capable after a few sessions.

Using hypnosis to gain access to subconscious processes is not as weird as it may sound. Firstly you need to realize that your subconscious is always 'on' but you are not aware of it until you need to be. You are mostly aware of your conscious mind (which is actually constantly being fed information from your subconscious senses).

If you think of your mind as being tuned to two radio stations but one is in the background, then what the hypnotherapist does is help you to turn down the conscious station so that you can hear the subconscious one properly and then you can communicate with it in order to very quickly establish some new ways of thinking and behaving (which can be as quick as when you learned that fire is hot).

It has been said that the definition of insanity is doing the same thing over and over and expecting a different result. I would say that a better definition is doing something different but expecting the same result.

Change something and see if an improvement comes about.

Your multidimensional mind can give you a better life – embrace it and above all, learn from it.

A word of advice here. If you do seek help from a Hypnotherapist first check if they offer CBT or Mindfulness. This will tell you that they are working with the conscious mind and this is **not** what you are looking for.

Part Three - More Past Lives

17. Martin Deacon – An American in the UK during World War 2

On many occasions I held meetings with up to twelve people in attendance, most hoping to be regressed to see who they might have been. On this occasion David had intended to simply accompany his wife but his response to a demonstration of the power of the subconscious showed him to be a very good hypnotic subject and he agreed to be part of the experiment. This is his first time under hypnosis and he is Lancashire born but as you will hear when you play the recording he soon has an American accent.

As usual I began by establishing some safety procedures and checking that all five senses could be used when recalling events, then we went to his childhood and then earlier.

What can you see?
A Police Station
A Police Station? Do you know where it is?
In London
Can you see it clearly?
No
Not clearly, what can you see of it? Tell me what you can see of the Police Station.
A lamp
Is the lamp on?
Yeah
What colour is it?
White.
And what does the building look like? What colour are the bricks?
Stone
Are there any policemen about?
ARP

ARP, Air Raid Police, is that what it says on their shoulders?

Helmets

It says it on their helmets does it? Do you know what year it is? Can you remember what year it is?

No

Never mind, it'll come, it will get clearer later on. What's your name?

Martin

Martin what? My name's Jim, what's your second name Martin?

Deacon

And how old are you Martin?

23

Where do you live, do you live in London?

Now

You don't?

Yes

Oh you do <u>now</u>. Where did you live before you lived in London? Do you remember?

No

Do you know if you've been in London for very long?

A year

And what do you do? Do you have a job?

Yeah, I'm a printer

Where do you work, which printing works do you work at?

Southwells

That's in London is it?

Yeah

And you've been there a year. Is that your first job?

No, I've been there four months

Oh, what did you do before then?

Nothing

Nothing? Didn't you go to school?

No

No? When did you leave school?

Oh I haven't been to school since I was... came back

Since you came back?

Yeah, from the States

In the States, what were you doing in the States? Is that where you were born?

I don't recall where I was born

You don't, where do your parents live?

My parents are dead

Oh, I'm sorry about that, was it a long time ago?

I guess so

You don't remember them

Oh I remember my Daddy. We had a farm in Illinois

And how old were you when you left there?

I don't rightly remember, I guess maybe about 15.

And how did you get to England

Came on a boat

Do you remember what it was called? It was a long time ago I know.

No it ain't

It's not a long time ago, how long is it?

Well it's only a year, I've only been here a year

Oh that's right, I forgot. But you left the farm when you were 15?

Yeah, when my Poppa died

Oh I see, where did you go from there, I'm just interested in your background?

I think... I don't know why he died, I mean.. I had to go.

You just had to go? Did you go to a town; did you go to any city?

I don't recall.

When you came from the States a year ago, do you remember the name of the boat?

I think it was Dankworth

Dankworth?

I think sir yes

Was that the HMS Dankworth?

Uh uh!

No, what was it?

SS I think

What did it cost to come over?

I don't know, I didn't pay the fare

Who did pay it?

I was.. I work.. I worked

Oh, you worked your passage

No

No? Go on, you tell me

I come over from the states for the war

For the war

Yep

I see, and where are you based?

I'm not uh, I live in London

You live in London, but you're not in the army?

No sir

*Oh I see, so you came over for the war, but what connection do you have
with the war?*

Correspondent

Oh, which paper?

It's not a paper sir, it's a magazine

Sorry, which magazine is it?

Times

Times Magazine

We're doing a supplement

You're doing a supplement on the war. What year is it?

We do the best

You do the best

Yes sir

What year is it now, how far has the war gone?

Well.... it's been on all the time I've been here

Yeah

No trouble here really

No, nothing happening in London itself

No, not yet, it's quiet

Where is the war going on, tell me a bit about the war

France, Germany, I'm hoping to go to France

You wouldn't go to France?

I'm going to France

Oh, you're going to France are you?

Yes sir! I want to be in the front line when it gets going good

I see. Has the war been on very long?

Well it's been on all the time I've been here but where exactly it started before I came I don't rightly reckon

Who's involved in the war, which countries and which people?

Germans

Yeah, who is leading them?

Don't rightly wanna say his name – fascist pig

But surely you have to write about it don't you?

Yeah, these Nazis

And who is leading the British, or the French

Oh it's DeGaulle

What do you think of him?

Well I don't really know cos I ain't never met him personally

What about his tactics though

Oh, I ain't got involved in tactics

Oh, what do you actually write about, what side of the war do you write about? Have you written?

I've only just come to England to hope to get to France. Don't know a lot about the war yet

I see, you've only been working for four months isn't it?

Four months here yes sir

And the war was on before that was it?

The war started before I came to England

What did you do before you were at the printers?

I didn't do much

So were you .. you were sent by the Times Magazine?

Yes sir

And did they not send you for a specific assignment?

No sir, I was sent over here in case a position came up to get me over to France

Oh I see, how have you managed to get to France then, how have you been allowed to do that?

I've not been to France yet sir.

Oh, is there a situation coming up where you could be able to go

Yes sir, for the last four months I've been working alongside the printers, finding out what stories I'm going to get

Have you written anything yet?

Nothing really interesting, just hearsay

What kind of hearsay

Well, it's mainly about Hitler, some people reckon he's mad.

Yeah, have you written that?

No sir.

No

Not yet

You will be though eventually

Don't wanna get in too deep

I see

Don't start making stories like that, or you'll be in the ... it's political

I should think war is fairly political isn't it?

Yeah but you've got to keep a close...

Yeah I suppose coming from the states you have to... How involved is America in the war?

Not a lot, we've got reserves more or less ready but we haven't called them up yet

You haven't, so there aren't any Americans over in England

No sir

Only correspondents like yourself

Correspondents, yeah

Are there any apart from you? Did you come on your own or with somebody else?

I came on my own

Who is the head of the Times magazine in America?

John Franklin, he's the editor

And who owns the paper, the magazine sorry

Can't remember his name (struggling a bit)

Name is on the tip of your tongue is it?

The name Woodrow

Woodrow, is that his first name or his last name?

Can't recollect sir

And whereabouts in America is the headquarters

New York of course

What street?

42nd

And has it got a number?

It's all 42nd street, the whole shebang

How many yards long is that? Or how many miles long is that?

I would say it's a good 1000 yards

1000 yards long, and it's all the Times Magazine?

Yes sir, 16 stories and then you got the top buildings. 16 floors editing & printing, then you got the guys upstairs who pay the wages.

What sort of wages do you get?

15 dollars

What's that, a week or a month?

A week

15 dollars a week, is that good money?

Not really, some guys get 30 dollars

Do they, what do they do?

They are top reporters

Who is considered to be the top reporter on the Times Magazine?

Well we have two or three

Can you tell me their names?

Well, there's John Simmonds

What does he do, what topic does he cover

Most things. Carlos Epta

Carlos Epta

Zepta, Zepta with a zee

And what does he do?

He does a lot of political, not war correspondence

The White House

Yes, that's America (as if to say 'well done')

That sort of thing

Yes sir. He's a good friend

You know him well do you.

Well he's about my best... he taught me

And he's hoping you're going to get a good story while you're here is he?

Yes sir.

Who else is there?

Well, there are so many guys

Those are the two main ones are they, that you know?

Yes sir, there are so many people, they are the biggest magazine in the country, in the whole states. Three and a half million per week!

Three and a half million per week. That's a lot, how many states do you cover? Do you sell in all states?

Most states. We're not getting into Canada yet though.

Why is that?

I don't know, it's something to do with the Government.

The Canadian Government doesn't agree with the US Government?

No sir

So they won't let you print your magazine there?

No sir, we print things that we want to say, they don't like it, no sir they don't.

Have they got a magazine like the Times themselves?

No, not as good as the Times

What sort of thing do they read then, over there?

Crap!

So the Times is the best?

Yes sir! No other magazine like the Times

Do you get it over in England, can you get it here?

Yeah but you gotta pay for it

How much does it cost?

Well it depends cos it's difficult. You know, by the time they get a copy here its weeks old

Yeah, I guess it would be, but how much would you have to pay for one, if you wanted to go out and get one? What would it cost me?

Normally 50 cents,

And if I wanted to get one here?

Oh you'd pay three dollars.

What's that in English money, do you know?
Well, three dollars is about 15 shillings.
15 shillings?
It's about that price
It's pretty expensive isn't it?
It's the best
It is the best
Yes sir
I'm afraid I've never read it, I wish I had. I'll certainly read it now.
Yes sir, you don't know what you're missin'.
No. I've got some.. there are some other people here with me, I'm sure they'd like to talk to you. I wonder if you.. you'll answer them won't you?
I'll try
Do your best
Mmm hmm
(Other questioner) Martin, where are you staying in London
Well, it's only a little pokey hole
Do you know what it's called?
It's just a boarding house
What district of London is it Martin?
Hackney
Hackney? Near the Lea Marshes? Near the River Lea?
Well I don't know sir, I ain't too familiar with the district. Got to be careful you know, don't stray about, no sir it's rough.
What's the name of the road Martin?
It's Marsh Lane
Marsh Lane? Isn't that near Tottenham?
No sir, it's Hackney
(Jim) Do you remember what year it is yet Martin, do you know what the date is?
I don't rightly recall sir
Who's the Prime Minister?
We don't have a Prime Minister in the States
No I know but you're in England now aren't you
It's a fat man

Does he smoke a cigar?

Yes sir

Must be Winston Churchill

That's the guy

Yeah, just had to jog your memory a bit.

(Martin growls)

Who's the President? .. Oh grrrr was that a Bulldog?

Yeah he does that all the time. See it on... get it on the relay

On the relay?

Yeah, we use it to get to the States

Oh

(Other questioner) Do you drink Martin?

No sir

You don't?

(Jim) What religion are you?

Methodist

And who's the President at the moment?

I think it's Roosevelt

Do you know which Roosevelt it was, has there been more than one?

There's Franklin, Theodore

Who's the President now, or do you know who his opposition is?

No sir

Which party is he?

Don't know sir

You don't know, are you sure?

I think he's a Democrat. I ain't too keen on politics

Oh, you just like the war do you?

Yes sir

Have you covered any other wars?

No sir

No, but you're looking forward to getting up to the front if you can?

Yes sir. I wanted to be a pilot

You wanted to be a pilot?

Yes sir

Did you try?

Well, I did but I was turned down

On what grounds

My eyes

(Other questioner) What kind of planes did you fly Martin?

I didn't sir, I never got in

You never got in to the Air Force at all?

No sir

Even to train?

I can't get into any force, because of my eyes

(Jim) They're bad are they?

Yes sir

Which way, short sighted or long sighted

I'm just blind

You mean you can't see very far

No sir

What kind of planes would you have flown if you'd got in? What did you want to fly?

Well, there was the old SuperMarine, I really like the old planes, better than the new types sir. I just wanna fly

(Other questioner) Was that the Spitfire you were talking about Martin, the SuperMarine?

Yes sir

That's an English plane isn't it?

Yes sir but we have some in the States. The SuperMarine waterplane was developed in the States, developed from the Spitfire. Not totally British you know, we Yanks do have something

(Jim) I didn't know about that

Yes sir, designed the pontoons and the underwater carriage.

You sound as if you know a lot about planes

Well sir I don't know a lot but I'm just interested in them and seeing them, looking at them

(Other questioner) Well you're not talking about the fighting plane though Martin, you're talking about the racing plane?

Yes sir, broke all the records

(Jim) Did it? Where did it break all the records? How fast does it go?

Uh, well, I think when it broke the first record, um, it was 87.6 knots

87.6 knots when it broke the first record?

I think so sir

Has it gone any faster than that now?

Yes sir, it's up to about 128 knots

128

I think so sir, I ain't too sure

Do they have to do anything to it to make it go faster?

Slightly, slight modifications, ain't too bright on technicalities, I just like the planes

(Other questioner) What was that trophy they flew for..

(Martin quickly interrupts)

Schneider Trophy sir

That's it

Yes sir, I don't rightly know the speeds

(Jim) But they won that did they

Yes sir, more than once if I recall. Beautiful plane, it's blue

Blue all over?

Yeah, it used to fly in Atlanta

In Atlanta?

Yes sir, Georgia

How many people does it hold?

Well it's a two seater but I think in the speed trials there was only one man aboard

What's going on right now, tell me what's happening right now

I'm talking to you sir

Yeah I mean what's going on around about us, where you are, can you still see the Police Station?

No sir

No, what's happened now then

I don't see much sir

You don't see much, you're just talking to me

Yes sir, I guess when I get talking about planes my mind goes.

Relax, relax and come forward 12 months. Can you see where you are Martin, can you see where you are?

Yes sir
Where are you?
Still in London (seems fed up)
You've not got to France yet
No sir
You sound a bit fed up
I'm sick
Why couldn't you get to France
No transport, I can't arrange transport, we're not allowed civilian
transport
You have to go with the Army?
Yeah but the limey's won't let us go.
The limey's won't let you go?
No sir, it's their war they say, they take all their own correspondents
And they won't let you go?
No sir
What are you going to do now then?
Well, I don't know
Are you going back home?
I guess. Just have to wait and see what uh.., I still wanna go
You still want to go, but if you can't get there you might as well go home
Well if I don't they may stop paying my salary
Have you done anything while you've been in England?
Not a lot.
Not a lot of work, have you done anything socially?
Well, I like going to the dogs
Where do you go to the dogs?
Hackney
Which nights of the week?
I go Wednesdays and Fridays
Do you win?
I guess, other days I break even, some days I lose
Are there any other dog tracks you go to?
No sir
Are you still in the same lodgings?

Yes sir

Do you remember where they are?

Still in Marsh Lane, the old bag

Oh, what's her name?

Mrs Oliver

Isn't she very nice?

No sir

What does she do wrong?

What does she do right?

Can she cook, or does she cook for you?

Yes she cooks, if you call it that. I don't like the English

You don't like English food, what kind of food does she do?

Egg and bacon, chips, egg and bacon, chips.

That's all is it? Doesn't sound like a very varied menu.

It's really greasy. Egg and bacon, chips, that's about it, not much imagination

No, not much. Relax, relax, drift off and come forward to the last things that Martin remembers. Can you see where you are? Where are you Martin?

I'm back in the States

How long have you been back in the states?

A long, long time

How many years?

Twenty odd, maybe thirty

What year is it?

1967

Who's the President?

President sir?

Yeah, do you know who the President is?

No sir, I don't get much involved

Where are you living? How old are you Martin?

52

What year were you born in?

1915

And where were you born, what town were you born in?

I wasn't born in a town, I was born on a farm in Illinois
What was the name of the farm?
It didn't have a name
It was just Deacon's Farm?
No name sir, just our home
And what are you doing now?
I'm just sitting here in my rocking chair, soaking up the sun
Come forward a few minutes, to the very last things that Martin
remembers. Where are you Martin, still in your rocking chair?
Yes sir
What's happening?
I don't feel too well
What's the trouble?
I just, I just ain't gonna last
What are the symptoms of you not feeling well?
Can't breathe
Are you in pain anywhere?
In my chest
What does it feel like? Is it hot or...?
Oh it's a vass sir
Fast?
A vass, it's like it's in a vass
Oh a vice?
Yes sir
Feels tight?
It's getting tighter all the time
Just relax .... ended session

Checking the story

Martin said	Research found
Location and Timing	
He was in Hackney and saw a Police Station with a white lamp outside	There was a Police Station at 2 & 4 Lower Clapton Road, built in 1904 and still there as a listed building (no longer in use). It is mainly red brick but the main entrance is stone. It has a classic police street lamp outside, with blue glass but the word Police is in white.
He saw Air Raid wardens with ARP on their helmets	There would have been ARP wardens there at the time as they were set up in 1937 and by 1940 there were 1.5 million in operation and it was anticipated that Hackney would be a target for German bombings. In 1940 they would have worn their own clothes but would have a steel helmet with a W on it (for Warden) and a badge or armband with ARP on it (Air Raid Precautions).In May 1941 they were renamed Civil Defence and issued with uniforms and rifles.
In respect of time period it seems quite specific. From the information gleaned it seems likely that the time is between late May and July 1940. There is no trouble in London, but there is in France. DeGaulle is leading France.	Between August 1939 and May 1940 the war consisted of Germany invading various countries with their opponents protesting but being defeated away from Britain and France, then France was invaded on May 10th and defending armies were pushed back. The French Government agreed an armistice (surrender) but DeGaulle led the Resistance and later a provisional Government (after liberation in June 1944). The Battle of Britain was an air battle from July 10th to October 31st 1940, in which the German air force was repelled.
America is not involved at this time.	From September 7th 1940 the heavy bombing attack on mainland Britain started and the Blitz lasted until May 11th 1941. America did not fully join the war effort until Dec 1941 after Pearl Harbour was bombed, though they had provided some support (arms, naval blockades, protestations) earlier.
Times Magazine	
He works for the Times Magazine. The HQ is on 42nd Street, New York, in a big building of 16 stories plus some 'top buildings'	We assume this to be the New York Times. The Sunday Magazine was launched in 1896 and was based at the Times Square building from 1913 until 2007, which was an 18 storey building on West 43rd Street (very close to 42nd Street) but it did not take up the whole street, just

	most of a block.
He earned $15 a week but some got $30	The $15 salary was fairly low as journalists were well paid in those days and could have earned two or three times this figure so $30 is more likely for official staff (Martin is probably freelance).
Circulation was 3.5 million per week	The circulation of the Magazine never got above 790,000 so his claim of 3.5 million was highly exaggerated.
The magazine cost 50 cents but $3 in Britain (equal to 15 shillings at the time).	In 1939 the Sunday paper cost 10 cents and the Magazine was included. In 1940 $3 was worth £2 and 7 shillings so not the claimed 15 shillings.
Canada had disagreements with the USA	Canada and the US co-operated well during the war although the USA was initially neutral whilst Canada was more involved because of its links with Britain. At the time we caught Martin there may have been some resentment that the USA was not supporting Europe as Canada was.
The editor of the Times Magazine was John Franklin and key reporters included John Simmonds and Carlos Zepta.	I contacted the NY Times to see if they could assist and they informed me that from the 1920's to the 1950's the editor was Lester Markel. There was no John Franklin, John Simmonds or Carlos Zepta. It was interesting that Martin needed to tell me "Zepta with a zee" which was an indication of authenticity in accent.
There were other foreign correspondents in the UK and France	There were a number of USA and Canadian journalists (I found 36 vie Google) covering the war in various places but perhaps the timing of the Battle of Britain and the Blitz made travel to the front problematic. At least one journalist (Ralph Waldo Barnes) was killed - in a 1940 air crash while flying to cover Mussolini's invasion of Greece.
Where he lived	
Living in Hackney, renting from Mrs Oliver on Marsh Lane (though here we must note that another questioner had just mentioned Hackney Marshes and this is leading)	There was a Marsh Hill that was a 100 yard stretch of High Street, Hackney and there was a Marsh Lane just north of Hackney Marshes but this was a small lane and unlikely to be an area for boarding. There was also a Marsh Lane near Tottenham but he said this was not the one and it is about 10 kilometres north of Hackney. It has not been possible to trace Mrs Oliver.
He went to the dog track on Wednesday and Friday	Hackney dog track is about 50 yards north of Marsh Hill and was operational at the time.
Politics	
Winston Churchill was UK Prime Minister and Roosevelt	Winston Churchill had become British PM on May 10th 1940. Franklin Roosevelt had been the US President

was USA President and was a Democrat. He named Franklin and Theodore Roosevelt.	since 1933 (and would go on until he died in 1945), he was a Democrat. Theodore Roosevelt had been President from 1901 to 1909 and Franklin was not a close relation.
Communications	
Martin mentions the 'Relay' as a news source	The Relay was a network of amateur radio enthusiasts, formed in the US in 1914 and which became international in 1923. It worked by 'relaying' news from operator to operator as there was no long distance means of transmission. In WW2 the government took over in order to transmit information and journalists may have had access via contacts. One odd thing is that from 1936 to 1940 the President of this network was E.C. WOODRUFF and Martin named Woodrow as owner of the Times – a coincidence or a confusion?
The SuperMarine and the Schneider Trophy	
He would like to fly a Super Marine, a racing seaplane developed in the US from the Spitfire. The Super Marine won the Schneider Trophy more than once	The Super Marine and Spitfire are very strongly linked, though the Spitfire evolved from the Super Marine. The Schneider Trophy is real, it was established in 1913 and ended in 1931 when the Super Marine won it for the third time in a row and then owned the trophy. I had never heard of it so the questions were (in hindsight) scant.
Martin claimed that records of 87.6 knots and 128 knots were set.	The 87.6 could be an early figure but I can't trace it, the 128 is equivalent to 237kph and in 1922 the winning speed was 235 so pretty close. Speeds went up each race as engines were developed and by 1931 the figure was 548kph.
The plane was blue	The trophy is now in the London Science Museum along with the winning plane, which is blue.
He mentions that it flew in Atlanta	Although Americans joined the RAF and did pilot Spitfires in the Battle of Britain the development of the Super Marine and the Spitfire was almost entirely due to R.J. Mitchell in the UK. The US Army Air Force did buy Spitfires and operated them in Europe but I can find no evidence for flights in Atlanta though there was an appearance 800km north of there (maybe they were secret?).
Question: Did he get this information by watching old films?	The significant achievements of R.J. Mitchell were celebrated in the 1942 film "The First of the Few" in which he was played by Leslie Howard, who also

	produced and directed. This covered the Schneider Trophy and Spitfire development. David Niven was in it and played a composite of the three race winning pilots and Jeffrey Quill, the Super Marine chief test pilot. In 1941 Quill flew a Spitfire disguised as a prototype for the aerobatics shown in the last 15 minutes of the film. Quill went on to write "Birth of a Legend" about the development of the Spitfire, but this was in 1986, eight years after Martin's session. If he did see this film then key information like the Spitfire being developed from the Super Marine would surely have been recalled.
Other items of note	
He said he worked at Southwells printers	I have not been able to identify this company but perhaps they were specialists in newsprint as he seemed to be waiting there for news.
He came to the UK on the USS Dankworth	I have not been able to trace this vessel
He did not drink alcohol and was a Methodist	Methodists did not approve of alcohol.
He talked of 'Limeys'	Of course, Limey is American slang for a British person but this is well known.

Here is the winning plane, followed by the Trophy

Thoughts and conclusions

There were points at which other people asked questions and this allowed a few 'leading questions' to be asked. The problem is that potentially the subject would pick up on these and the resulting information would be weaker than information which came directly from them. For this reason I try to keep my questions to the "What is happening", "What can you see", "Where are you" type.

It has to be understood that a lot of the information I have discovered recently has come from internet sources that were not available at the time of the session, the internet hardly existed even 10 years after the session. The fact that there was information I could not confirm does not necessarily mean it was wrong, if anyone can add to my knowledge please feel free.

Finally of course, Martin quotes the year as 1967 and his age as 52 which fits with his birth date as 1915. The person in my chair was in his late twenties so born in about 1950 and therefore 17 years old when Martin died. This is the only case of an overlap that I have encountered but those supporting the spirit possession theory would not find it a problem – as I said earlier it is the evidence we must follow before coming to conclusions.

So, in spite of Martin having an authentic mid-American accent for the entire session (not the Lancashire one belonging to David) and there being a considerable degree of plausible information and no time for any preparation, and the fact that he had actually intended only to accompany his wife that evening, we are left to conclude one of two things.

This was either a fabrication stitched together on the spur of the moment from odd bits of information in David's own memory banks, or it was a fabrication created by the memory of Martin Deacon, who was not a reporter at all but someone living out a bit of a fantasy for a stranger who stopped him one day in Hackney and asked him some questions.

He may have been a boastful yank out to impress a limey. He may have been mindful that 'Careless talk costs lives" (a publicity campaign that began in early 1940) and so became careful about what he said. He knew more about planes than he knew about the war and his own knowledge and memory would not be perfect of course.

The point to make here is that this was an interesting regression, with a mixture of good and bad information that flowed quickly, but it may be a good example of cryptomnesia and creativity. Without searching for evidence it might have been assumed to be genuine. Sadly David decided not to pursue the experience further so there was no opportunity to build on the information but it is still an important part of the research.

18. Jenny Cockell - Who re-united an Irish family

This is my most well known case to date. Jenny had been having dreams about a life before her own since she was young and in late 1987 she heard about my research into regression and attended a group meeting of about 60 people. We briefly discussed her situation but she did not want to participate at that time.

She approached me again at the start of 1988 and asked to attempt regression to see if we could clarify, add to or help understand the experiences. I arranged for her to join an early January meeting of a dozen or so members of a women's group who were also interested.

Jenny was hypnotised and described a cobbled street, market stalls and her death. Very much a repeat of the dreams. She cried and felt the fear, guilt and pain as Mary had.

It was agreed that we would conduct further research, purely for mutual interest. Jenny wanted to see if it would confirm and clarify her thoughts and my interest was in seeing if regression was to provable lives. We met on several occasions over the following six months and the sessions are reported in this chapter.

Some amazing things resulted over the next couple of years and Jenny wrote a book about it called "Yesterday's Children" (Piatkus Books 1993), it was featured in the television programme "Strange but True?" in 1993 and was dramatised in an American film also called "Yesterday's Children".

You will note that some years have passed since the above events. Jenny's book focused on the aspects of the story that interested her but my primary interest has always been to seek evidence of reincarnation and it is only recently that Irish census records for the early 20th century have been released so until now a proper search for Mary (the name she gave in regression) could not be made. Here I present the regressions for your examination and the results of my more recent searches will follow.

As always with regressions some parts are more interesting than others and it can take a long time to get to the interesting (possibly checkable) parts. I have summarised some of what happened under hypnosis and only the more interesting parts appear as the original conversations.

Mary - Session 1

Some minutes spent relaxing, establishing a good level of hypnosis, and at 5 years old.

Back through time...

She tells me she can smell grass, is 17, pretty, does not have a boyfriend. Has an apron on, a skirt which comes to the floor, and a blouse over which there is a jacket without sleeves. She is resting before returning to work in the big house, which belongs to the Lett family. The Letts do not work, there is an oldish woman and her son, who rides and is about 30. They have less money than they used to, "they don't have the land". The girl cleans the grates and things, lives in a room at the top of the house, alone. There is a cook – "Good at pastry". The house is out from the village (where her father lives) which may be called Boscottle or similar (not very sure). Her mother died a few years ago and her father used to work on the land, "He has strong arms but he's not so good now". She went to school when she was little, with some other children in a room, and someone taught them.

What is your name?
Mary
And your last name?
Sullivan
Do you know what year it is Mary?
1915
And what is happening in the world?
Something's not good but I don't hear much here.
Which country is this?
Ireland
Has anybody been called to go from here. Anybody you know?
I think so, I think that's what happened with the land, the English.
How long have you been working for the Letts?

About nine months.

Do you know where they get their money from, or what they do?

I think they just have money, they always have.

None of them go off to the city to earn their living?

They get it from the land.

What is the biggest place you've ever been to?

I haven't been to a big city.

Haven't you. What about the village, just think of yourself walking in the village and tell me what you see?

The crossroads, built on all sides, some nice cottages, there's a big barn at the end, a Smithy.

What street is the Smithy on?

It's got two names, Wall Down.

Is that one of the crossroads?

Yes.

What is the other one called?

The name Williams comes, I don't know why, perhaps it's somebody who lives there.

Do you know some of the people who live there?

Yes, I think it hasn't got a name.

How far is the Smithy from the crossroads?

Only a short walk.

Is there anything between the crossroads and the Smithy?

There's a big house on the corner that takes people in.

A Hotel?

Well, a Pub but they have one or two rooms above, I don't know, I don't go up there.

And if you go past the Smithy, what is beyond there?

There is a shop; it's someone's front room.

What do they sell?

Ribbons, and other things but they sell ribbons.

Ribbons for your hair?

Yes, and on your dress.

Do they sell hats?

No

Where are the food shops?
They sell food too.
And Bread?
Sometimes, it depends if they've baked.
Do they bake it there or somewhere else?
Somebody bakes it for them, but we don't have that much bread, its potatoes
And they sell potatoes at the shop?
We grow them.
Oh, what else do you grow, any particular crops or animals?
I think there are some chickens, I'm not sure if they're ours. They're in the yard at the back running free, we might share them.
How far is the village from the coast?
A cart ride I think, it's too far to walk.
Do all the people in the village earn their living from the land?
The Pub doesn't, and the shop, the Smithy, and some don't seem to work, and some are at sea.
What are they doing, are they fishing or in the Navy?
Some are away a long time.
Whereabouts does your father live, he's in the village isn't he?
Yes, when I come down from the house, on the big hill, it's just in the village on the right.
Do you know what the address is, if you wanted to write to him?
I'd just put his name. I can't remember his name, I just think of Mrs Williams.
His last name must be Sullivan?
Yes, he's just 'Father'.

I move her forward three years.

Where are you now?
In the town
Which town?
Malahide.
Is this what you used to call the village?

No
What's Malahide like?
Quite smart. It's quite big.
Where are you at the moment, in the middle of the town?
I'm walking over the top, near the High Street.
What are you passing as you go along?
Houses on the curve, on my right, a letter box on the corner.
What kind of houses are they, what construction material?
These ones are dark brick, proper brick.
They aren't black and white houses?
Old-fashioned houses? Not on the bend there, no.
Are there any black and white houses here?
I don't know what you mean.
Tudor style, beams and white areas?
There are some with wood but not with white.
*What sort of roofs do they have, or special chimneys, or are they just
ordinary houses?*
In town they've got hard roofs, slate, not like the cottages, which have
thatch or turf.
Some have turf do they?
Yes, lots with turf.
What is it about Malahide that makes it smart?
It's got lots of shops, I'm dressed up anyway.
You're dressed up, what are you wearing?
I've got some smart things, a skirt with a dark border, and petticoats.
Why are you dressed up?
I've got a man.
Is he with you now?
Yes.
What's his name?
Brian.
And his second name?
I don't know.
*It will probably come to you in a minute. When you remember it just let
me know. Does he have a job?*

Yes, he works for a man cutting wood, timbers for building.

How long have you known Brian?

Not very long.

Where is he taking you?

Just into Malahide for a walk.

Is there anything to do in Malahide?

There are shops to look at.

What shops, can you see their names?

The one at the top is a Butcher, it has lots of windows, then there's a very dark shop, I can't see in.

What do they sell?

I think they sell fabrics. I'm not sure the next one down is a shop at all, they're on the right as we go down.

And what street is this?

Main Road.

Can you see a name above a shop, so that I can find it?

There's a – I can't see it written there but there's a name comes – O'Donnell.

What year is it now?

1919.

Do you know what is happening over in England?

No

Do you ever hear stories or news about the King or Parliament or anything like that?

There's a lot of talk but I don't really listen, the work's better on the land, work is better.

Who's in charge of Ireland?

Goodness knows.

Is it someone from England?

I don't think so.

Have you got a separate King or Parliament?

Yes.

Can't you think of any names, or do you ever see newspapers?

I've seen some.

Do you remember which one?

Sorry, I looked at the pictures, people's faces.
Do you go to church?
Yes.
Every week?
Nearly every week.
Where do you go to church?
Now or where I used to?
You've changed have you?
Yes, sometimes now I come here.
Where do you go when you come to Malahide then?
There's one in the back street behind the main road, but it's quite a
proper church
What's that one called?

(Recall difficult, moved to be looking at the church)

It's very tall.
Does it have a spire or a tower?
At the front, I can just see the front and it is a big long wall that comes to
a point, and there's a little cross on top of the point. It's a flat wall and it's
stone and there's a door. At the back it's much smaller but the front wall's
very big and stands proud. I don't know if there's a spire.
*Is there a nameplate on the wall, to tell you which church it is, and
perhaps to give you the name of the Priest?*
There's a board for notices and it has writing in the wood, up, across, and
down and it has some writing on the top in different letters. Up and down
it's like a prayer to Our Blessed Mary, and across the top it's St Mary's.
Can you see the name of the Priest anywhere on there?
No.
(We go in.)
There are some benches both sides. At the front it's not a table, it's
smarter, I think this is a proper church.
Have they got any stained glass windows in there?
The only place I can see any colour is right at the other end but I'm not
sure, there's quite a lot up that end – bits and pieces.

Are there any statues?
Not big ones no, just little ones. There's a little one there.
Is it of Mary?
Yes, half stooping, bent forwards with a child.
What was your other church like, the one you used to go to?
Wooden.
Do you remember what that was called?
Just Church, it was really quite small, this one is much better.
Has anybody you know come back from the war?
Older people I'd say.
What about Brian, did he have to go?
I think he must have done because he wasn't here before.
Has he said anything about the war?
Not a lot.
Do you think he's been abroad?
I think so
Perhaps he'll tell you one day.

(Move forward five years)

Where are you now?
In a little cottage near Malahide.
Are you married?
Yes
To Brian?
Yes
Do you have any children?
A little girl called Cathy, she'll be three soon.
Has she been Christened yet?
Of course she has.
Where?
At Mary's
Do you remember the date?
Date, 4th February
And what would the year be?

I have to count the years, I can never remember, twenty two.

When is her birthday?

I think that was her birthday, I think I answered the wrong question.

What year is it now?

Is it 26 or...

Do you remember when you were married?

I remember the day, I don't remember the date.

What were you wearing?

White and flowers across the front of my hair

Let's go back to that moment?

It's very frightening

Why, you don't have second thoughts do you?

No. People watching me

Is your father there?

Yes

And relatives?

Yes, Auntie and a few cousins

What is going to be your name when you've married Brian?

I've still got that name Williams in my head

Does the priest tell you what your name is going to be?

No

Do you have to go and sign a certificate?

Yes, a big book

And which church are you in?

Mary's

What date is it today?

June 16th 1921

And if you think about Brian and when he writes his name in the book, what does he write?

O'Neill.

(Move forward ten years)

The kids are in the way!

Are they, what are they doing?

They won't go in the yard, and I'm cooking.

How many children have you got?

Cathy's the oldest, and after her there are two boys, and then another girl.

What are their names, the boys?

(Some difficulty here)

I keep thinking Neil but that's wrong.

Never mind, perhaps you'll remember later. What about the young Girl?

Peg or Pat.

What is Brian doing now?

Well, he's out but he's coming back tonight

What does he do for money?

On the boats

Where do they sail to?

They just go out to sea, where the fish is, I don't really know.

Do they catch a lot of fish?

They can get a good catch or a bad one

Are they trying to catch Herrings or something?

They get a lot of Herring and some Mackerel too.

Where do they sell them?

Well, it's the man's boat, he sells them, they take some for part of their money.

So you eat a lot of fish?

We do, but it's good.

What are you cooking at the moment?

Potatoes mostly, there's an onion in there, and dry peas.

Do you hear much about the world?

Not now, not a lot, no.

Would you know who's the King of England?

George, one of them.

Are you not sure what his number is?

Not really, something keeps saying four but something else says that's not right.

How's your Father?

He's not bad, not bad. His breathing's not so good though, he's a bit fat, his big shoulders gone to his stomach.

Are you alright for money?

Not really.

What do you do with the children, do you clothe them alright?

We try.

Do they go to school?

Yes, the boys and Cathy, they go, the little one doesn't.

Where is the school they go to?

It's in Malahide, they have to walk.

So it's not very far away?

Not too bad.

What is it called?

I haven't thought about a name.

Is it just the Village School?

Yes, we've only got one school.

Is it run by the Priests, or the Nuns, or someone else?

I don't know if it's run by the Nuns but there are Nuns there, and there are other people who are not Nuns there. There's quite a smart teacher there, a lady.

What's her name?

Ooooh.

Do you think she's clever?

She's very neat, got some money.

What does she teach?

I don't understand.

Did you say she was a smart teacher?

She's very tidy, she just teaches children.

Oh, I see, she teaches everything?

Yes

(Forward ten years, nothing there, back five years, nothing, back another two years)

I see something, going away.

What's that, what do you see going away?

I'm going away.

How old are you?

39

And what year is it?

1937

What's happening to you?

I'm just going away (very weak).

Have you been ill, have you seen a Doctor?

I don't remember.

Where's Brian?

I think he's here now.

And your children?

They're somewhere else, not here now.

What symptoms do you have?

Very, very weak, can't hold any food, it's too late now.

Are you hot?

Just shivery. My chest.

How long have you been in bed?

Too long now.

Is there any pain?

Not any more.

(She is in tears now)

What are you thinking about?

It's unfair, I'm too young, it's not me, it's the children, they don't deserve it.

You won't be there?

I know what it's like.

What, not to have a mother, because that's what happened to you?

Yes

Do you remember what happened to your mother when you were young?

She just went, I don't remember.

Brian will see that they're right though won't he?

He's a good man.

(Forward one day)

I don't hurt.
Are you still there in bed?
It's empty, I'm not there now.
Where are you now?
I don't know, I'm just lifted.
What can you see around you?
I can see down, he's by the bed.
Brian?
Yes, I think he's praying.
Did a Priest come to you?
I don't know.

(Forward five years, looking for any memory)

There's nothing, I want something.

Relax now, drift away from the memories of Mary.

End of session.

Mary - Session 2

Think of the year 1920, where are you now?
I can smell the sea. There's a small wharf and a beach. There's a little jetty, not very long. There's some timber and rubbish.
What are you doing there?
To look.
You've gone to look?
There's a reason, waiting for somebody.
Are you, who are you waiting for?
They're talking about something.
Are you married?
No, not married, to be married.
Who are you going to be married to?
Brian.
Is it Brian you've come to see?
He's seeing someone.
Oh, he's seeing someone?
He's with somebody, talking.
I see, do you know what he's talking about?
Not really.
Who has he come to see?
A man.
An important man or just a friend?
I think its business.
Is it, what does Brian do, what is his business?
Cleavers.
And you've come with him have you?
Yes, it's important.
Why?
Work.
Is he going to make something with the timber, this man wants him to make something does he?
I don't know, I don't think so.

How long have you known Brian now?

It's been quite a while, a couple of months I think.

Whereabouts is the port, the bay that you are in?

Not a place with a lot of houses, but it's busy, with a lot of stuff in wooden boxes.

What have they got in them?

Nothing, they're just stacked.

Do you know what they are for, is this a fishing port?

Mmm, could be.

What sort of a day is it?

A bit cold and damp.

And are you on the beach or are you somewhere else?

I'm just looking out to sea, I'm on a rock near the jetty raised up on a wall.

Are there any lighthouses near, can you see a lighthouse from where you are?

No.

Is it dangerous water there?

I don't think so.

Is it near to Dublin where you are?

Yes, it's down that way, down on my left.

Do you hear much about Dublin and what goes on there?

Oh, plenty goes on there.

What sort of things?

Men and Politics.

Yes, what do you hear about that?

People arguing.

What are they arguing about?

What should be done.

What sort of things though, there are a lot of things that should be done, are they thinking about anything in particular?

I don't know, it just seems so foolish, they can't do anything so why argue.

Do they argue about what taxes to set, or how to run the country or whether to go to war, what sort of things do they talk about?

They talk about the land, and money, and who should do things.

Who actually runs Ireland?

Dublin, somewhere in Dublin.
And is it connected with England at all?
Not from Dublin, there's lots of English but they're not in Dublin.
Have you been to Dublin?
No
Have you learned about Dublin?
Well, I seem to have an idea, and I've seen pictures.
Does Brian ever go there?
I think he probably has.
I suppose if you are in business you need to go there?
I think he's been lots of places.
Are there any mountains near you, or landmarks, rivers, anything like that?
Not mountains, there are hills, there are always hills if you go inland.
What about rivers, what's the big river near you?
Don't have a big river.
I think there's a river in Dublin isn't there?
I never thought of that, we've got water but it's just little streams.
When you're at home do you have any electricity?
No
How do you light your house, what do you cook on?
There's a big cooker, it's always hot.
What sort of fuel do you put in it?
It's some black stuff.
Is it coal?
No, I think it must be... there's the peat or there's wood.
Is that cheaper than coal?
Yes.
Could you get coal if you wanted it, if you had the money, or isn't it as good as peat?
You must be able to get coal because I've lit fires with coal.
But normally you don't use it?
Not in the cooker.
Do you put it on the fire?

Not in ... At a house that has big metal fireplaces and they have coal and you light a coal fire in the big rooms.

Is that the house where you work?

Yes.

Do you still work there?

I don't think so now.

How do you get money then, what do you do for money?

I don't know, I think there's a problem.

You've got some money though, haven't you?

I think father has some.

Have you got any money with you now, have you got your purse with you?

I'm looking, only coppers, I've got a few.

Can you look at them, what do they look like, what pictures have they got on them?

They're just pennies. This one says 1919, there are lots of lines on it in the middle.

And what's on the other side?

I'm fighting but I can't see it.

Never mind, have a look another time. Has Brian finished his business?

No.

Still talking is he,

Alright, just relax. Drift away and go back three years to 1917.

Where are you now?

In the big house.

What was the people's name?

The Letts. There's Richard Lett.

Is he the master?

Well, it's his mother's house.

I see, and he's a younger man?

He's not so young, he's about 30, he's a smart dresser.

They own the land do they?

Mm, they own quite a bit round here.

What do they do with it all, do they farm it themselves?

No, they've got people to farm it, and lot's of men to work it.
And do they work it for the Letts or do the Letts let them have a piece of land for rent and they live on it and farm it for themselves to pay the rent?
I think they just.. there are men who look after bits of it and men who work for them.
What do they grow mainly, or what do they do with the farm area?
Oh, there's vegetable crops and there's sheep and I can't see much else.
Any particular vegetables?
Well its potatoes mostly, and some green stuff.
And sheep, any other animals?
Some cows, the meadowlands are wet, you can't grow by the streams.
And is the soil generally good in other places?
It is.
Do they have any pigs or chickens?
We have chickens.
Yes, what about pigs?
Don't think so, I don't like pigs.
How old are you now?
19.
When was your birthday?
August, at the end.
Do you know what your birth sign is?
.....
Do you know about those things?
No.
You don't know if you're a Pisces or an Aries or something?
No.
Do you ever read any newspapers; do you see any that the Letts have got?
I see their papers, I use their papers for the glass and for the fires.
You use it for the glass?
To polish the glass and mirrors.
Do you, with newspaper?
Mm, it gets the grease off.
Does it, and do you ever get a chance to see what's in the papers?
Sometimes.

Has anything happened recently that's been big news?
They put silly things in newspapers, about someone's bull.
What, a prize one or one that escaped from somewhere?
No, it was just a heavy one.
What about news from Dublin, has anything happened in Dublin recently?
Oh, there's always news from Dublin.
What's the biggest thing that's happened in Dublin in the last year say?
A lot of argument.
What happened, tell me what you can remember about that?
I don't understand it, there's something to do with the English and it's
making people angry, I don't understand it. People are getting worried.
You're a Catholic aren't you?
Yes.
Do you do anything special at Easter time, Good Friday and Palm Sunday?
I don't know.
*I heard there was something special about Easter last year and I wondered
if you had heard about it?*
There's something, I keep seeing a dress, very full skirt.
(She is struggling to get it clear)
*Never mind, think about something else, you went to school didn't you,
how old were you when you left?*
12.
And you were being taught all sorts of things by one person weren't you?
Yes, in a little house, in that place there's a child hasn't any shoes.
Why is that?
I think they hadn't got a big brother to pass them on.
And what kind of shoes do you wear?
They come up past my ankles and they lace, they're good.
Where did you get those?
I think the Letts gave me them.

(Move to ten years later)

Where are you?
Walking down the lane.

Is it you and Brian?

No, I've got the children, it's in the daytime.

Where are you going to?

Just a walk, I thought we were going to market but we're not, we're dressed nicely.

Brian must be doing well if you're dressed nicely?

I think he does alright.

How old are you?

I'm gone 30.

What about your children, how old are they at the moment?

Cathy is 7, she's got a new dress, a newish dress.

Does she go to school?

Yes.

She's not going today?

It might be school, it's either school or Church. If it's Church I don't know why Brian's not here.

And which other children have you got with you?

I've got the boys.

What are they called?

There's Harry.

How old is he?

Five.

Does he go to school yet?

I think not yet, I think I wish he had.

And what about his brother?

No, he's only little, he's only three and a half, he doesn't go yet.

Have you only got three?

Yes.

And do you think you're going to Church?

Yes I think we might be, I don't know why Brian's not here.

What sort of things does Cathy learn at school?

Kind of poems, and she does the words.

Does she learn any history?

They do the Bible stories.

I was wondering if she'd learned what happened to Ireland, if anything had changed recently?

I think she's a bit small for that.

Yes, of course she is. What's your father doing now?

Moaning, he once had too much to do and now he hasn't got enough. He's on his own now.

You live fairly close to him don't you?

Yes, it's not too far, you see, we have to walk unless we can get someone who is going that way.

Do you have any friends who've got cars?

No.

Aren't there many cars around where you are?

No, I've seen them coming through the town. I think... well, perhaps people in the town can have them.

Have you got any money with you at the moment?

Yes.

What sort of coins have you got with you?

There's a sixpence.

Have a look at it and tell me what's on both sides of the sixpence?

Well I think on one side it's like a clover and the other side has mostly got writing around the edge with something big in the middle but they feel nice, very thin.

Do you have any bigger coins?

No.

Have you ever seen a half-crown?

Yes.

What was on it?

I'm sorry, I can't make sense of the picture, there's a very complicated picture on one side.

Have you remembered where Brian is at the moment?

He should be back, it's a calm day, he should be able to get back, he was in a boat.

What was he doing on a boat?

Fishing.

Fishing, I thought he was involved in wood?

That was a long time ago.

And he fishes for a living now, not just for fun?

Yes.

Which sea does he go out into?

The sea off... there's only one bit of sea.

Oh, what's that called?

Just sea, I don't know.

Do you ever get boats coming from England?

Yes (angrily).

You don't like that?

No, we've enough trouble.

What do they do then?

I think they've always got money.

Why do they come?

Some of them come just to look, to walk, to drive about.

Can they bring their cars with them?

Yes, I think either they bring them with them or they... some of them have cars so they must bring them with them.

They must put them on the boat. Are the potato crops alright?

We don't farm now, we...

Have you moved house?

Not for a while.

I just wondered, do you live down near the docks?

Not very near the docks, we live up behind the town, up along the lane, a bit away from the town, it was where we could get a house.

Do you know what the name of the street is?

Salmon, I don't know why.

Perhaps people fish for Salmon there?

Not round here you can't I wouldn't have thought.

Are there any rivers nearby, any streams?

There's the brook.

But you probably wouldn't get Salmon in that. Is there a river in Dublin where you might get Salmon?

Not in the town.

Coming down from the hills?

Quite possible.

I was thinking about the potatoes because I know that a while ago there was trouble with the potato crop?

I don't know when that was.

Do they talk about it?

I think people like not to talk about it.

Do you think that was a long time ago?

I think it wasn't a very long time ago. I think it wasn't so... I can't remember my having trouble. I can remember why, perhaps it was when I was growing. There might have been some problem then. There were other problems then as well, it wasn't always very good. I think it's better having someone fishing rather than having someone farming.

Always plenty of fish in the sea?

They always come back with something.

As long as they come back, have there been any people lost, or boats that didn't come back?

There were some that didn't.

Alright, just relax and come forward.

End of session.

Mary - Session 3

Usual beginning. Going straight to Mary. In a room.

What are you doing Mary?
My baby died.
Your baby died. Which baby, did you give your baby a name?
No.
Do you have any other children already?
Yes.
How many?
Four.
You've got four and this was to be your fifth?
Yes.
Was it a boy or a girl?
Boy.
What was wrong, how long were you carrying?
It was full.
You carried him for the full time. What went wrong, do you know?
No.
Was he the right way up?
I don't remember.
Has it just happened, are you still in Bed?
Yes.
And is anybody there with you?
Yes.
Who's with you, is your husband there?
No.
Who's there?
A lady.
Who is she, where does she come from?
I don't know.
How old are you?
35.

Is that a good age to be having a baby?
It's not unusual.
Is it the first one you've lost?
Yes.
Where are the others?
Not sure.
Do you think they might be at school?
I'm not even sure what time of day it is.
You're weak?
Tired.
Was it a long delivery?
I can't remember.

Alright, relax and go back one year.

Where are you Mary?
In the kitchen.
What are you doing today?
Cleaning.
What do you use to clean?
A rag, and I'm cleaning off with a damp rag from the tops of cupboards.
What about knives and forks and things, what do you clean those with?
Lumps of... its soap but it's in chips.
Not the same stuff you wash your clothes in?
No.
What do you wash your clothes in?
We have a block of soap, you scrub on the stuff.
And where do you do that, do you do it in the house, or outside?
Inside mostly, can't outside.
Have you got hot water?
No.
So do you wash them in cold water?
No, you can heat the water up.
And what do you do that on, a fire or have you got a cooker?
On a big stove.

Where are your children today?
School.
Are they good at school?
Well, that varies. Cathy's good.
Is she good at anything in particular?
Books.
Reading?
Writes.
She writes does she, what about arithmetic, do they teach her arithmetic?
I've not noticed if she's good.
Do they ever get into trouble at school?
Boys do.
What, fighting and things?
Yes.
Which school do they go to?
I keep thinking Kir something.
Do you ever visit them there, or ever go and look at their work?
Yes.
What are the desks like?
Just little single desks.
What do they write on, have they got writing books and pens and pencils or do they use something else?
They've got pencils and I think she's got a book.
They don't have to write on slates?
It's possible but Cathy's got a book.
How old is Cathy now?
She must be 9-ish.
Tell me a bit about yourself, what do you do all day, what do you think about, what do you believe in?
I think about people, I sometimes think things about people I couldn't say, they wouldn't understand. Sometimes I can see when people are doing things when they can't.
What sort of things do you mean?
Just watching them, sometimes people argue and don't see how silly they are.

Why don't you think they would understand?
People see things the way they want to see them, and don't look round corners.
And what do you think is round the corner?
How you really feel.
What do you think really matters in life?
Giving, the children.
Do they seem happy?
It's easier with some than others.
What do you think they'll be when they grow up?
Cathy could be a nurse, she's got the patience.
Is there plenty of work?
There's enough about.
If she was a Nurse would she stay in Dublin?
Plenty of work in Dublin I should think.
Has there been any call for Nurses?
Yes they need Nurses.
What about religion, what do you think about religion, are you a good Catholic?
You have to be careful what you say, you can upset people.
What do you think happens to you when you die?
I think that you wait.
How long do you wait for, or do you wait for anything in particular to happen, and then something else happens?
I think you wait like a flower might wait for spring.
What do you think about heaven then, when you've waited long enough do you go to heaven or do you go somewhere else?
It's silly, if some go some place and some go another place it makes no sense.
You don't think there's a place for good people and a place for bad people?
Who's to say who's good?
Isn't everybody going to be judged though, when they die?
So then we'd all be bad.
Except for the Priests?

Hmm, No, there's bad in there.

Must be a lonely place, Heaven. Have you ever thought about what happens to you when you die, do you think you come back here again?

No.

Have you ever heard of anybody coming back?

No, people wouldn't say that.

Do you think you've been on earth before?

Sometimes I feel very old.

What's your husband's name again?

Brian.

What's Brian doing today?

I think they're mending today, cleaning and mending.

Do you know how much money Brian gets a week for his work?

No.

Doesn't he tell you?

No.

Does he give you money to pay the bills and buy the food?

Yes, some.

How much does he give you?

Its coins, some shillings.

Do you ever go out with Brian, to special occasions?

No.

Or down to a pub?

No.

Does Brian go to any pubs?

Yes.

Where does he go?

It's in Malahide, there's an anchor, I can't find where it is but I can see an anchor in the picture, and there are some stars laying in the anchor.

And what year is it now?

1934.

Alright, just relax, and go back 20 years, you are 20 years younger, it is 1914 or 15 and once again you can see where you are clearly and fully, you can tell me the things that are going through your mind, you can tell me the thoughts that come across your mind, where are you now?
I'm sitting in the garden, I can see the water and right down across the hills.
Have you gone out for a walk or are you having a rest?
I'm out for a walk.
Do you work?
Not today.
Today's a day off is it?
Yes.
Where do you usually work?
I'm just starting work, stuck in a house, cleaning all day.
Don't you like that idea?
Not really.
What would you rather be doing?
I'd like to walk and walk.
Are you on your own?
Yes.
Do you have any family?
Yes, my father and brothers.
What do your brothers do for work?
Two brothers had to go away for work, had to go a long way.
What, over to England?
Don't know.
And have you got any more brothers?
Yes, I've got another brother, and I think he's talking of going.
Isn't there any more work around locally for them?
There's only farming and there's not a lot of work.
What are the people you work for like, what do you know about them?
I like the Lady, she dresses very nicely, speaks very nicely, she wears pearls.
What's the house like, if you take a walk around it in your mind how would you describe it?

There's a round pillar by the front door, a big wooden door, behind that is a hallway and to the right of that is the main room, a big room which is beautiful with mirrors and a big carpet.

How big is that?

It's big enough, you'd take a walk across it.

Do they hold parties in there?

No.

Don't they do very much entertaining?

No.

Seems a waste of a house?

She doesn't like too many people.

And what's in that room?

Lots and lots of things there, mirrors and chests, writing desks, and chairs with arms.

Do they have a library, a place with books in?

I think so, I'm trying to find it.

Is there anything on the other side of the hall?

The stairs, and the hall narrows. It goes to the kitchen, you turn off right to get to the kitchen and that's the dining room there, you can go through it, the kitchens on the side.

Is there anything downstairs?

This is all downstairs.

Is there a cellar?

No.

Do they keep wine anywhere?

I don't think she likes a lot of wine.

So, when you go upstairs, is there one storey upstairs or more than one?

There's more than one, you go to the top of the stairs there are the nice bedrooms, there's another set of stairs to my little room, there's not much else up there, it's very small.

How many bedrooms are there on the first floor?

I'll have to count the doors, there's one door facing and then three doors along the landing, so there are four rooms and there's something else at the end, or a big room at the end.

What sort of facilities have they got for washing and cleaning?

There's no water upstairs.

So what do they do when they want a bath?

Must be downstairs, I'm looking. There's a bit of the house I can't get into, that might be the bathroom.

Is it near the kitchen?

Yes.

Perhaps that's where the water comes from?

Yes, I think there's only water in the kitchen.

How do they keep the house warm?

Fires.

Is there a fire in every room?

Yes.

Even the bedrooms?

Yes.

Is there a fire in your bedroom?

Yes.

What about outside the house, have they got any other buildings?

He has horses, there are no buildings near the front of the house, it's very tidy. Round to the right at the back are a lot of long low buildings and its untidy round there, lots of stuff.

Do they go hunting?

Perhaps that's why they go riding, I don't know much about hunting.

Do you ever see groups of people on horses?

Well they travel two or three at a time but not big groups.

Any dogs?

I think there are dogs, they're his dogs and they are not allowed in her room.

Are they allowed in the house?

No.

They stay somewhere near the stables, outside?

I think so, he's a funny man.

What makes you say that?

He's got all that, and he's got a temper on him.

Perhaps if he's got money he hasn't got any patience?

Well, she won't stand for it.

Do you know about their history, where the money came from and where Mr Lett went?

He's not been here for a long time, they had the house built a long time ago. I don't know what they had before. She's English.

Do they have anywhere special to be buried; do they have a place reserved in the church?

I don't know what church they go to.

Have they ever done anything special with their money, bought anything in the town or donated something special?

I think that's right but I'm looking, I think there's a fund but there's not a building, a charity fund but not a place.

Is the fund a general one or is it supposed to help somebody in particular?

Particular I think.

Do you know what kind of people it is?

Widows.

Is that because Mrs Lett is a widow?

Could be.

At this point I took the focus off Mary and asked Jenny to move to different times and see if other memories/lifetimes could be found. This would be useful in terms of seeing if anything more significant could be found, testing the chronology of memories in general and at the same time breaking the focus on Mary to make it more difficult to 'weave' a story if imagination was at play. We did reveal several 'lives' but these are not included here because we did not visit them often enough to justify research.

A few weeks passed before the next session.

Mary - Session 4

Back to around 1918.
Where are you Mary?
Wooden room.
You're in a wooden room, what room is this, are you at home or
somewhere else?
Somewhere else, in a loft.
What are you doing in a loft?
I don't know.
Is there anybody with you?
No.
Why have you gone into a loft?
I don't think I should be here/
Whose loft is it?
The Letts.
That's where you work?
Mmm
What's in there, what do they keep in the loft?
There's not a lot, there's some hard wood and a chest.
What's in the chest?
Sort of sawdust, long bits.
What do they do with this room?
I don't know, not a lot.
Why have you gone in there, are you cleaning it?
I only meant to look.
Where should you be at the moment?
Upstairs.
Can you read?
Yes.
Do the Letts have a library?
Not a library, they've got books.
Have you ever looked at the books?
No.

Have you seen the covers though?

Yes.

Move to a time when you are looking at the books and tell me any of the titles you can see?

Some words, garden.... it's not very clear.

Never mind, do you have any books at home?

Not many.

What is your favourite book?

I can see one with pictures, its Bible stories but with pictures. That's all I can see, I think it's the only one with pictures.

Have you seen many cars?

Not in the village, not really, not up here.

Do the Letts have one?

I've only seen him with the horses.

Don't they travel very much?

She doesn't, I'm sure they ought to have one but I can't see one, I just see him with the horses.

Who are the other people who work in the house?

There's the cook, she's older than me, she's .... I can't find her name...

Is there anybody else or is it just the two of you?

Only two in the house.

What about outside?

The people who work the farm, there are some who sort the stables, sort the horses, there are not that many horses.

Do they breed horses?

No.

They just keep them to ride?

Yes.

Have you got a boyfriend?

No.

How old are you?

20.

Have you ever had a boyfriend?

No.

Aren't you pretty then?

Alright.

Don't you have the time?

There's only one person here that's... he's too busy, he's not uhh... I'm too busy.

Who are you talking about?

It's not really allowed.

Not Mr Lett?

Mmmm

Really, have you been out with him at all?

No.

Do you think he knows you like him?

No.

Does anybody come to see Mrs Lett, is she ill, she seems not to do very much?

Ladies come.

What about Doctors or people like that?

Yes, there's a Doctor who comes.

What's the name of the Doctor, do you know him?

I just saw a 'D' but then it went. They talk, he's a friend as well and he's a nice man.

What does he bring with him when he comes?

Just his bag and I think he has a car.

Does he, do you know what kind of car it is?

I don't, I see a black car, it's very square, very shiny.

Where does he come from when he visits?

I'm not sure, he comes from the other way to the village, he comes over the hill way.

Is that from the west?

Yes, more or less.

What's over there then, is there a town over there?

There are some more villages first, you can get to Dublin from that way I think, but I'm not sure if he comes from there. I think perhaps... I'm not sure what's over there.

What does he wear, does he wear any clothes that are different from normal people?

Very, very tidy. He has a hat and a black coat, well not it's not quite black, it's dark.

What kind of a hat is it?

It's soft to touch but it's a firm shape with a small brim and a dip in the crown.

What about his legs, what does he wear on his legs?

He wears trousers.

And his shoes?

He wears shoes that stop at the ankle, not boots.

Does he carry anything else as well as the bag?

I'm not quite sure, sometimes I think something else but not something big. Sometimes he carries a paper and he talks about the horses.

How often does he come?

About twice a month.

Is it a regular thing or is he actually called for?

No, he comes.

He just comes regularly, what about in an emergency, if they had to get him quickly what would they do?

I'm not sure, I think she has a phone.

Do you know where that is?

In her room.

In her room, and do you go in there?

No.

You don't go in there at all?

Only to clean.

Do you clean the phone?

Yes.

Does the phone have a number written on it?

713 maybe 4.

Is it just 4 numbers?

I think so, perhaps some more but not in the same line.

7134?

I think so.

And maybe some other numbers as well. What does she have in her room?

She has a carpet that has lots of colours in it and it's nearly white round the edge and it has a fringe on two edges, and a tiny pattern round each edge with colours – a little bit of blue, mostly dark colours against a bit more white-ish, not white, near white, very soft and she has...., it's a narrowish room and she has a fire on the outside wall, on the other side to the door, and it's quite big, it's against the long wall. On the right there's a desk. She sits near the door on the other side with a little table next to her. There's a picture behind her, and you come up to the other end of the room, turn to the left, the room goes back a bit, there's an L-shaped recess and there's books at the end. There are lots of bits of small furniture, she likes little tables with legs like animals. There's no window on the wall with the fire, they're at the ends, quite big windows with stone bits running down between the panes. There's a lot of stuff at the end, the right-hand end, a big plant. It's a funny thing – where she is I don't know if there are not many chairs but everyone seems to stand up in front of her when they are talking to her, she's just by the door and they open the door and they walk in and they stand in front of her. Where are the chairs, there are some but they're a bit far away, perhaps people don't think it's polite.

And does she sleep in this room or another one?

No, there's no bed.

So this is her day room and she stays most of the time?

Her bedroom's almost exactly at the top.

How does she get up to her room, can she walk?

Yes, I think she's not very good though. I think she doesn't like it very much, I see someone helping her up.

Where does she keep her clothes?

In her room.

Do you help her with those?

I don't.

Who helps her with those then?

I don't know, she doesn't like too much fuss.

What about ironing them, do you do them for her?

Yes.

What do you do, how do you do that?

In the kitchen, by the fire, there's ummm.. we keep the iron – one, two three but that's not a very good one – we keep them warm.

You've got three irons and you keep one of them warm, and what do you do with the other two?

One of them you keep warm but it's got a rough edge, it's not really safe, it can tear, but you use one, keep one hot, have a cloth on the ...

The one that's hot you use and while that's being used you heat another one up?

Yes.

I see, and what's the third one for?

Well you're supposed to have two heating but I can't use that one, it's not...

Oh, because it's rough?

Yes.

How about washing, do you do the washing, do you wash her clothes?

I hang them out so I must wash them.

What do you use to wash them?

All I can see is just a lot of mess and there seems to be stuff everywhere. It's off the kitchen, there's um..., it's actually not a very nice room. You just use loads of soap and sometimes, some of the things - you have to be a bit careful with them.

Does she buy new clothes very often?

Not now, she doesn't really have to, she's got lots.

How's your father?

He's alright.

Does he still work or has he stopped?

He had a problem with work, he's not working much, he's working a bit but I don't think he's very happy about it.

Do you see him very often?

I always see him when I'm not here.

Does he give you Christmas presents or Birthday presents?

I'm not sure.

When is your Birthday?

August.

Which day in August?

Two.

Second?

Yes.

And which year were you born in?

98.

So, August the second, 1898. Alright, just relax, relax and come forward a little way, to your wedding day, and come to the point where you and Brian are signing your names, can you see that?

Mmm

Can you see the book?

Yes.

Can you read any of the other names in the book?

Dindall it looks like, that's a strange name.

When you write your name, what do you have to write, do you just write your name or do you have to write other things?

Well, there are lines going down in the book and rows going across, and the lines going down are darker. There are several things, I think I just signed it, not much more.

Did somebody put a date in?

Yes.

What's the date on yours?

Date today.

Yes.

It's the 16th of June.

And what year is it?

1922.

16th of June 1922. And does somebody have to witness your signature?

Yes.

Who has witnessed it for you?

It's someone I don't know, someone Brian knows I think.

Do you know what their name is?

Ian.

Was your father at the wedding?

Yes.

Did he give you away?

Yes.

Good, now come forward 10 years, where are you now?

I'm in the house, but I'm often in the house.

Where are your children?

All over the place.

Are they, how many have you got?

Four.

Four, what are they called?

Cathy.

How old is Cathy?

About 8 or 9.

Who's the next one?

James.

How old is James?

He's nearly two years younger than Cathy.

And who's next in line?

There's another boy, he's not much younger, he's about a year younger, I can only find the English name, it's Henry.

Henry?

Mm, doesn't sound quite right.

And what's your other one, your fourth one?

It's a little girl.

And what's her name?

She is another Mary.

Another Mary, I see, and is she just little?

Mmm, well she's 3 or 4.

How's your father?

He doesn't work.

Doesn't he?

He's alright though, he's always got a joke.

Does he drink?

He doesn't drink too much.

What does he drink when he does drink?

Whisky when he can get it.

Is it short?

Well it is a bit dear.

How much would you pay for a bottle of Whisky then?

I don't know, something more than a Sherry.

Where would he get that?

Well I don't see it in the village shop but I think they could get it.

Does he buy it in bottles or does he just buy it by the glass?

I see him drinking in the house.

So he must have a few bottles then, does he ever get Potcheen?

Don't know about that.

No, or Porter, do you know what Porter is?

No.

Do you ever go into pubs?

I don't.

Session ended.

Mary – Session 5

Jenny was very quietly spoken in this one and I had difficulty hearing some of the recording so apologies for the occasional omission. After the event it is not often possible to go back.

Going straight to Mary at the age of 23.

Tell me what you see
It's busy, there's a lot going on
What's busy? Tell me about it
We are working to finish a dress.
What is the dress for?
A wedding
A wedding, which wedding?
My wedding
Your wedding! When is that going to be?
1921
What date?
June the 16th
June 16th you are going to get married. Who are you getting married to?
Brian
And what is Brian's last name, what's going to be your new name?
O'Neill.
Where is the marriage going to take place?
The reception is here
What, in your house?
No
Oh, so what is here then?
The dress makers, we will be at the church
So it will be in the church in Malahide
Yes
Which church will it be?
 St Mary's.

Who is going to perform the ceremony?

Michael

Where are you going to live after you marry?

There's a cottage, there's a man who owns it and you work for him.

Is that where Brian is going to work?

Yes, he sorted that out

So he's going to work for this man. What sort of thing is he going to do?

He works with timber so it must be something including that

Where are you living now?

Back with my father

And where does your father live, what is your address?

I'm not sure, it's something like Dowers hill cottage. It is a short name.

And what does your father do?

He is in farming, it's a small farm, with sheep

Where's your mother?

She died

When did she die, do you remember what year it was?

1908

What did she die from?

There were some problems and she had a stroke.

Tell me about your brothers and sisters

No sisters, just brothers

What are their names, and ages?

Maybe Charlie, Peter, Shaun (answers not really audible)

Do they have jobs?

(answers not audible)

Are they coming to the wedding?

(answers not audible)

What will happen at the wedding, will there be a big celebration?

(answers not audible)

Do you still work?

No, I'm not sure what happened, something went wrong and it stopped.

What happened to the house then, have they left?

No, they're still there but um...

The lady is on her own is she?

I assume she is, I don't know

She doesn't need any help, do you think? What was their name?

Lett

And there was a woman and her son?

Richard

And do you know what her first name was?

Lottie

That's an unusual name, or is it a good Irish name?

She isn't Irish

Isn't she, where does she come from?

She's English

And you're getting married in June are you, when is your birthday?

August

What part of august, what day is it?

The 2nd.

When you go to the church to get married, what religion is it?

Protestant

Is Brian a Protestant?

Yes

Are you?

Yes

What's your last name at the moment?

O'Donnell **(up to now her name was Sullivan)**

Where did you go to school when you were small?

There's a room in the village, just a few children

And what year is it now?

1921

Do you know who the King of England is?

George something

Do you know which George it is, there have been a few Georges?

George 4th or 5th

Is there anything in the news at the moment that's worth talking about?

There's always trouble somewhere else

In Dublin?

Yes

Do you ever go to Dublin?
No
Do you remember telling me about Mrs Lett and her boy, what happened to Mr Lett?
I don't know, I never met him
You never met him. Do you think he used to be there at one stage?
Yes, I'm sure
How many children do you want?
I don't know
Haven't you thought about that? There's no danger of you uh... you're not having one now are you?
She is quiet
Is that anything to do with why you're getting married or are you just getting married because you love each other?
We want to be married
And you're not pregnant?..... Are you not sure?.....Are you living at the moment with your father?
Yes
And what's your father's full name
Two names, something – not clear
And what is his last name
O'Donnell
Do you know anyone called Sullivan?
Yes
Who do you know called Sullivan?
(answers not audible)

Come forward one year, where are you now?
(Sounds like) Rope prayer frame?
In the cottage?
Yes
Do you have any family?
Yes
What have you got?
A little girl

What's her name?
Cathy
When was she born?
February
She was born in February was she, can you tell me when her birthday is?
2nd
2nd of February, and you were married in August?
In June
In June, oh. What happens in August then?
My Birthday
That's your birthday. So you were married in June and your daughter was born in February, that's about right isn't it? Is she pretty?
Mmm
How old is she now?
She's a couple of months
Is she any trouble?
No, she's a good girl
Has she been ill at all, are there any problems?
No
That's good

Come forward 10 years now, where are you?
Outside
Going somewhere or just outside?
I must be going somewhere, I've got a smart coat on
It's a smart coat is it, are you alone?
I can't see anyone
Where are your children?
In school I think
How big is your family now, how many children have you got?
Some boys and some girls
What are the boys names?
James and Henry
How old is James?
About 9 or 10

Are they both the same age?
No
Oh, how old is the other one?
Henry is a bit younger
Is there anybody else, anybody even younger?
(answers not audible)
How old do you think she is
(answers not audible)
Yes, there's another girl
What's her name?
Sarina (or something like that)
How old is she?
(answers not audible)
And how old is Cathy now?
Oh gosh, 10 maybe
And then who is the next oldest?
And then Mary
(answers no longer audible)

As this session closed (in mid 1988) I suggested that we should stop for a while as I felt it was becoming a strain for her and because we should not realistically expect to discover more useful information. Jenny told me that because she felt compelled to discover what had happened to the children she was likely to follow some enquiries she had made in Ireland and I also felt that this may have a negative impact on the value of what we had achieved.

If you read her book you will see that starting in 1988 she made contact with several agencies in Ireland and visited Malahide in June 1989. Someone she met told her about a family called Sutton and that the mother had died in the 1930's leaving a number of children. This became the focus of her search and led to a remarkable and positive sequence of events as in September 1990 she met Mary Sutton's first son and later met others from the family, being instrumental in re-uniting them many years after they had been parted after Mary Sutton had died.

The development of Jenny's book took some time after this and was published in 1993.

Jenny and I met again several times in late 1993/4. We did not investigate Mary but at Jenny's request spent some time examining future 'lives'. You can read about them in her 1996 book "Past Lives, Future Lives".

The direction that Jenny took was related to her wish to understand where her dreams had come from and how the situation had ended.

My objective has always been to see whether the information produced by volunteers in regression could be verified.

In my initial version of this book I included this case because it was an important part of my own experience. I dealt with it in the same way as the others and included an analysis of the prominent parts and an overall conclusion.

The more forensic analysis that follows was prompted by contact from Jenny which made me question whether I had done all that I could to provide readers with the best information possible.

Investigating the story

My first step was to create a list of potentially verifiable information from the regression sessions, plus the information I got from Jenny before we began the sessions, and from Jenny's account of her experiences in the book "Yesterdays Children". It was also necessary to research the Sutton family (which had no part in any of the regression material) to substantiate or otherwise the claim that this was the family that Jenny was a part of in a previous life.

I used the following resources to check what I could:
- Census.nationalarchives.ie Irish household/street data 1901 and 1911
- Civilrecords.irishgenealogy.ie where records of Births 1864 to 1919/Marriages 1845 to 1944/Deaths 1878 to 1969 are available
- OSi.ie > geohive.maps.arcgis.com Ordnance Survey Ireland for maps from 1829, 1841,1897,1913
- Malahideheritage.com   for photographs about 100 years old
- The Irish Historical Picture Company - again for old photographs
- Google Maps for current maps and calculating distances

It must be noted that almost none of this was available in 1989 so Jenny did not have the opportunity to research in the way that I have.

Anyone can use these sources and find the same information that I found.

Historical data is not perfect. Not every birth was registered, not everyone completed census forms or did so correctly or perhaps even truthfully, people emigrated and immigrated or were not in their own home on census day and it seems that not everyone was sure of their age or that of their children. Research is hard but we do what we can.

There are five specific information sources relevant to this investigation.

1. The regressions that I conducted with Jenny.
2. The letter describing her dreams that I asked Jenny to provide before we began using hypnotic regression.
3. Thoughts that came to Jenny when she was awake and which are described in the early part of her book.
4. Information Jenny found on visiting Ireland and afterwards until her book was written. This is covered in her book.
5. Research I was able to carry out in 2020 because records from the period had become available.

In my analysis I have drawn information from these sources together in order to focus on the areas of main interest.

One major point to hold in your mind is that there was no reference at all to Mary Sutton until she was suggested as a possible fit to Jenny during her own research. Neither she nor any part of her history was mentioned in dreams, letters, regressions or flashbacks. She was, of course, a real person so information about her was easier to find.

At the time the regressions were conducted the census records and those for births, marriages, deaths and other data was either not available or extremely difficult to reach, so it is no surprise that at the time neither I nor Jenny was able to discover anything about the people she mentioned.

Very little detail was produced anyway, with the only usable names being for Mary Sullivan, Bryan O'Neill, their children Cathy, Henry, James and Mary and in the first regression Mrs Lett and her son (who she named as Richard in session 2). The only places named by Jenny were Malahide (to which she was 'drawn' whilst map reading in childhood) and Dublin.

In regression research the first thing I would normally seek to discover is whether the person being recalled was real. So that is where I began in 2020.

Looking for Mary Sullivan

In the first regression session she gave her name as Mary Sullivan so I began by trying to find her.

There are thousands of Mary Sullivans in Ireland and without details like parent names and locations it is impossible to search specifically. The 1901 census shows 604 Mary Sullivans aged between 1 and 8.

Trying to trace an individual is always problematic but particularly so in Ireland, where the 1911 census reveals that one in every five females was named Mary – approximately 450,000. Looking at birth records showed that in each year between 1895 and 1900 about 11,000 baby girls were named Mary.

I made no assumption that Malahide would be correct so my searches initially covered all of Ireland.

Here is a birth record for Mary Sullivan born 2.8.1898 matching the date given in regression

But she died on 22.11.1899 aged 15 months.

Jenny's dream provided no maiden name but suggested a married name of O'Brian. The 1911 census records only 3 O'Brians in Ireland but 13 O'Bryans and 4,447 O'Briens so it is much more likely to be O'Brien. Between 1915 and 1923 there were 3,856 O'Brien marriages (including spellings O'Bryan and O'Brian) and taking just those in 1923 as a sample there were nine where the bride was named Mary so I estimate that of the 3,856 around 350 would involve a Mary.

This wedding is a close fit but it is not Brian and not in June. They also seem to have mixed up the fathers.

Spreading the net to cover 1920 to 1924 and possible name confusions would have meant examining 1,200 O'Neill (which came up later in regression 1), 1,200 O'Brien and 1,600 O'Sullivan marriages (including spellings like O'Brian, O'Bryan, Sullivan etc).

I did do a considerable amount of searching but came to realize that whilst I may get some close matches there was not enough information to allow confidence in any of the results.

The most specific information relates to Mary's death which at the end of session 1 is given as 1937. I searched more widely and death records show that between 1929 and 1940 thirty-six Mary O'Briens aged between 30 and 40 died. Fifteen were spinsters and one was a widow.

Tuberculosis (TB) was a major cause of death but at least three died of a haemorrhage after premature childbirth. Death records do not give the maiden name but most give the occupation (often "wife of a labourer") and the husband's occupation where applicable.

If she died in the 1930's at the age of about 35 then it may be possible to link a death record with birth, marriage, census and other records to get to information about other family members and generally about the life.

Most death records only give the name of the deceased (and this being the married name if married), the location or residence at time of death, the age or estimated age, and the cause of death, plus very rarely for married people the name of the spouse.

The lack of maiden name makes it very difficult to trace to a marriage certificate which if found would add such details as the location of the wedding, addresses and occupations of the bride and groom, the bride's maiden name, bride and groom's fathers names and occupations, plus some witness names that may be relatives.

I did manage to establish links in this way to six marriages and two births in which a Mary married an O'Brien but this is a very small fraction of the potential total. The next useful piece of information would be the names of any children from the marriage.

Records of children that are said to be born are not available through online sources for 100 years unless they died young (then they are in available death records) so this cannot be checked without proof of a relationship.

The marriages I managed to link to all took place after 1920 so I could not trace any children. I did establish that on average nine children per year were born in an O'Brian family in Ireland.

Pause for a moment to consider - the last three pages illustrate why it is so important to gather much more information about the life history, geography and relationships connected to a regression experience before attempting any research. The regressions were intended to seek out such information but Jenny did not want to pursue these.

I also made notes about 400 or so Mary Sullivans listed in the 1901 and 1911 census' that would be about the right age. Whilst doing this I saw that there was a very distinct geographical pattern in at least some Irish surnames.

More than 85% of 31,000 Sullivans were from the south west whilst 50% of 17,000 O'Neills were from the north east (particularly the six counties of what is now Northern Ireland).

I also discovered that searches such as this are confounded by the fact that several thousand census entries can be listed with no name, or a ?, or initials. These relate to people that were stationed in barracks as part of the military or the police, those in hospitals, workhouses, orphanages, asylums, prisons and convents. The names may not have been recorded either for security or personal privacy reasons or simply because the writing was not clear but it means that some people that existed can't be found in census records.

Looking for Bryan (or Brian) O'Neill

This is not a common forename in Ireland. It is more usual to use saint names like John, Patrick, James or Michael. In fact taking 1879 to 1895 only three of 13,452 O'Neills were named Bryan but there were over 1,000 Johns.

Again, without more detail a search is very arduous.

There was a Bryan O'Neill Driscoll that was a private in the East African Mounted Rifles from 8.8.1914 until decorated and discharged unfit on 22.7.1919 and awarded a Victory medal for service as a 2nd Lieutenant in the Royal Field Artillery on 8.6.1922

Not related but it shows what can be discovered

No other Birth, Marriage or Death information about this man, but....

On Dec 3rd 1898 a Bryan O'Neill was sent to prison in Louth (Ireland) for 7 days for assault.

On April 23rd 1900 Bryan O'Neill was sent to prison in Louth (Ireland) for 7 days for being drunk in charge of a horse.

They are probably the same man, a carpenter living in Tullykeel, Louth.

The 1901 census has a 30 year old Farm Steward listed, about right and one of just four in all of Ireland.

Alone in his 3 room house he looks after 25 buildings for Denis Brown. The buildings make up the largest farm in the area.

Things soon change as in the 1911 census he is 38, has been married for seven years to Elizabeth and has five sons (one of them is a two year old called Bryan). He now lives in a different house (four rooms, no buildings) and someone else manages the farm.

Another of the Bryans came from Wexford and was 46 in 1901. A third was from Kilkenny and was 68. In the 1911 census the first was 56 and the other was not listed but there was a new one, aged 70 and from Kilkenny. Finally came a 13 year old Bryan O'Neill in the 1901 census, living in Carlow with his parents and seven siblings. I found records of his birth, marriage, address, family names and that he was not in the 1911 census so may have left the country.

Interesting and distracting it certainly is but none of these Bryans is the one we seek.

Looking for Mary O'Neill

If Mary O'Sullivan married Bryan O'Neill she would be Mary O'Neill and records may still be found.

Deaths recorded from 1929 to 1940 show eighteen Mary O'Neills aged between 30 and 40. Of these eight were spinsters, three died of TB, three of heart failure and four were accidents or unspecified.

Trying to be exhaustive I ran a similar search for Mary O'Brien in case names were confused in Jenny's mind. I found a few records that led me to dig deeper but with the same result – there was not enough corroborative evidence to provide confidence in a link.

You may recall that in session 5 Jenny gave a different surname – O'Donnell. In session 1 she said the Malahide Butcher was called O'Donnell and I always felt that this was just a slight confusion. In spite of this I did search using this name but had similar results so I have not included the details here.

Looking for the Lett household

One of the first things Mary said was that she worked for the Lett family in about 1915. In summary, when she was 17 she worked in a big house, which belonged to the Lett family. There was an oldish, smart woman and her son Richard (who Mary liked). He rode horses and was about 30. They had been better off in the past. Mary lived in a room at the top of the house (possibly attic space), alone. There was also a cook. They had animals (horses, dogs, cattle, sheep and chickens) and people to tend them. They also grew vegetables.

It was a smart three storey house with several rooms on each floor. Outside at the back there was a range of buildings but none at the front. She said that Mr Lett had not been there for a long time. The house was built a long time ago. The woman was a widow and was English.

She also said the house was "out from the village where her father lives, which might be Boscottle". A quick Google search eliminated Boscottle, the closest match being Boscastle in Cornwall, England.

Armed with this information I set out to identify potential households.

Fortunately Lett is not a common name in Ireland. The census of 1911 has 111 people with the surname Lett and they are in 46 households, mainly in Wexford with a few in Dublin. I looked at all of their details and after eliminating those whose homes were too small, or that had no servants, or where occupation was clearly not compatible, I was left with just one.

The Lett household

In 1911 this was a family of five, the head being Anastasia (a widow aged 63) with a son called Richard aged 31, plus another son and two daughters. They employed ten people.

The property was a hotel and general merchant but in addition to its 20 rooms there were 28 outbuildings for horses, other animals and storage, details of which are shown a couple of pages further on.

In the 1901 census there were six in the family as Anastasia's husband Robert was alive and aged 75. Robert also owned 23 other buildings which were not owned by the Letts in 1911 so perhaps they had needed to sell them after his death to support a restructured business.

According to this Robert Lett was born in 1826 but he died on 2.12.1901 aged 78 so could have been born in 1823. There is probably an entry for his birth in parish records but I don't really need to find it.

Also Anastasia Lett is shown as 50 so would have been born in 1851 but she died 26.4.1917 aged 70 so could have been born in 1847 or 1848.

In the 1911 census her age was shown as 63 so that would confirm 1848.

Robert Lett and Anastasia Murphy married on 30.5.1876. He was a widower and hotel keeper.

Richard was born on 18.1.1880.

In the 1901 census Richard was described as a farmer but by 1911 was managing the business.

He died a bachelor on 3.11.1915 aged 34 of TB at The Dell, a short distance west of Ferns. He had become a farmer again.

Searching all Irish records this is the <u>only</u> Richard Lett that can fit the case.

Mary had described some discussion between Richard and his mother, perhaps he moved away to farm as a result.

More about the Lett business and its location

The preceding information shows that they lived in Ferns, County Wexford.

The 1901 census lists 115 houses in Ferns Town, on 8 pages, so I just show the 8th page here which includes the Letts.

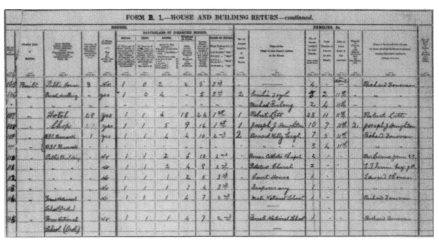

No 107 is a hotel with 23 rooms and 28 outbuildings owned by Robert Lett. An associated form shows that the additional buildings were mainly related to farmwork.

(these figures actually come from the 1911 census because the 1901 page is missing, there are still 28 outbuildings)

Census information does not reveal addresses. The numbers are references and not house numbers but it is possible to estimate house location based on the surrounding buildings.

No 108 is next door and is a shop with 10 rooms and 29 outbuildings, owned by Joseph Haughton, who also owns 10 small houses.

No 109 is the Royal Irish Constabulary Barracks, 10 rooms. Next on the list are two churches, the Court House, a dispensary and the boys and girls schools.

Going the other way, 106 is a house, 105 is a pub with no occupants, 104 is a shop with 9 rooms, then two houses and at No 101 is another pub.

At 86 is a 26 room hotel with 23 outbuildings, owned by John Bolger. 70 is a pub with 14 rooms and 17 outbuildings, owned by Edward O'Connor. 57 is the Post Office. 55 is a pub of 11 rooms owned by Aiden Foley. 33, 34 and 6 are pubs and 4 is a spirit grocer.

The 1911 census shows (now referenced as house 38 on Mainstreet) the Letts business ten years later, five family members and now ten servants/employees who reside there. Eldest son Richard has become the manager.

It can also be seen that one housemaid is 19, which means she was born in 1892 – and her name is Mary.
Here is her marriage certificate.

In regression Mary Sullivan worked for the Lett family from 1914, perhaps replacing this Mary?

The 1911 census lists 53 buildings on Mainstreet, starting with a Public House owned by Mrs White but occupied by Aiden Foley, an unoccupied house, two shops, then 12 very small houses owned by George Chapman, and the Post Office.

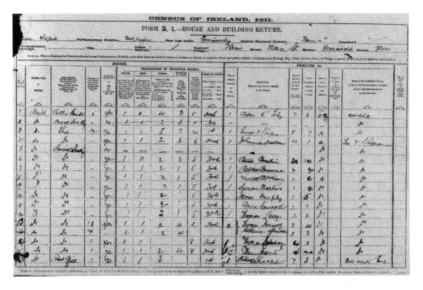

Starting from building 17 we now see another Pub (occupied by Edward O'Connor), the Courthouse, Dispensary, and 12 more small houses.

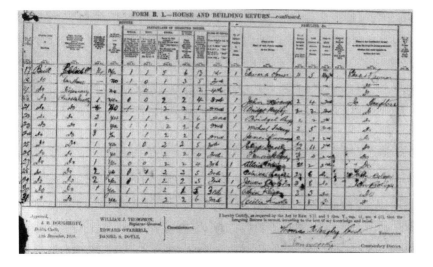

From building 32 we have a small house, followed by several large houses and at 38 the Letts 20 room house. Next is another pub occupied by James Doyle and owned by Richard Donovan (who owns 8 of the properties), then a shop, two small houses, and another pub.

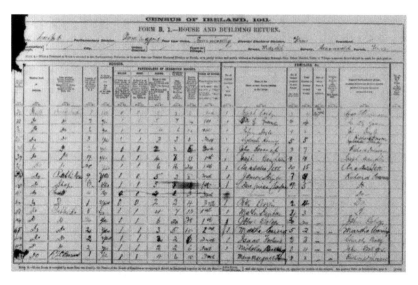

House 44 is shown as a private house owned by John Bolger but it has 30 rooms with 20 residents. The next 4 are moderate houses, then an RIC (Royal Irish Constabulary) Barracks.

Finally building 49 is a school house and then there are 3 medium houses and a shop owned by Richard Donavan.

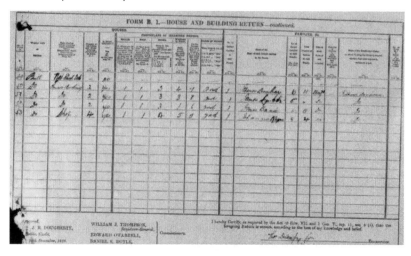

This information from both census years can be used to reveal locations.

The 1840 OSi map of Ferns shows substantial buildings on the lower road, called Fernstown in the 1901 census and Mainstreet in 1911.

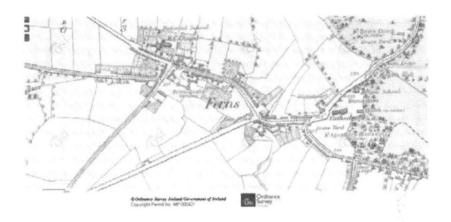

The 1913 OSi map shows significant change and building around the hotel (housing the tenants?). There is also a new hotel on the opposite side of Main Road to the east. The Church, Post Office, RIC barracks, Court house, dispensary, Schools, and hotels are labelled. I added the numbers.

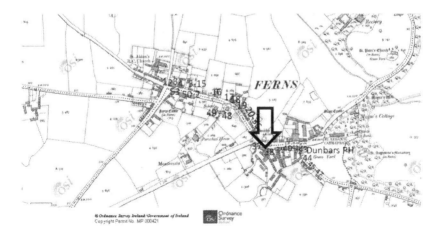

In Ferns, the Letts hotel and business is now O'Laughlin's public house. On mapping sites you will see it is a large two storey building but there will be rooms in the attic as well.

A little more about the Bolgers. House 44 is Bolgers Merchant shop.

The household return form only shows 15 of the 20 people living at 44 but clearly it is a significant General Merchant run and owned by John Bolger (who also owns the houses 28 to 31 and 47).

The 1911 census reveals that the Letts no longer own any other property so may have sold it to support the hotel and shop (Mary Sullivan said things had become worse for them as "they don't have the land").

There was clearly a link between the Letts and the Bolgers and Patrick Lett married Margaret Bolger in January 1914.

We cannot complete all the links in the story but a lot that was said by Mary Sullivan about the Letts was true.

New Lives, Old Souls 259

Turning now to Mary Hand/Sutton

Hopefully you will recall that Mary Sutton was identified by someone Jenny contacted after her visit to Malahide in early June 1989.

In Autumn one of her contacts informed her of a Mr Mahon who owned buildings on Swords Road, which she had decided was the location of the house she felt she had lived in. She wrote to ask him if he knew of a family that lived on that road with at least five children whose mother died in the 1930s. He replied that the only woman fitting that description was a Mrs Sutton, who had been married to a soldier and whose children were sent to orphanages after her death. He also told her that the husband had returned to the UK to train soldiers in the 2nd world war.

This set Jenny down the track of trying to find this family rather than the one she had remembered.

I needed to carry out my own research.

Finding out about the Suttons, which is not easy even though we know they existed.

Mary Sutton's life

Jenny was told about Mary Sutton dying in the 1930s so the trail starts there, and quickly ends as only one person fits the profile.

She died on 24.10.1932 at the Rotunda Hospital, Dublin. She lived at Gaybrook with John, a labourer. She was 35 so born around 1896/7.

As I said earlier a marriage certificate would give her maiden name so that a birth certificate could be found. In addition a marriage certificate will give her father's name and occupation and other useful information that helps in a search for her early life.

She could have married between 1912 and 1932.

There were 20 John Sutton marriages in that period, three to a Mary.

One was on 20.2.1924 to Mary Murphy and she gave her age as 21 so would have been 29 in 1932 so too young.

One was on 21.4.1918 to Mary Dunne and she was a widow aged 27 so would have been 41 in 1932 so too old.

The last was on 22.7.1917 to Mary Hand.

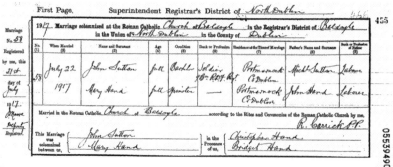

She did not give her age so I needed a way to get a birth date and to confirm it was the right person.

Her father is a labourer called John.

The witnesses are Mary's family members.

Her husband John is a soldier of unknown age whose father is a labourer called Michael. He and Mary both live in Portmarnock which is 2 miles south of Malahide. We will look for him later.

In the 1901 census there were six Mary Hands aged from 4 to 6.

I found the birth records and all the mothers were called Mary, three of the fathers were called John.

I found this one that was not in the census

Born 29.4.1896 in Castleblayney Workhouse, near Ballybay and the N.I. Border. John and Mary Hand (related?). She would be 4 yrs 11 months on the 1901 census so perhaps round up to 5?

I looked at all the census records. One had Bridget and Christy as family members (they witnessed the marriage later).

The Catholic household that Mary Hand at five seems part of in 1901.

Father John was born (if correct) in 1857/8, mother Mary in 1855/6, sister Alice in 1889/90, brother Christy in 1891/2, sister Bridget in 1893/4, Mary herself in 1895/6 and brother Michael in 1898/9.

Father is a platelayer on the railway – responsible for maintaining a section of track. They live in house number 15 in the census, other pages in the census tell us more - later.

Placing the Mary Jane record amongst the other Hand children confirms that her birth fits in with the others and she would be five in the 1901 census.

It is worth noticing that all the writing is done by the registrar and that the last four are all by the same one. These are not John or Mary's signatures.

The first two children were born in Kinsealy (sometimes called Kinsaley) but Bridget, Mary Jane and Michael John were born in Portmarnock after the family moved there in 1892 (roughly).

Mary's parents lived in Kinsaley (1 mile west of Portmarnock) and married on 27.11.1888 in Baldoyle (2 miles south east of Portmarnock).

Strangely, Baldoyle is close to Sutton, on the way to Howth.

St Dolough's is a church 1 mile south of Kinsaley. Everything is very local.

The birth certificates and census records tell us that Bridget, Mary and Michael were born in Portmarnock and they all live there but it would be good to know at which house.

Form B of the 1901 census shows that Thomas Plunkett owns most property but that John Hand lives with six others in the property labelled as 15 which is a three room dwelling house in Portmarnock owned by the Northern Railway. The building labelled 19 is Portmarnock Station and 20 is Portmarnock Church.

The 1911 census shows that Mary Hand grew up in Portmarnock

The main residence (18 on the 1911 list, 1 in 1901) is Portmarnock House, where the Plunketts live.

Almost every house is still owned by the Plunkett family.

I saw that there was a Nicholas Sutton in the 3rd house listed but a search showed no son called John, though his 35 year old wife was Mary.

I wondered if John might be related and lived there at the time he wed Mary but no Nicholas marriage or birth certificates exist so I can't tell if his father was called Michael.

The building labelled 11 is Portmarnock Church and 17 is Portmarnock Station. Remember that the reference numbers are not house numbers.

The additional buildings form shows No 18 to have 24 buildings for stabling and farming.

The Hand family of five live in the 21st house counted which is a four room house in Portmarnock not said to be owned by the Northern Railway but by the Plunketts.

A closer look at the Plunketts and Portmarnock

The Portmarnock area in 1840

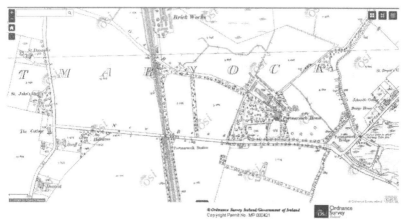

The Plunketts owned the very successful brickworks, supplying building materials for many Irish houses that would be built in coming years.

The Portmarnock area in 1913

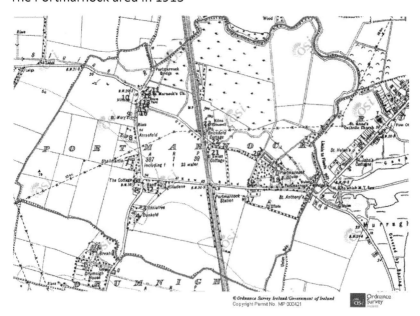

Significantly more housing can be seen in Burrow (to the east).

The numbers are my estimates about which house is which in 1911.
Perhaps the Hand family lived at Swiss Cottage.

Home of the Plunkett family, Portmarnock House burned down in the
1950's.

Portmarnock House

Could it be that this is where 'Mary' worked as a maid around 1912 to
1917? Jenny named Lett but did she mean to say Plunkett? That is quite a
stretch and the evidence does not fit Plunkett anyway. This house is also
very much larger than the Lett house Mary described.

The 1901 census shows three staff and no sons.

Further searching for a Richard Plunkett found none near Portmarnock.

In 1911 a family of five (no sons). Maud is listed so was perhaps just away in 1901. There are four live-in staff, none of whom are farmers.

Age is variable – Thomas has aged 14 years in just 10. Elizabeth is not "very old" as Mary described Mrs Lett.

Thomas and 'Lizzie' married in 1876

Thomas Luke Plunkett died on 28.9.1927 at Portmarnock House, aged 77, married. If Mary had been a servant there she would have known of him.

Birth and death records for wife Elizabeth were not found but -

Thomas left his wife and daughter well off. So she was still alive in 1927.

PLUNKETT Thomas Luke otherwise Thomas of Portmarnock House Portmarnock **Dublin** died 28 September 1927 Probate **London** 24 January to Elizabeth Plunkett widow and Elizabeth Plunkett spinster. Effects £28466 10s. 2d.

Daughter Elizabeth died in 1948, never married.

Elizabeth was Irish. They were both at Portmarnock House well after the period when Mary Sullivan worked for the Lett family so –
this was not the Letts.

What of the other Plunkett girls?

The census suggests Caroline was born in 1880. Actually 1879.

She married in 1919.

The other daughter, Maud, was born in 1885 and was at home in 1911

I found no other certificates for either but they were left nothing in Thomas' will so had they died by 1927? Another mystery.

Back to the Suttons

This is the Sutton family at house 3

Perhaps John was a relative of Nicholas and visited?

There were no Suttons listed here in 1901.

Clearly a second marriage for them both in 1909 (it says they have been married 2 years), Nicholas bringing four children and Mary (Griffin?) bringing three.

We may conjecture that John Sutton was living or staying with this family when he married Mary Hand in 1917 but Nicholas would be 54 by then so could have been an uncle but without significantly more research I am not able to find a connection.

The household that Mary Hand at 15 was part of in 1911.

Father John was born in 1855/6, mother Mary in 1855/6, sister Alice is not there and as shown John and Mary had 5 children but only 4 are alive – Alice died but her death certificate was elusive until I discovered she was listed as Mary.

Brother Christy is also gone and would be 19. Sister Bridget is now 17 so born in 1893/4, Mary herself is 15 so born 1895/6 and brother Michael is 12 so born in 1898/9.

All correct apart from father who is now two years younger than he should be. He is still a platelayer on the railway. He and Mary married in 1888/9.

Daughters Bridget and Mary are not shown to be scholars or to have jobs. At age 15 years and 5 months Mary was not a maid.

Linking to John Sutton

Referring back to the marriage certificate Mary Hand/ John Sutton married on July 22nd 1917. She had no job.

He is a soldier in the RDF (Royal Dublin Fusiliers, 9th Battalion), age unknown except that John and Mary are both over 21 ("Full").

Mary's father is John Hand. John's father is Michael Sutton.

John may have been based with the RDF at Devoy Barracks, Naas, 20 miles south west of Dublin so how they met in Portmarnock is unknown.

If you are interested, there is a lot of history on the RDF fighting in the Great War but that is not of relevance here.

They all live in Portmarnock, which is two miles south of Malahide.

They married in Baldoyle, which is 1.9 miles south of Portmarnock, at St Peter & St Paul Roman Catholic Church

Mary's siblings Christopher and Bridget were witnesses so alive in 1917.

Jenny was told they lived with her parents for a few years in Kinsaley, which is 1.7 miles west of Portmarnock. Her parents lived in Portmarnock at that time so this is wrong.

Finding John Sutton

Which John Sutton?

Searching for John Sutton's birth with Michael as father, a labourer, between 1880 and 1902 produced three birth certificates

Number one

Chapel Lane, New Ross is 75 miles south of Portmarnock but father is Michael and a labourer and John would be 20 at the wedding. Perhaps Mary was named after mother-in-law?

Michael Sutton and Mary Curran of New Ross were married on 13.4.1896 and John was born seven months later.

Number two

Born 1.7.1883 in Dublin North. Father Michael is a labourer. John would be 34 at his wedding.

I could not find a marriage certificate for this one.

Number three

Born 9.7.1881 at 136 James St, Dublin South but father Michael is a Vanman and John would be 36 at his wedding.

Michael Sutton of 39 James St, Dublin S. (now a labourer) and Grace Marsden were married on 10.5.1874 and John was born seven years later.

Searching for John Sutton's death as a widower between 1931 and 1969 (later records not accessible) I only found one record. He died on 27.11.1967 in Thurles (85 miles south west of Malahide), a 73 year old (so born around 1894) who never married. Circumspect but perhaps he moved closer to his birthplace and did not want to admit the history so told people he was single? Or perhaps this is not him and he went to the UK as Jenny was told but I could not find him there either.

I thought Number one was the most likely John Sutton as he would be 20 at the wedding. They probably are his parents but sadly I then found this:-

He died of TB five months later. This Mary seems confused and put her husband's occupation in. Bullawn is a three minute walk from Chapel Lane, where he was born.

Searching for John Sutton in army records I found this possibility.

He signed up on 13.10.1914 for the 9th Royal Dublin Fusiliers. This matches John and Mary Sutton's marriage certificate.

He was 34, single and a labourer from Dublin. It says he was born in the parish of Cabinteely, south east of Dublin but perhaps he didn't really know.

This would mean he was born in 1880 and aged 37 when he married Mary.

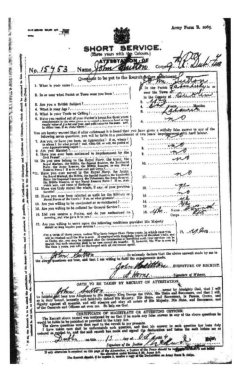

Close enough to be the second or third birth I found but more evidence is needed to be sure.

John Sutton is very elusive.

At around this point you may be thinking that it would be good to be able to link various pieces of information together without relying on relatives names and ages to be found. With many people sharing similar names the one thing that could help would be the signatures on marriage certificates, death certificates, armed forces documents and so on.

Unfortunately most documents available on-line are copies completed by an official looking at the original so handwriting is unlikely to be that of the desired individual.

The signature on this document is a little different from the names written elsewhere on it so perhaps it is authentic.

I searched widely but could not find a credible record of John Sutton. I think he is the soldier above but nothing else seems to exist.

A couple of points about the census. It was distributed by the Police and meant to be completed by heads of households but I believe often the Police actually completed it. In 1911 Anastasia (Lett) was spelled Anastatia and I can't imagine that she got it wrong herself. Also looking at the handwriting in 1901 and 1911 for several households shows significant differences. A further problem, though perhaps not a large one is that the suffragette movement encouraged women to refuse to participate so some are missing.

The next step is to try and find out -

Who lived at Gaybrook Lodge?

The name Gaybrook has cropped up several times. It is marked on the old maps in the part of Swords Road contained in an area west of Malahide called Yellow Walls.

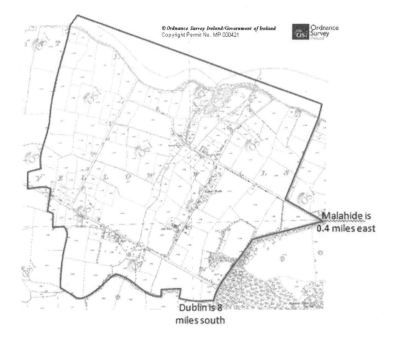

© Ordnance Survey Ireland/Government of Ireland
Copyright Permit No. MP.000421

Ordnance Survey

Malahide is 0.4 miles east

Dublin is 8 miles south

The 1911 census showed 236 people living in 55 houses in Yellow Walls, most of them on the north side of Swords Road.

The census data reveals the names, ages, religion and occupations of people along with the number of rooms in their homes and how many outbuildings they had but it does not include addresses (unless it is a presbytery or similar) so matching occupants to buildings is hard.

I had not found any mention of Gay Brook in the searches I had made, and assumed it was derelict as I knew from current maps that it was knocked down to make way for the current estate. I now needed to find a starting point to identify who occupied the houses, particularly Gay Brook and the Lodge.

Using the census information for large houses with outbuildings it is possible to match some and by inference place the others fairly well. This was not as easy as the same exercise I completed for Ferns.

The 55 houses take four pages in the census. Other pages provide more detail about any outbuildings.

All small houses so far. House 17 has 9 people living in two rooms.

House 26 has 11 rooms, 3 outbuildings and only 2 occupants.

House 29 has 15 rooms, 13 outbuildings and 5 occupants.

33 to 49 are all small houses.

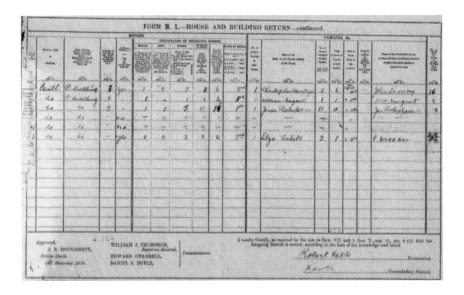

House 52 has 11 rooms, 9 outbuildings and 10 occupants.

The house is owned by 52 year old James Robertson and the household census form shows that he is a seed merchant living with his wife, three daughters and a son. They employ a Governess, a Nurse and two servants.

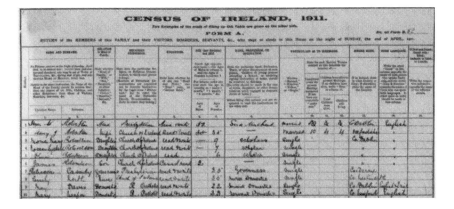

Birth, Marriage, and Death certificates sometimes include parts of an address so I found his death certificate which showed this not to be Gay Brook but La Mancha, which is shown on the map so now I know that house 52 is in the bottom right corner.

There will be more about La Mancha soon.

The other large house was number 29, with 15 rooms and 13 outbuildings, clearly a farm. Mary MacMahon lived there with her family and a servant. The 1901 census shows a husband and two more daughters.

The husband, Edward MacMahon, died at Gaybrook (now not known as Gay Brook, unlike on maps of the time) in unfortunate circumstances on February 22nd 1910.

Mary MacMahon died at Gaybrook on February 23rd 1937, attended by Rose (one of her daughters on the 1901 census, then aged 7).

Thomas MacMahon died at Gaybrook on February 22nd 1959, attended by Rose.

Clearly not a good idea to be at Gaybrook on February 22nd but proof that the family occupied the house for many years.

House 29 was definitely Gaybrook.

The eagle-eyed among you will have spotted that on the census page Mary MacMahon is shown as the owner of house 29 and is also the owner of house 28, lived in by the Rodgers family of seven in 1911. This was brick built, had 2 rooms, 2 front windows, a slate or tile roof and no outbuildings.

Looking at other details I worked out that the other large house (number 26) must be Mill View which is also named on the map. I worked out the route that the census taker must have followed and allocated house numbers to buildings. I have put a few on the map to illustrate this.

Yellow Walls with a selection of deduced house locations

© Ordnance Survey Ireland/Government of Ireland
Copyright Permit No. MP 000421

The Lodge at Gaybrook has to be number 28, owned by the MacMahon family and probably occupied by lodgers or employees until about 1959.

The people living at Gaybrook Lodge in 1911

I wanted to know more about the Rodgers family so I got their household form (a search not helped by the different spelling of the surname).

Thomas (aged 37) was an agricultural labourer (likely to be working for the MacMahons) and with wife Anne (aged 33) they had two sons and three daughters, aged from 9 years to 9 months. They had been married 11 years and had lost no children.

This is Thomas and Anne's marriage certificate. Maggie is her sister (1901 census).

I think a mistake was made about his age on the census, he should be 34.

Their birth certificates show he was almost 2 years older than her.

Turvey is an area a couple of miles north of Swords/Malahide, just west of Donabate.

I wondered where they lived, and discovered her at house 25 in Yellow Walls with her mother but she may be visiting or living there if Thomas is away doing army duties. She has a 3-month old son named James.

I noticed that Ellen is a widow so I looked for her husband's death certificate which must be 1900 as he was at Annie's wedding in August.

I found the certificate but he died on July 22nd, a month before Annie's wedding. They clearly forgot to write "Deceased" on the certificate unless something seriously paranormal was going on.

My next move was to see if house 25 was a large one.

On the relevant 1901 census page we see that it was a two room house with 10 people in it on census night. We also see that it was owned by Edward McMahon of Gaybrook.

The result of this somewhat diversionary searching is that we now see that the Rogers family was well known to the MacMahons and it is likely that when Thomas and Annie wanted a place of their own the MacMahons agreed to rent the Lodge to them.

It is just a matter of context and there may be a link between this and John and Mary Sutton moving to the Lodge. So now I need to know when Ellen Lowery died.

An Ellen Lowery died in Malahide aged 75 (though she could have been 80) on 13/2/1935. Her son John was present and she was the widow of a labourer. I can't be certain that this is the same Ellen but I could not find a better match.

Unfortunately this does not tell me when she left the Lodge so I can't cross reference a time when the Suttons moved in. It was worth a try and has provided some insight into life in Ireland at the time.

I must return to La Mancha

I said I would come back to La Mancha (house number 52).

Here I am reproducing a story from the Irish Times of 1926 which they reprinted in October 2017 and they have given permission for it to be included here.

"When Henry McCabe arrived to work on the gardens at La Mancha, a large country house in Malahide, Co Dublin, he quickly discovered things weren't right.

It was shortly after 8am and smoke billowed from each of the chimneys, but there were no signs that his employers, the McDonnell siblings, were awake.

"It soon seemed to him that the smoke issuing from the top of the house was excessive and he made to go in at the back door," reads a report in The Irish Times a day later, on April 1st, 1926. "He saw flames and other signs that things were not as they should be, and he set off at once for Malahide to call the fire brigade, and, on his way, told men whom he met that the house was on fire."

La Mancha was a prominent building on about 30 acres of "prime land" and was "pleasantly situated and well-kept residence, not of mansion proportions".

Four middle-aged siblings of the McDonnell family had lived there for about six years, after retiring from a successful grocery, drapery and general store business in Ballygar, Co Galway. The house had recently been put up for sale, with the first mention of the house in The Irish Times appearing days before in a short advertisement.

Before the fire brigade arrived, a Garda sergeant and a local man reached the house and broke into a basement room - that of the family's yardman, James Clarke. They found him partially dressed on his bed and on dragging him out through the window, saw he was dead.
James had what looked like defensive wounds on his forearms and one deep wound across the left front of his skull, "and from later indications it would seem that his head had been opened by the blow of a poker or some such instrument." He had been dead for some time.

Firefighters arrived just before 9am and lines of hose were laid from a nearby pond, according to early reports. Water was pumped into the rooms and over the roof of the house, but "the whole of the roof was eventually burned and fell in". Most of the interior, too, was gutted.

The remains of the McDonnells - Annie (56), Joseph (55), Peter (51) and Alice (47) were recovered, along with that of Mary McGowan, a house servant. The two sisters were found in the same room and were nearly indistinguishable - the rest of the bodies were found throughout the house.

"Four of the bodies were burned, and actually were being charred by the flames when the Fire Brigade arrived; another body bore marks of violence, and the sixth was found stripped," reads an early report.

Fire poker
Peter McDonnell's body was "entirely unclothed, but a woollen singlet and a pair of pants were lying loosely over it. This circumstance is one that gives a peculiar depth to the mystery." He seemed to be the last in the house to die, yet the "garments had the appearance of having been placed over his body by the hands of another."

A fire poker, which had what looked like brain matter on it, was found near Peter.

From the outset, reports point to "mysterious circumstances".

All over the house - and the observations of the firemen as to the course of the burnings were to the same effect - it is plain that fires were started in many separate places, apparently by the spreading and lighting of some inflammable spirit."

The rumours began. Neighbours theorised as to possible culprits within the house - with "peculiarities" mentioned about Alice in particular. Those close to the family would roundly dismiss any conflict between the siblings and deny there was "real evidence of any predisposition to such an extremity of madness" among any of them.

The mystery drew the close attention of newspapers and holiday makers; hundreds travelled to the house to get a look. A week of fruitless searches ensued and no hard leads could be formed. Subsequent medical reports discovered trace amounts of arsenic in some of the bodies; not lethal doses, but enough to make them weak. Each victim had died before the fire was set, by about 5pm on the Monday, one doctor said.

At the inquest, a family friend named Martin Wall further dispelled any idea of friction within the family. As to whether they had any enemies, he said: "They couldn't have. . . they were too harmless for that," according to a report on April 10th.

Suspicion turned then to the gardener, Henry McCabe, who lived with his wife and nine young children in Malahide. He was first detained on April 2nd, three days after the fire.

While in custody, he made a statement to police, detailing a story about a safe which had been hidden on the La Mancha property. Shortly after the McDonnells arrived in Malahide, McCabe said he and Clarke were ordered to bury a box near the front porch. Three years later, they were ordered to dig it up and put it in the store.

McCabe was later found to have the keys to the same safe in his pocket when he gave a statement. When police searched the house on the morning of the fire, they found no valuables and it was said some possessions were missing.

Det Sgt John Mooney gave evidence of an encounter with McCabe on the morning of the fire. When he arrived to the scene, he found McCabe standing near the house, smoking a cigarette.

New trousers
"This is an awful business," the detective said, according to a report on June 29th, to which McCabe replied: "It is, and I after being up all night. They were all right when I left here last night, and when I got here this morning, I got an awful fright: the back door was broken in."

The door was indeed broken, though it seemed the damage came from the inside. On the same morning, McCabe was also found to be wearing a pair of new, grey trousers that had belonged to Peter McDonnell.

On the day he was officially charged, April 12th, a garda named Hayden asked McCabe how he was: "It is all up with me now," the gardener said. "I am going to Mountjoy in the morning, and it is all over the pants I have on me. Would I be able to get out and tell my wife to say I got the pants some time ago in a parcel which the McDonnells sent me?" The garda made no reply.

More than 60 witnesses gave evidence of comings and goings to the house over the last days of March. It seemed that McCabe had, on a number of occasions, steered visitors away and said the McDonnells were unwell.

Other evidence included bloodstains on McCabe's shirt, as well as his access to weed killer, which contained some amount of arsenic. The defence would dismiss the blood stains as common among manual workers and argue that he wouldn't know how to extract the arsenic from the weed killer: "was McCabe such an expert chemist that he knew?" asked the defence council at the closing of the six-day trial on November 15th, according to a report in the *Examiner*.

The prosecution's case, the defence argued, was largely circumstantial. The prosecutor, "could not make bricks without clay, and out of the rotten rubbish and half-baked clay, he was not able to build the house of the prosecution."

After less than an hour, the jury found McCabe guilty of the six murders.

Asked why he should be spared the death sentence, McCabe, who protested his innocence throughout the trial, said: "All I have to say is God forgive them. I am the victim of bribery and perjury."

He was sentenced to hang on December 9th, 1926.

The last mention of Henry McCabe in *The Irish Times* comes seven years later in October 1933, when a boy named Denning found jewellery inscribed "James Clarke" and "J McD" while digging in a garden on Church road, near where McCabe lived (at Parnell Cottages). The executed gardener had also reportedly planted the shrubs that were growing in the same garden."

This is what you find if you search for McDonnell deaths in 1926.

It is gruesome.

Their story is significant to my story in that Gaybrook Lodge is the closest neighbour to La Mancha and anybody living there in 1926 (as Mary Sutton was) would certainly have been aware of these events.

Fleshing out the Sutton family tree

When Jenny contacted the Sutton family in 1989 she first spoke with the oldest child "Sonny". I searched but there has never been anyone named Sonny. It is a nickname.

Is this Sonny's birth on 7.4.1919? Parents John Sutton, a soldier and Mary Sutton (nee Hand) living at 15 Bath Avenue, SandyMount, Dublin, near the Rotunda Hospital which specialised in maternity.

Is this Mary, the second child? No birth certificate (1922 is not yet 100 years ago) but a marriage and death (of TB) that fits.

The addresses are 10 Marrowbone Lane and 55 Pimlico (now a block of flats) which are adjacent in Dublin 8.

Mary's mother died aged 64 on 17.3.1927 at Gaybrook, making her birth date 1863 so she should have been 38 in 1901 or 71 at death? Husband John is described as a labourer.

Mary's father – John Hand died 17.10.1930 in a workhouse having moved from Gaybrook.

Aged 69 would mean born in 1861 but could have been 72 which would match the 1901 census.

It appears that Mary's parents were living with her until they died.

Just for completion, this is Nicholas Sutton's wedding.

Whilst a soldier in the Royal Dublin Fusiliers based at Collins Barracks, Dublin he married Catherine O'Connor from 55 Pimlico, about 2km south, on 25.8 1941.

John M Sutton was his father.

Here is Catherine's birth certificate.

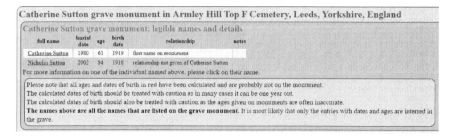

Suddenly 55 Pimlico takes on more significance
- Catherine O'Connor was born there 9.9.1918
- She married Nicholas Sutton whilst there. Perhaps they lived there for a few months. He was at the RDF Collins Barracks nearby.
- Nicholas' sister Mary at age 19 married Thomas O'Callaghan on 28.12.1941 whilst living at 10 Marrowbone Lane, near Pimlico.
- It appears that Mary and Thomas took over at 55 Pimlico at the end of 1941 and Nicholas Sutton and Catherine O'Connor left for England in 1942.
- Catherine died in 1980, Nicholas died in 2002 and they are buried together in Leeds.

Catherine Sutton grave monument in Armley Hill Top F Cemetery, Leeds, Yorkshire, England

Catherine Sutton grave monument: legible names and details

full name	burial date	age	birth date	relationship	notes
Catherine Sutton	1980	61	1919	first name on monument	
Nicholas Sutton	2002	84	1918	relationship not given of Catherine Sutton	

For more information on one of the individual named above, please click on their name.

Please note that all ages and dates of birth in red have been calculated and are probably not on the monument.
The calculated dates of birth should be treated with caution as in many cases it can be one year out.
The calculated dates of birth should also be treated with caution as the ages given on monuments are often inaccurate.
The names above are all the names that are listed on the grave monument. It is most likely that only the entries with dates and ages are interred in the grave.

- Mary O'Callaghan died living there on 9.7.1947

Jenny was told by Sonny that he had joined the Irish Free State Army in 1936, married, gone to England and joined the RAF, then his wife died and he remarried. These statements do not stand up well under scrutiny. The Irish Free State Army disbanded in 1924. He was a bachelor in the RDF when he married Catherine in Ireland in 1941. He might not even have been in the RAF.

We can be certain that Nicholas was 'Sonny' Sutton.

Family trees compared

On the following two pages I have summarized some of the birth, marriage and death data.

The first page shows the basic information coming from Jenny's dreams, the five regression sessions, plus the actual Sutton children.

The second page shows the three generations of Suttons involved in this story.

Most of these details about Mary's children were published in Jenny's book. I saw no reason to try and verify this information with the exception of "Sonny".

The number of children, their names and dates are significantly different between dreams, regressions and official records.

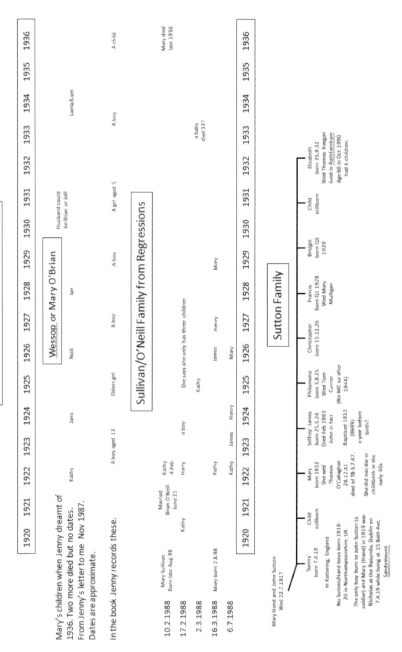

Dream, Regression and actual family details

Mary's children when Jenny dreamt of 1936. Two more died but no dates. From Jenny's letter to me Nov 1987. Dates are approximate.

In the book Jenny records these.

Wessop or Mary O'Brian

	1920	1921	1922	1923	1924	1925	1926	1927	1928	1929	1930	1931	1932	1933	1934	1935	1936
			Kathy		Jane		Neill		Ian		Husband could be Brian or Jeff				Liam/Liam		
				A boy aged 13		Eldest girl		A boy		A boy		A girl aged 5		A boy			A child

Sullivan/O'Neill Family from Regressions

	1920	1921	1922	1923	1924	1925	1926	1927	1928	1929	1930	1931	1932	1933	1934	1935	1936
10.2.1988	Mary Sullivan Born late Aug 98	Married Brian O'Neill June 21	Kathy 4 Feb														Mary died late 1936
17.2.1988		Kathy	Harry	a boy		She says she only has three children								a baby died 33?			
2.3.1988						Kathy											
16.3.1988	Mary born 2.8.98		Kathy				James	Henry		Mary							
6.7.1988			Kathy	James	Henry		Kathy	Henry		Mary							

Sutton Family

Mary Hand and John Sutton Wed 22.7.1917

	1920	1921	1922	1923	1924	1925	1926	1927	1928	1929	1930	1931	1932	1933	1934	1935	1936
	'Sonny' born 7.4.19	Child stillborn	Mary born 1922 She wed Thomas O'Callaghan 28.12.41 died of TB 9.7.47. She did not die in childbirth in the early 40s	'Jeffrey' James born 25.5.24 Died Feb 1993 John in fact Baptised 1923 a year before birth?		Philomena born 3.8.25 Wed Tom Curran (No MC so after 1944)	Christopher born 15.12.26		Francis born Q1 1928 Wed Mary Mulligan	Bridget born Q3 1929		Child stillborn	Elizabeth born 25.9.32 Wed Thomas Keegan lived in Rathfarnham Age 60 in Oct 1990 had 6 children.				

In Kettering, England

No Suttons/Hand boys born 1918-20 in Northamptonshire, UK.

The only boy born to John Sutton (a soldier) and Mary (Hand) in 1919 was Nicholas at the Rotunda, Dublin on 7.4.19 while living at 15 Bath Ave., Sandymount.

Additional historical family details

Hand/Sutton Family Tree

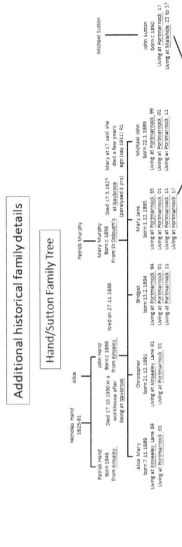
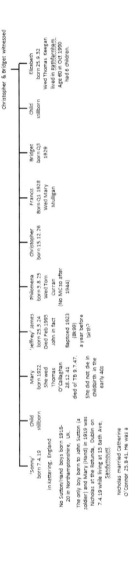

Michael Sutton

John Sutton born c 1850
Living at Portmarnock 17
Living at Malahide 23 to 3?

Patrick Murphy

Mary Murphy Born c 1856 From St Doolcath's — Died 17.3.1927 at Gaybrook (paralysed 3 yrs) — Mary at 17 said she died a few years ago (say 1911) R1

Nicholas Hand 1825-81   Alice

John Hand Born c 1856 from Kinsaley — Died 17.10.1930 in a workhouse after being at Gaybrook   Wed on 27.11.1886

Patrick Hand Born 1845 from Kinsaley

Alice Mary born 7.11.1889
Living at Kingsailey Lane 89
Living at Portmarnock 01

Christopher born 21.12.1891
Living at Kingsailey Lane 91
Living at Portmarnock 01

Bridget born 13.2.1894
Living at Portmarnock 94
Living at Portmarnock 01
Living at Portmarnock 11

Mary Jane born 1.12.1895
Living at Portmarnock 95
Living at Portmarnock 01
Living at Portmarnock 11

Living at Malahide 23 to 32
Died 24.10.1932 at Rotunda Hospital
Living at Gaybrook a labourer's wife

Michael John born 22.1.1899
Living at Portmarnock 99
Living at Portmarnock 01
Living at Portmarnock 11

Wed 22.7.1917 in Baldoyle.
Both are >21 and live in Portmarnock.
He is in the RDF, joined 1914.
Christopher & Bridget witnessed

Elizabeth born 26.9.32
Wed Thomas Keegan
lived in Rathfarnham
Age 60 in Oct 1990
had 6 children.

'Sonny' born 7.4.19

Child stillborn

Mary born 1922
She wed Thomas O'Callaghan 28.12.41
died of TB 9.7.47

'Jeffrey' James born 25.3.24
Died Feb 1993
John in fact

Baptised 1923 (8699)
She did not die in childbirth a year before birth?

Philomena born 8.8.25
Wed Tom Curran
(No MC30 after 1944)

Christopher born 15.12.26

Francs born Q1.1928 Wed Mary Mulligan

Bridget born Q3 1929

Child stillborn

1901 Census shows John (43), Mary (45), Alice (11), Christy (9), Bridget (7), Mary (5), Michael (2) Hand at property 15 (3 rooms, railway owned) in Portmarnock. Station is 19. Church is 20.

1911 Census shows John (55), Bridget (17), Mary (15), Michael (12) Hand at property 21 (4 rooms, Plunkett owned) in Portmarnock. Station is 17. Church is 11.

So confusion about age for Mary's father John. Alice has gone (she died but no DC) and Christy has gone

In Kettering, England

No Sutton/Hand boys born 1918-20 in Northamptonshire, UK.

The only boy born to John Sutton (a soldier) and Mary (Hand) in 1919 was Nicholas at the Rotunda, Dublin on 7.4.19 while living at 15 Bath Ave, Sandymount

Nicholas married Catherine O'Connor 25.8.41. He was a soldier in the RDF.
Father John, a labourer.

Left for England 1942, joined RAF? Catherine died 1986, Nicholas died 2002 and they are buried together in Leeds

Comparing dreams and regression with the facts

Where you see R3 it means the data came from Regression 3. Bk9 means page 9 of Jenny's book. BC means birth certificate, MC means marriage certificate, DC mean death certificate, other references should be clear.

Was Mary O'Neill (nee Sullivan) really Mary Sutton (nee Hand)?

Early Life	
Mary Sullivan	Mary Hand
She said her birthday was 2nd August 1898). R4 and R5	Her birthday was 1st December 1895. BC
She said she had no sisters but two older brothers. R3 and R5	She had two older sisters (though one died when Mary was 11) plus one older and one younger brother. 1901 and 1911 census
She finished school at age 12. R2	Leaving age was 12 from 1899 to 1914 when it changed to 14. Right
Aged 17 she said her father used to work on the land. R1	Father was a platelayer for the railway. 1901 and 1911 census
She said the house was a good distance from the beach (a cart ride). R1	The house in Portmarnock was a 15 minute walk to the beach and actually not feasible by cart
At age 20 (1918) she said Ireland was run from Dublin and there was no connection with the English. R2	Ireland was all one country and part of the UK. Dublin was the capital but Ireland was governed from England at that time.
She said they did not have electricity at home. R2	Electricity came to Malahide in 1929 and Portmarnock in 1936. Right
In 1919 she describes a church. It is very tall, the front is a big, long wall that comes to a point with a little cross. It is a flat, stone wall with a door. Does not know if there is a spire.	Jenny drew a picture of this after the session. Most churches look like this.

There is a board for notices and it has writing in the wood up, across and down and some on top in different letters. Up and down it is like a prayer to Our Blessed Mary, across the top it is St Mary's. R1	The one she identifies in her book is St Andrews

Later Life

Mary Sullivan	Mary Hand
Worked for the Lett family as a maid in 1915. R1	No record of working anywhere but Jenny suggests the Plunketts as a possible alternative
The Letts	**The Plunketts**
There is an oldish woman and her son Richard of about 30. On the first floor are nice bedrooms, then stairs to another level where her room is and not much more. There may be five rooms on the first floor. R3	The Plunkett home (Portmarnock House) had 27 rooms and 24 outbuildings. It was much larger than Jenny's drawing. It was never mentioned by Mary Sullivan, she just said she worked for the Letts. 1911 census
Mary says the woman is English. In R5 she calls her Lottie	Jenny said Elizabeth Plunkett was English, she was Irish. 1911 census
Mrs Lett was 67 in 1915	Mrs Plunkett was 60 in 1915
She said Mr Lett had been gone a long time. She had never met him. R3 Robert Lett died at the end of 1901.	Mr Plunkett died in 1927. If Mary had been working there she would have known him.
At the Letts she said there were hills and slopes and the back of the house faced south west. R3 and R4 Ferns is quite hilly so her descriptions fit better there	Portmarnock is flat. The back of Portmarnock House faced north. The area around Malahide is flat, being coastal. Old OS maps
Mary said there was a pub in the village where the Letts were. R1	Portmarnock was a simple village, consisting mainly of private homes. There was no pub or hotel. Census.
The Letts are not the Plunketts. Father was alive well after Mary died and there was no Richard. The Ferns Letts fit better.	

The family	
Mary Sullivan	Mary Hand
She meets Brian in 1920. R1	She wed John Sutton in 1917. MC
She thought he may have been to the war or abroad as he had not been around earlier. R1 Jenny says he was from a different area of Ireland. Bk20	They were both born in Portmarnock. MC
In 1920 he is a 'Cleaver'. R2 (A Cleaver is either a specialist carving knife or the person who decides how best to split a rough diamond.)	In 1917 he is a soldier in the Royal Dublin Fusiliers. MC
In 1920 with Brian at a Jetty. She does not see a lighthouse. R2	She would see two lighthouses in Howth from the jetty in Portmarnock. Early OS map
Brian worked with wood for a while but then was a fisherman. R1 and R2	John was a labourer after being a soldier. MC and on daughter Mary's MC and Nicholas' MC, both in 1941
Mary Sullivan said she and Brian were Protestant. R5 (Jenny thought they may be Catholic)	Mary Hand and John Sutton were Catholic. MC
Their Marriage	
Mary Sullivan married Brian O'Neill on 16.6.1921. R1 (In R4 she says 1922)	Mary Hand married John Sutton on 22.7.1917. MC
They married in St Mary's Malahide. R1 There is no St Mary's in Malahide.	They married in St Peter & St Pauls, Baldoyle. They both lived in Portmarnock. MC
She said her father, an aunt and a few cousins attended the wedding. R1	Her father and at least one brother and sister attended. MC
Mary Sullivan's witness was Ian, who Brian knew. R4	Mary Hand's brother and sister witnessed her signature. MC
There was no mention of Brian being violent.	In the 1920's John beat his wife and children, according to Sonny. Bk125

Their children	
O'Neill	Sutton
In regression Mary only had 4 children plus one that died. Her dream had 6 plus 2 that died.	Mary Sutton had 8 children plus 2 that died (no DC though because stillbirths do not require to be registered).
This is the birth information about children, notably Mary O'Neill's first child was a girl.	

Dream	Regression	Facts (mainly from Jenny's book)
		"Sonny" 7.4.1919 (BC)
		Stillborn child
Cathy 1922	Cathy 1920/2/5	Mary 1922
A boy 1923	James 1923/6	
Jane 1924	Henry 1922/4/7	Jeffrey (John) James 25.5.1924
		Philomena 3.8.1925
Neil 1926	Mary 1926/9	Christopher 15.12.1926
Ian 1928		Francis 1928
		Bridget 1929
A girl 1931		Stillborn child
		Elizabeth 25.9.1932
	Lost a baby	
Liam 1934		

Aged 35 she lost a baby (the first she has lost) and has just four other children. R3 The lost baby was full term so would need to be registered.	In the book Jenny says all but the second stillborn baby and Elizabeth were born by the time Mary was 35.
Dates, names, number of children, siblings do not match Suttons	
According to the book Jeffrey was born after his baptism (1923). Bk99	

Their marital home	
It was the first house in a hamlet of 10 to 12 houses. P3, P5.	It was the first along Swords Road but the next house was Gay Brook Farm and there were no more for half a mile. Old OS Maps
The cottage has small windows at the front and a few outbuildings. R4	Gay Brook Lodge had two windows but had no outbuildings. Census

She said there was a stream to the west. R5	There is a stream 50 yards west. It is actually Gay Brook Stream and links to the estuary to the north. Old OS maps
Mary said the land on the other side of the road is boggy and no use for anything. R5	Land north of Swords Road was reclaimed from marshland in the 18th century and by the 1840's there were houses, farms and a school on this land. Old OS maps and History of Yellow Walls.
	1911 census and maps show The Lodge to be a single building to the east of Gay Brook, a large house. The owners also own the Lodge.
	The house is let from the MacMahons with no land. Tenants probably worked as gardeners. Census
In 1915 Mary said her mother died "long ago". R1 Her mother died in 1908 of a stroke. R5	Mary's mother died at Gaybrook Lodge in 1927. She had been paralysed for three years. DC
In 1931 she says there is only one school in Malahide. R1	There was St Andrews, St Sylvesters and Pope John Paul II.
In 1932 her father was still alive. R4	Mary's father also died at Gaybrook, in 1930. DC
Mary O'Neill died in 1937, aged 39. R1	Mary Sutton died on Oct 24th 1932, aged 35 in the Rotunda Hospital, Dublin, with husband John present. Both lived at Gaybrook. (DC)

The Suttons definitely existed and lived at the Lodge.

Information coming from "Sonny" (all in her book)	
Sonny tells her that his father's name was John	A name Jenny had never mentioned.
At their first meeting (23.9.1990) he told her that soon after marrying Mary and John had lived in Kinsaley before moving to Gaybrook Lodge. BK124 Later (perhaps 1992) he told her that soon after marrying they had moved from Kettering, England to her parents house in Portmarnock. Bk 135	Her parents had left Kinsaley before she was born so she could not have lived there with them after marrying. Sonny is clearly an unreliable source.
He identified Jenny's Molly friend as Mary Monahan	Jenny accepted this in spite of the different name.
He told her she had a sister they used to visit. Jenny did not remember her.	This is Bridget, a year older than Mary and a witness at her marriage
He told her the market she described was Moore Street in Dublin	She accepted although it is not cobbled and was enormous.
He told her that when young she lived at the Station House in Malahide, her father being station master.	Her father was a Platelayer and they did not live in the Station House but I guess Grandad might have lied to Sonny.
He told her that Mary's brother died aged 19 at Lucknow.	He was 28 at her wedding and Lucknow saw no action in the war. There was a siege there as part of the Indian Rebellion in 1857.
He said his grandfather was a Yorkshireman.	He was born in Co. Dublin.
He never mentioned that his grandparents lived with the family, and died at Gaybrook.	

He also told Jenny that Mary (the eldest daughter) had returned to Gaybrook to look after John but eventually married and left but died soon after in childbirth.	She probably did go back for a while but married in 1941 and died of TB (not childbirth) in 1947. DC
He told Jenny he was born in Kettering, England.	Sonny has never been a real name in Ireland or England. His birth certificate suggests Nicholas and that he was born at the Rotunda, Dublin. Confirmed by a marriage certificate.

Other observations

The Sutton family was suggested by a stranger and accepted too easily

Mary Sullivan never mentioned –
Surnames Hand, Sutton, Plunkett, MacMahon
Sibling's names Alice, Christopher, Bridget, Michael
Parent's names John or Mary
The name of any of Mary Sutton's children except Mary (a much used name)
Place names Kinsaley, Portmarnock, Baldoyle, Swords, Yellow Walls, Gaybrook, St Sylvester's or St Andrew's Churches
Road names Swords Road or Church Road (the largest road in Malahide)
She did mention Malahide but Jenny was already aware of it from her maps so we can't give significance to this.

The Suttons that Jenny found say they lived at Gaybrook Lodge and paid rent to Mrs MacMahon and indeed they did, but Mary would know the house she spent every day for about 10 years in much better than Jenny described.

The incidents at La Mancha in 1926 would surely have been known to Mary, being the closest neighbour and walking past the scene on every trip to Malahide. Sonny was almost seven years old and he would have remembered this but never mentioned it.
What he did tell her was that the garage now on the corner of Swords Road had been built some time after a fire in 1926 and Jenny said that must be why she didn't recall the garage. Bk131

In 1928 we try to look at a sixpence. On one side she sees a clover. And says the design on a half-crown is too complicated to describe. R2 Until 1922 there were just English coins but at this time all coins had a harp on the front, a 6d had a wolfhound on the back and the half crown had a horse.
There was a three month gap before the final regression session and in her book Jenny describes getting very anxious to investigate though knowing that there was insufficient information really. In 1988 Jenny obtained a detailed map in the midst of regression sessions and sent a letter and copy of her drawn map (having added the names Malahide, Swords and Gaybrook to it) to several O'Neills listed in the Dublin telephone directory. (Thereby limiting the credibility of further regression memories).
The BBC were planning to feature the story but dropped it in September 1990 claiming it was because they could not find the cottage. Was it really because they realised it was false? The family reunion story was clearly the 'hook'. When this happened it prompted Jenny and Sonny to review the researcher's notes together, negating the possibility that they could provide independent corroboration. Only after the book came out in 1993 did the television programme "Strange But True?", made by a different company, feature the story and Jenny and I appeared in it.
In the Postscript of her book Jenny talks of her visit to the area in 1993. She found Mary Sutton's marriage certificate and seems entirely unconcerned that the date and place was different from her memory and the brother she said had died five years before was one of the witnesses. Bk145

Examining the geography

Before starting with the regression sessions I asked Jenny to describe the recurring dream she had been having since childhood in writing so that any research I might subsequently conduct would have some information that could not be considered to have been created by the hypnosis. Earlier parts of this chapter have used some of this but the description of where Mary Sullivan lived needs to be compared against Malahide.

Jenny's dream	Research
The main street was uneven (cobbles?). Going north she passes many market stalls on the left, selling fish and vegetables. Feels it is a busy, small town.	This should be Church Street (or Road) but it ends at a crossroads with The Mall and New St going north to the estuary and Irish Sea. Photographs about 100 years old on the Historical Picture Archive show Church Road to be quite smooth.
The stalls end at the top of the street at a T junction.	There were never market stalls here. The Police Station, other official buildings and good houses are here.
The right turn goes nowhere. In front of her are two large wooden gates, the land beyond belongs to the railway and there is a brick wall. The trains don't run that way but just stop there.	Turning right is The Mall and the main Coast road to Portmarnock. Mary Hand was born in Portmarnock and lived there when in 1917 she wed John Sutton in Baldoyle. She would have known the way from Malahide to home.
She turns left past a tall post box on the corner. This would be the south east corner.	There was a green free standing post box about 4' 6" tall on the NW corner of this crossroads from 1900 to 1910.

	A green post box was set in the wall on the NE corner of this crossroads from 1940 to 1960. No post box on the SE corner
	Turning left at the crossroads (also called the Diamond) leads to Main Street (for 75m) and this becomes Malahide Road at the junction with Old Street and then Dublin Road after the Cricket Ground (on the south side of the road).
She passes the station, set back across the road on the other side.	The station is in the early part of Malahide Road and set back sideways (north south) on the other side (to the right).
There is traffic on this road, which widens as it turns to head south. This is the road to the city, some distance away.	On the 1913 OS map Dublin Road widens a little shortly after the station but narrows again before turning south towards Dublin.
The lane home heads left off this main road, a bit after the bend. It is a straight lane and a rough wall begins on the left at this point. It is needed to stop landslides.	Turning left leads into a footpath to Malahide Castle. The road home (Swords Road) turns right off Dublin Road when going south. It would be seen as left if viewing a map.
She goes along the road for a mile. At their cottage now, a stone wall and wooden gate posts but the gate has gone. The house is side on to the road with the front pointing towards town (Malahide?) but the steep slope means it is hidden from the road. The ground has been moved to seat the house.	A mile (1.5km) along Swords Rd is where the straight section ends. The Lodge for Gay Brook House (a former Rectory) was just 480m along this road on the left on the corner of what is now Castle Downs Road, which on the 1913 OS map was the entrance way to the Rectory. There was no slope. Jenny put the house at 175m along the road in her book.

The type of map Jenny had in 1980

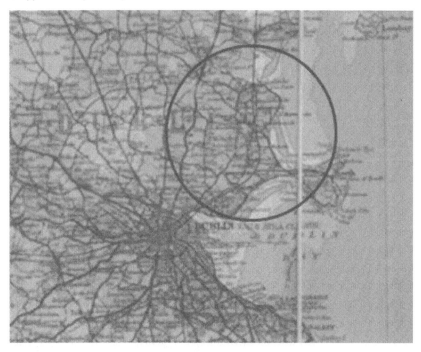

Looking at the shape of the road around Malahide it is arc shaped, which Jenny said. However, in reality the part to the right is a minor route round the coast to Portmarnock. The town centres on the Diamond at the top of Church Road by the railway, so going left from the first 'a' of Malahide the road is very straight. Only the map gives the impression of an arc.

Jenny produced drawings to illustrate where her cottage was in relation to the nearby town. She assumed this to be Malahide, which she had seen on the map. She enclosed one with her letter to me and the one in her book is generally similar.

When I lined them up with the actual geography and used reference points like the station and Gaybrook I found that the early drawing has Gaybrook 2 miles from Malahide centre and the later one has it at 4 miles. It was in fact 1.3 miles so there is considerable variation in the drawings that Jenny claims are highly accurate.

In early March 1988 Mr Coulter brought her a tourist map of Malahide so the last three sessions may be compromised. Jenny also obtained an even more detailed map in 1988 before the last session.

I mentioned that this quite exhaustive research effort was prompted by contact from Jenny and on completion I did offer to share the results with her to see if there was anything she knew which could add further clarity. Sadly she did not take up this offer and I felt obliged to publish to ensure that anyone that may have been misled by the story is now properly informed. Of course, Jenny could do this research herself.

Thoughts and conclusions

Almost nothing matches. Jenny Cockell was not Mary Hand/Sutton.

There will have been other cases of such family situations given that families were large and giving birth was more risky then. Many of the things that Jenny remembered may well have fitted a Mary Sullivan somewhere in the south west of Ireland but there is not enough information to allow research to verify that.

I do not believe that Jenny sought to mislead anyone. She simply got caught up in a story that became much more than it really was. It seems that even the things Sonny told her about can't be relied upon.

In reality all Jenny had was a dream about a woman called Mary who had died in hospital leaving a lot of children and some other thoughts that came when awake. She didn't know her children or her husband's names.

She had lived a life of poverty and the children had differing characters. They lived in or near a village and later in a larger place that had a station, a church and a butcher shop. She described a somewhat rundown cottage on a westward road with a picture of a soldier on one wall. A little further on was a stream. There was a major city further south. She had drawn road layouts of the area with the station, shops and the cottage marked.

The thoughts and images that were already in Jenny's mind before she used hypnosis to investigate were an opportunity to see if we could clarify and expand on these to identify potential evidence. She provided me with some notes about her dreams before we began but I did not look at them until we had completed the regression sessions to ensure that I had no influence on results.

On page 70 of her book Jenny writes about the potential conflict of interest in our goals and admits that mine was to research hypnotic regression and that she "had fallen on the offer of hypnosis like a drowning woman". Jenny seems to have similarly "fallen" on the Sutton family too.

The main difficulty that I believe we had was that Jenny's enthusiasm to find her own answers never really allowed her to be properly immersed in the sessions we had and it seemed that she was always checking in her mind to see if what she told me was aligned with her earlier thoughts. It would have been better had she simply allowed whatever was brought to mind to flow freely so that information could be detailed before any checking was carried out.

An additional factor was that Jenny sought to follow up on the various pieces of scattered information before we had really dug deeply enough to make it worthwhile. Her different sources and approaches to various individuals even including Mary Sutton's eldest child brought out information which was different to both the dream and regression experiences on a number of significant points but Jenny seems to have adopted what others have told her as supportive of her interpretation.

If we had been able to obtain more detailed information during the regressions I believe we may have been able to find Mary Sullivan and proved that Jenny was her in a previous life. There may have been another family that could have been reunited but we will never know.

19.   Janice   Kershaw   –   Who   had knowledge of part of Leeds that no longer exists

Sylvia was one of the four volunteers that were selected to appear on the radio programme mentioned earlier and her memories of Janice provide significant evidence of reincarnation but at first we didn't know what was to come.

After hypnotizing her and initially exploring the mid 1800's and a character called Frances, I directed Sylvia to move to 1930 or thereabouts and see what was there …..

What can you see, can you see where you are?
It's a big room.
What's your name; do you know what your name is?
Janice.
Janice. And what is your second name Janice?
Kershaw.
And what is this room you are in?
I work in there.
You work in there do you, what do you do? What is your job?
Guns.
Guns, you're something to do with guns are you?
Mmm
What part of the country is it, are you in the south or in the north?
In the north.
Near what town or in what town?
Leeds.
In Leeds, what's the name of the company you work for?
Crowther.
And how old are you?
19.

How much do you earn for doing this?
It depends.
What does it depend on?
How much work I do.
Oh, you get paid by the number of things you produce do you?
Mmm.
How much do you usually earn, what is your average wage?
Oh, I don't ... about £4.
A week?
Mmm
Have you got any boyfriends?
Sort of.
Sort of, why only sort of?
I don't like him very much really.
Don't you?
No.
Why don't you find somebody else then?
They're all the same.
What's his name?
Peter.
What does he do, does he work in the same place?
No.
What does he do then?
Can't think.
Alright, just relax and drift away.

Session ended, she was having difficulty answering and it did not seem very interesting at this time.

On revisiting her at another session things became more interesting so here I include all following sessions to show how the evidence built up.

Janice Kershaw - Session 2

It is worth stating again that sessions can be weeks or months apart and there is no notice of where we may go so it would be pointless to attempt to prepare and weave a checkable story.

Asked to go back to the memories of Janice.

What is around you, what can you see?
I'm in the street.
In the street, are you going somewhere?
No.
No, are you standing still or walking?
I'm playing.
You're playing are you?
Mmm
How old are you Janice?
14.
You're 14, what are you playing?
Just kicking a ball about.
On your own or with friends?
There's three of us.
Yes, are they all girls?
No, there's one boy.
One boy is there?
Peter.
Peter, and they're all about the same age as you?
No, Peter's a bit older.
Do you usually play football?
Oh I don't know really, not much to do.
Aren't you going to school then?
No, it's a holiday.
Is it?
Yeah.

Do you enjoy school?

Not a lot.

No, what are you good at?

Nothing really.

Oh, you must have a best subject?

No, I don't think I have.

What about Art, any good at Art?

Mmm

Yes, you like painting?

It's alright.

What's the name of the school that you go to?

St Bede's.

St Bede's, who's it run by?

How do you mean?

Well it sounds as if it might be some sort of religious establishment, is it?

Well it's Catholic.

But is it run by Nuns?

No.

No, just ordinary?

Yeah.

I see. Is it attached to a church?

Oh I don't know. I'm not all that bothered.

No. What town is it, where do you live?

Leeds.

In Leeds, and what is your address?

I live in Cooper Street.

Cooper Street, is that the street you're playing in?

No.

You're in another street are you?

Yeah.

What's this one called?

Carlisle Street.

And is it near Cooper Street?

Yeah, it's just round corner.

Just round the corner is it, and what number do you live in?

5.
Number 5 Cooper Street?
Yeah.
What does your father do for a living?
Doesn't work.
Doesn't he?
No.
Why not?
Oh, says he can't get a job, don't believe him.
Don't you, why, what do you think it is then?
Bone idle.
Just bone idle. Well where does your money come from then, to live?
Social.
From the Social?
Yeah.
And is that enough to live on?
Not really.
Does your mother earn any money?
Well, does a bit of cleaning.
Have you got any brothers or sisters?
Yeah.
How many?
Four.
What are they, brothers or sisters?
Two of each.
And what are their names?
Oh, Stuart, Freda, Barbara and Alan.
Do you like them
Freda's alright.
Is she?
Yeah.
How old is Freda?
15.
15, she's a bit older than you. Are the boys older or younger than you?
Younger.

Younger, oh so they're a bit of a nuisance then?
Yeah.
When do you leave school?
I've left.
Oh, you've left have you?
Yeah, this summer.
Are you going to get a job?
Might do.
Where do you think you might work?
Depends.
What on, who'll give you a job?
Yeah.
Have you got any qualifications?
No.
No, why, weren't you allowed to take any, or didn't you pass?
No, didn't pass.
Didn't pass?
Not interested.
What exam was it that you took, what was it called?
CSE.
CSE, what does that stand for?
I don't know really, some kind of certificate.
What kind of places are there for you to work, where could you work in Leeds if you wanted to?
Oh, mills, shops, don't know, that's about it.
Just Mills and Shops?
Mm
Do any of your friends work, does Freda work?
Yeah.
Where does she work?
At Mill.
At the mill?
Yeah.
Which mill?
Crowthers.

Crowthers Mill?

Yeah.

Whereabouts is that?

In Leeds.

What, in the centre or in the north or.. which side is it?

Oh, nearby.

Near your home?

Yeah, not far.

Alright, just relax.

End of session.

Janice Kershaw - session 3

Taken to Janice's time.

Can you see where you are?
Yes.
Where are you Janice?
At home.
At home, what are you doing?
Nothing much.
Have you been to school?
No.
Do you still go to school?
No.
Oh, you've left have you?
Yes.
Which school was it you went to, I've forgotten, I can't remember which school it was?
St Bede's.
And who was your favourite teacher there?
Didn't have one.
Didn't you, well who did you like the least then, which was the one you hated most?
Oh, he taught us maths.
The one who taught you maths, you didn't like him?
No.
Was that because you don't like maths?
No.
It's just because you don't like him, what did he do to make you not like him then?
Don't know really, kept telling me off.
Did you have any good friends at school?
Not really.
Nobody you'd call your best friend?

No.

What about the children in your class, what's happened to them now, do you know?

Not much.

Have they all got jobs?

Some of them.

Do you keep in touch?

Well I see them now and again.

Have you got a job?

No.

You just stay at home do you?

Yeah.

And what do you do most of the time?

Go down't shops, have a look.

Are you looking for anything in particular?

No, just having a look.

Have you got any boyfriends?

No.

Why, are you too young?

No, I don't really like them.

Do they like you; do they ever chase after you or call after you?

Not really.

What do you look like, what colour hair have you got?

Brown.

Is it long or short?

Short.

Is it straight or curly?

Straight.

And what colour are your eyes?

Brown.

Are you pretty?

Oh, don't know really, I'm not bothered.

Has your father got a job?

No.

Does he stay at home as well then?

Well he goes down the pub a lot.
Does he, which one does he go to usually?
It's just around the corner.
Has it got a sign out at the front?
No, it's just written over the door.
Who makes the beer, do you know?
No.
Do you ever go in there?
No.
Aren't you allowed to?
Me dad would kill me.
What's it called, this pub?
The Nelson, it's a bit of a dump.
But he goes in there every day does he?
Yeah.
What time?
Dinner time and night time.
Whenever it's open?
Yeah, I don't really see him much.
What does your mother say about that?
Oh, tells him off, doesn't do any good, might as well save her breath.
Does he drink a lot or does he just go there for the company?
He drinks a lot, he's always drunk.
Where does he get his money from?
Dole.
How much does he get, do you know?
I don't know really, he boozes it all, we never see it.
Have you got any brothers or sisters?
Yeah.
What are their names and how old are they?
Freda – she's 17, and Stuart – he's 14, Alan's 12.
There's a lot of them!
I'm not finished yet.
Keep going then.
Susan – she's 10, that's it. **(Susan was Barbara last session)**

That's it is it, that is a lot isn't it?
Yeah.
Do they all get in the way or do you play with them?
They're a bloody nuisance.
Are they, you don't like them a lot then?
Well, Freda's alright.
The rest of them just cause trouble do they?
Yeah, always mithering.
How many of them go to school?
Stuart, Alan, and Susan.
And Freda stays at home does she?
No, she's got a job.
She's got a job! Where does she work?
Crowthers.
What does she do there?
She's on winding.
Winding is she, does she tell you much about it?
Not really, she doesn't like it, it's hot, she's always warm, always moaning.
Where else could she work?
Don't know really, she's not so clever.
Aren't there any other factories around that she could work in?
There's a little one, Crowthers is quite big, they pay better money.
Oh, I see! There's a little one though.
What does that one do?
They do cardboard.
Make cardboard do they?
Yeah, it's only a little one.
Do they make it out of paper, or rubbish & stuff or do they make boxes out of cardboard?
Boxes.
They make boxes, I see, do you know what that is called?
Fairbrothers.
Have you tried to get a job there?
No, he's right mean him.
You know him a bit then?

Well, not really but everybody knows him, he never pays his bills.
Whereabouts is that, is it very far away from where you live?
No, it's not far, nearer than Crowthers.
What's the name of the street that that is in?
Fenton Street I think.
What does your mother do all day?
She goes down to the pawn shop, to try and get money, and she cleans a bit.

Relax, come forward 10 years, you're 25 years old.

Where are you Janice?
I'm in bed.
Is it night-time?
No.
Why are you in bed then, just tired are you?
No, I'm pregnant.
Oh, you're pregnant, when is it due?
Oh, about 4 months.
Four months from now but you're not feeling too well?
I don't want it.
Why not?
Can't afford it.
They don't cost all that much!
It does when you've got three already.
I see, well one more won't make much difference then will it?
Don't suppose so.
How old are the three you've got?
2 and 3.
You had twins did you?
Yeah.
What are they, boys or girls?
One boy, one girl.
Oh, the twins are a boy and a girl are they, or have you only got two?
Only two.

Oh sorry, I thought you said you'd got three?
No.
Are you married?
Yeah.
Oh good, I thought you were. What is your husband's name?
Peter.
And what is his last name, what is your married name?
Tomlinson.
*And what does your husband do for a living, how does he earn his money,
does he work?*
Some (she is groaning now)
How are you feeling?
It hurts.
Not feeling well? What sort of feeling have you got, where does it hurt?
In my stomach.
Can you feel the baby moving?
I don't know, feels funny.

*Alright, just relax, drift away and come forward one year, its one year
later, can you see where you are?*
All hazy.

Come forward another year, you're 27 years old, where are you?
I'm in a shop.
Are you buying something?
Yeah.
What are you buying?
Bread.
How many children have you got now?
Three.
What's the name of the last one that was born?
Tommy.
Did he give you any trouble?
How do you mean?
Was he easy when you were expecting him?

Oh not so bad. Oh God!

What's the matter?

She won't let me put it on the slate.

Why, how much do you owe her now?

Five quid, she doesn't like that.

And she won't let you have any more?

No, she did warn me, Oh God.

What are you going to eat now then?

I don't bloody know.

Does your husband work?

He goes out and he comes in.

What, goes to the pub and things does he?

No, he goes out, but I'm not really sure, I don't think I want to know.

Oh, how often does he go out, every day?

Not every day, goes out at night quite a lot.

Does he ever give you money?

Sometimes, when he doesn't lose it.

How do you get money otherwise, do you have a job?

We get some off the dole, not much.

What year is it now?

1947.

Did you do anything during the war?

Yeah, worked a bit.

What did you do?

Did a lot of munitions.

Where was that?

What used to be Crowthers.

What is Crowthers now?

Oh they're wool again.

They've gone back to wool now, I see. When did you stop working when you were in the war?

Oh I weren't doing it long.

You got pregnant did you?

Yeah.

Alright, just relax and come forward 2 years, where are you now?

I'm at my mum's.
What are you doing there, just visiting?
No, I'm living there.
What about your children?
They've come and all.
And your husband?
I don't know where he is.
When did you last see him?
About a year ago.
What happened to split you up?
He was in trouble.
What kind of trouble?
Coppers.
He'd been stealing things had he?
Yeah.
Anything big?
Don't know really, didn't ask.
Did they put him in prison?
I think so.
Do you know which one?
Quite a way away, I don't know.
So you live at your mothers now, is life a bit easier there?
Not really.
What do you do now, have you got to work?
I help out at the shop.
What shop, your mother's got a shop has she?
Oh no, no, it's nearby, corner shop.
And what do they sell there, all sorts of things?
Yeah, it's alright, she lets us have a few things.
Where are you living, what is the address where your mother lives?
Cooper Street.
Cooper Street, and what number is it?
Number four.
And what town is it in?

Leeds, it's a right dump, mind you ours weren't much better.
Where was yours?
Carlisle Street, it's just round the corner, next street.
It's a bit easier if there are a few of you living together I suppose. What happened, were you thrown out of your house?
No, I just left.
Were you renting it or did you buy it?
No, we rented it.
Who was the landlord?
Mr Jackson.
Does he own a lot round here?
Yeah, most of them.
Does he, does he own the one you're in now?
Yeah, doesn't do anything, they're wet through.
Are they, he doesn't look after them then?
No.
I see, still, somewhere to live isn't it?
Oh yeah, better than nowt.
Do you go to church?
No.
Were you christened?
I don't know, never asked.
Hasn't your mother told you?
No, doubt it.
Is your father still alive?
Yeah.
What does he do these days, still go drinking?
Yeah.

Alright, just relax, come forward two years, where are you now?

I'm at home.
Doing anything?
Yeah, helping Mum.
How old are your children now?

Tommy's 5, Janice is 8 and Peter's 10.
Which school do they go to, the ones that go to school?
St Bede's.
They go to the same one you went to, I thought you didn't like it there?
I don't, well I didn't.
Why do you send them there then?
Not much option.
Haven't you, aren't there any other ones?
No, they've got to go there.
Do they all go to school?
No
(She is moaning a bit here)
When you married, where did you get married?
St Marks (getting very weak)
Have you got any cousins, any relatives?
(No response except groaning)
What's the matter?
I don't know.
How do you feel, what do you feel?
I feel funny.
Where, in the head or..?
Yeah.
What's the matter, where does it hurt?
(Heavy breathing, moaning, no real response)
Come forward two hours, feeling any better?
No.
Just relax, come to the last things that Janice remembers. How old are you Janice?
31.
Do you know what the date is?
(Doesn't know anything, delirious)

Just relax.
Session ends.

Janice Kershaw - session 4

Taken to Janice at some point.

Where are you Janice?
I'm lost.
You're a bit old to be lost aren't you, are you going somewhere?
I think I'm coming back.
Coming back are you, have you had a nice time?
Oh, alright.
Alright was it, where have you been?
To't Zoo.
You've been to the zoo, where was that, which zoo, was it a big one?
No, no, bit small really.
Who did you go with?
High.
High up?
High something.
High something was it?
Oh God.
What town is it?
I don't know what to do, its pitch black and I've...
Where are you, are you in a street somewhere?
No, it's all open.
In the countryside is it, did you go to work today?
No.
Have you got a job?
No.
Can you see anything at all, can you see any light, are there any lights anywhere?
No, it's all fields.
And you are on your own, how far have you walked do you think?
Not far, it's.. I don't know where they've gone.
There are some others are there?

Yeah, there's a few of us.
Where were they?
They've buggered off and left me.
What were they, friends or what?
No, Freda and ...
Who's Freda?
My sister.
Your sister, Oh, you were with your family were you?
No.
Just Freda?
No, no, there were a few of us, from where Freda works.
Where does Freda work?
Crowthers, oh God, I don't know what I'm going to do.
Never mind, have you called, have you shouted for them, have you called out?
Well they're not there, they've gone.
When did you last see Freda?
Oh, about half an hour ago, thereabouts. I don't know, I just went for a walk and they've gone, I don't know where I am.
I expect you'll be alright.

Just relax, relax and go back in time 4 hours, its 4 hours earlier, where are you now Janice?

We're in the tea room.
In the tea room?
Yeah.
And who's there altogether, how many of you are there?
Five.
Yes, and what are their names?
Freda, Carol, somebody I've not met before, I don't like them.
And where are you, where is the tea room?
It's at the zoo.
At the zoo?
Yeah.

And which zoo is it, have you been to this zoo before?
No.
You haven't, this is the first time?
Yeah.
What sort of things have they got there, what can you go and see?
Got Monkeys and Birds.
How did you get here?
On our bikes.
You came on your bikes did you, what kind of a bike have you got?
Well it's a bike.
Well what make is it?
(No reply)
You don't know, what colour is it then?
It's a rusty thing, I don't know what colour it's meant to be.
And how far was it from where you live?
Oh, a bit away.
It's a what, a long way?
Yeah, a good bit away.
How long did it take you to get there?
Oh, we kept stopping for a rest.
Did you take anything to eat with you?
Yeah, a few butties.
And what day is it?
It's Saturday.
Is Freda married?
No.
Isn't she, how old is she?
20.
Is she going to get married, does she have a boyfriend?
Well, not a proper one.
When you say 'not a proper one' what do you mean, she's just got somebody who likes her?
Well, she goes out with a couple, anybody who'll pay for her.
She's not fussy?
No, don't blame her, they're a right mess.

Who, the boys?

Mmm.

Is there anybody you like?

Well, I go out with Peter.

Do you, who's Peter, where does he come from?

Oh, he lives not far away from us.

Which street, is it round the corner or a few streets away?

It's a few streets away – Kingston Street.

Do you send him Valentine cards and things?

How do you mean?

On Valentine's day, do you ever send him a card, or does he send you a card?

No.

Perhaps he will one day, what about on his birthday, do you ever send him anything on his birthday?

I've not known him that long really.

Haven't you, when's your birthday?

July.

What day?

14th.

What year were you born?

1920.

And how old are you now?

18.

And you live in Leeds is it?

Yeah.

Is it a particular area of Leeds you live in, is it called anything?

No, it's in Leeds.

Just Leeds?

Yeah.

Do you ever go shopping in Leeds?

I just go down and have a look.

Are there any big buildings or churches or anything in Leeds, is there a Cathedral?

No.

What about big churches, is there a big church, a major one?
Well, there's quite a big one right in the centre.
What's that one called?
St Mary's.
St Mary's, that's in the centre is it, and is there a University there?
Don't know what you mean.
A University, where people go after they've left school if they want to go on learning?
(Pause)
No, perhaps you wouldn't know about that?
I left when I were 14, I weren't bothered.
Were you any good at anything at school?
Oh no, I didn't like it.
Did you have any teachers that you liked?
No.
What about one that you hated the most?
Oh, he taught us maths – Mr Benson.
Mr Benson, you didn't like him?
No, he was awful, he used to chuck chalk at me cos I talked.
Well, they all do that if you talk. Who was the headmaster while you were there?
Mr Forsyth.
And which school was that?
St Bede's.
Why was it called St Bede's, was it a religious one?
Well, it were Catholic, that were it I think.
Was it in the centre of Leeds?
No.
Whereabouts was it?
It were near us.
Near where you lived?
Yeah.

Just relax and come forward 5 years, its 5 years later, where are you Janice?

At home.
What have you been doing today?
Been doing my work, bit of cleaning.
Do you work?
No.
You just stay at home do you, are you married?
Yeah.
What's your husband's name?
Peter.
And have you got any children?
Yeah, one.
Just one, is it a boy or a girl?
Girl.
What's her name?
Janice.
Called after you is she, how old is she?
Nearly two.
Have you ever had a job?
Not for long.
Why, didn't you like it, or did you get fired, or...?
No, I got pregnant and had to get married.
I see. How long have you been married?
About 2 years.
Where were you married?
In St Marks, I had to.
Are you happy now though?
Not really.
Aren't you, don't you like Peter?
(No reply)
What does he do, has he got a job?
No.
What does he do then, all day?
He's not in much really, he goes out. I don't really know, I'm not bothered, he's out of my way.
Has Janice been christened?

Yeah, I don't go in for all that really but Pete's mum, oh, she's a bit fancy and she wants everything to be just so and she's no better than the rest of us, she wanted it to be done.

So it's been done has it, Where was that?

In St Marks.

And was that shortly after she was born or not?

I think she was about 4 months old, about that.

Who did the christening?

Vicar.

What was his name?

Oh, I don't know, it's a bit ago.

Was it the same one who married you?

No, it's a different one.

Were you married in that church?

Yeah.

And who was the one who married you?

(Struggles but can't remember)

Do you go to church regularly?

No.

Only for marriages and christenings?

Wouldn't do that if I didn't have to.

What religion was the priest, the vicar?

I suppose it must have been Catholic.

Why do you suppose that, are you a Catholic?

Well, school were Catholic so they wouldn't have let me go if I hadn't have been would they?

I suppose not, was Peter a Catholic?

Well, he doesn't bother either.

You think he's probably Catholic?

Probably.

How far away is it from where you live?

How far is what?

The Church?

Only so far.

And do you walk there or do you have to drive?

We can walk, bit long but we can do it.
What's going on in the world now, is there anything happening?
The same as it's been for a bit really.
Oh, what's that?
Oh, this war.
There's a war, who's winning?
Don't know, I suppose we are but I don't know really.
Do you hear very much about it, has there been any trouble where you are?
Oh, we get air raids and what have you but...
Where do you go when there is an air raid?
Usually under a table or something. They have shelters and that but they are too far away, they are right in the centre.
In the centre?
Yeah.
Are they?
Mmm, by the time you get there you probably wouldn't be there any more, so we usually hide under a table someplace, it's not as bad as it was.
Why do you think they have air raids where you are, on Leeds, what are they after?
I don't know.
You don't know?
No.
How's Freda?
She's alright.
What's she doing now?
She's married.
Who did she marry?
Jack.
What was his second name, what's her married name now?
Barker.
And where does she live?
Oh, she lives a bit away now, I don't see a lot of her now.
She used to work at Crowthers didn't she?

Yeah.

What do they do now?

They're on the munitions.

Are they, what did they do when she worked there?

They did wool.

Wool?

Yeah.

And what did they do to the wool?

They made it.

I thought sheep made wool?

Eh!

I thought sheep made wool, you can't make wool, it's grown?

No, they treated it and everything.

They turned it into things did they, or did they just turn it into long strings of wool?

Yeah, they made it you know, Oh god!

Sorry, I'm a bit silly, I don't know much about factories. Did they make clothes out of it or anything like that?

No.

No, they just made it into balls of wool?

Yeah.

I see, and now they're on munitions are they?

Yeah.

And where are they, they're in Leeds are they?

Yeah.

In the centre?

No, it's out of the centre, other side.

The other side from where you live?

Yeah.

Is that the north or the south side?

I don't know.

Do you know what their address is, do you know exactly where they are?

No.

Do you know what road they are in?

It's a big road.

What number bus would you catch to get there, can you get there by bus?
How do you mean?
On the bus, double-decker buses or – you know what buses are do you?
No.
Trams?
Oh, yeah.
You can get there on the tram?
Yeah.
What number tram would it be?
I don't know really, I don't go out that much
(Tuts at this point)
What's the matter?
I'm trying to think of the name of that road, I can't remember, I've been
trying to.
Never mind, what are you having for tea?
Don't know, whatever I can make up.
Have you got a ration book?
Don't get much.
You don't get much?
No.
You've got a book though have you?
Yeah.
What's it like, I've never seen one, is it full of tickets or anything?
Well, you've got different coupons for different things, it depends what
you want.
Are they different colours or do they just say different things on them?
Well, they're like, numbered.
And have they got a special number on to show that they're yours?
Well, they're stamped in the top right-hand corner, don't know whether
that's it or not.
And have you got an identity card?
No.
Haven't you, has Peter got one, has anybody got one?
Don't think so, why, are you meant to have one?

I don't know, I just wondered if you'd got one, I think some people have got them?

I thought he might have got one and lost it, it'd be just like him.

He might have done. What kind of coupon do you use if you want to buy some meat?

Well, you just take your book in, they rip it out and that's it.

So they just take what they want, or what it costs?

Yeah, well it depends what you get, I mean so many coupons cover what you get, they do it like that.

Which butcher do you go to when you buy meat?

Oh, I have to go right into Leeds, it's a right trek.

And which butcher do you go to when you get there?

Batemans.

Is that a big one?

No.

Is there a lot of meat about, do you find any trouble getting meat?

Oh, you have to queue, it's bloody awful, I hate it when I have to go there.

And what about other kinds of food, how difficult is it to get food?

Depends what days you go really, if you play your cards right you're not so bad.

What about fruit and bread and that sort of thing?

Oh, you can't get fruit, mind you I couldn't afford it anyway.

How much is it, how much are oranges?

Don't know, it's that long since I looked really.

Alright, just relax.

Session ends.

Janice Kershaw - session 5

Not a very clear session so these are summary notes

Taken to Janice at 8 years old.

It is a cold day in November.
She has not been to school today, is not well.
She goes to St Bede's, where Mrs Campbell teaches.
The Head teacher is male
I ask how she gets to school.
She goes to the end of the road, Cambridge Road, turns right onto a big road, crosses it and turns left, cuts through a few streets it is there.
She has a whip and top, ball to play with.
Julie lives at 121 Cambridge Road, she has a rope.
I ask if she has ever been to a Cinema, swimming, roller skating, or a pantomime. She says no.
Father works at a Glue Factory, goes to work by tram.

10 years later, aged 18

Strange problem with her throat so moved to 1 year earlier.

She is with Peter, walking, been to Leeds, went round the shops, bought some stockings in Castle's.
Could have got a number 43 tram.
Going past Carr Mills off Meanwood Road. There are some gas tanks around and maybe a shoe works.
The year is 1937.
There is a Dole office near the city centre.
Left school, is not working.
We talk about the house, colour etc. It has two stories.
They have a bath, but often go to the baths to bathe. It costs 6d and she goes once a month.

Talk of neighbours, she doesn't bother with them.
Talk of crime, Police etc.

<u>3 years later (1940)</u>

At home in Cooper Street, Number 4.
Not yet married, due soon as she's pregnant.
Doctor is Mathews, about 5 tram stops into Leeds.
Is in St Mathews Parish.
There's a war on. Blackout in operation.
There are army bases near Leeds.
There is a Cinema in Carlton Street.

<u>Forward to 40 years old</u>

Can't see. Back 10 years, trouble finding memory.
I asked her if she knew where these memories had come from (books, films etc) – no result.
End of session.

Janice Kershaw - session 6

Taken to Janice.

What are you doing?
We're walking.
Where are you going, tell me what you're going to do today?
I think we're going to the shops.
And what are you going to do at the shops?
Well I think she's going to buy something.
Is she. What sort of a day is it?
It's alright.
Is it sunny?
No.
Is it raining?
No.
It's just alright?
Yeah.
Is it the morning or afternoon?
It's afternoon.
Where's the rest of your family?
I don't know, they're not here.
As you walk along, what can you see?
Well, houses.
What do they look like?
They're houses.
Are they a lot of separate houses, or are they joined together?
No, they're joined together.
What's the name of the street you're on?
It's a big road.
Do you know the name?
(Tries but no success)
Never mind if you can't think of it, do you go to school?
Yeah.

Where do you go to school?
Near where I live.
And what's it called?
What, the school – St Bedes.
What kind of a school is that, who runs it?
Teachers.
Do you like it?
No, not really.
Have you got any friends there?
There's Julie.
And how old is Julie?
Like me I think.
Where does Julie live?
Bit higher up than us.
In the same street?
Yeah.
What street is that?
Cambridge Road.
What number do you live at?
23.
And she lives higher up, at what number?
I don't know, I just go and call for her to come and play.
What sort of games do you play?
Skipping, Julie's got a rope, I haven't. Freda had one but it broke, mind she wouldn't let me have it anyway, not unless I give her something for it.
What have you got that you could give her for it?
Well, toffees.
What else do you play with?
I've got a ball.
Do you play any special games?
No, just throw it and kick it around, not much to do really, we sometimes go to the playground.
What do you do there?
They've got swings but big kids chase us off.
Where is the playground?

Not far away.

How do you get to it from your house?

Well you can get to it a couple of ways. You go down the big road.

Is it on the left or the right?

On the right near the top.

Do you sing?

What?

Do you like singing?

What do you mean?

Well, are there any songs around at the moment that you like, have you got a radio at home?

No.

Do you hear people singing songs?

No.

Can you see other people in the street?

Yeah, there are some walking along.

Can you look at one in particular and tell me what they are wearing?

There's a lad, he's just got... ordinary.

Has he got a hat on?

Cap.

What colour is it?

Brown.

What kind of shoes is he wearing?

They're dirty.

What about his shirt, what colour is that?

It looks grey but it might be dirty.

Does it have a collar, what's it like round his neck?

Well it's like a scarf.

Do you hear much news, is anything going on in London say?

Don't know.

FROM HERE I HAVE SUMMARISED

School holidays are 3 weeks in summer, 1 week at Christmas, and odd days.

Forward to 12 years old.

At School, standing in a corridor, been sent out.
Mr Benson, maths teacher is always picking on her.
They have tests at the end of each year.
Still St Bede's
St Micheal's church is near the school.
Living at 4 Cooper Street, been there a couple of years.
Family ages:- Freda is 14, nearly ready to leave school, Stuart is 11, Alan is 9, Susan is 7.
Father worked at glue works once, it is a fair walk from home, quite a few tram stops.
It is 1933.

Forward to age 21.

Had to get married, baby due any time.
Married in St Mark's on Woodhouse. Uncle Bob was there, lives in Samuel Street, is mother's brother-in-law.
Mother's maiden name is Williams, first name Edna. Father's name is Frank Kershaw.
Lives at 6 Carlisle Street now, with Peter.
Worked at leather works at the bottom of Lovell Street.
Food is rationed, it is wartime.
No air raids yet, no gas mask.
Ration tickets, description vague, just have a value.
Session ends

NOTES.

Sylvia was involved in my research for some years, and discovered several sets of 'past life memories', including one which seems to have been the cause of her violent recurring nightmares, which stopped forever when she found that particular memory.

Whilst we are still not certain that every regression actually enables us to find memories of previous lives, as there may be other explanations for what happens, it is easier to describe the case as though it were a life. This does not mean that I always believe it to be so.

At the age of 31 she complains of head pains, and dies in late 1951.

Sylvia was born in 1952.

Checking the story

Over several sessions we went to various times in Janice's, and other characters 'lives' in order to clarify what detail we could before doing any checking into what was said.   When I did start checking it involved considerable effort and some very obscure sources. Here is what we eventually found:-

Janice said	Research found
At age 7 she is in Leeds. Her name is Janice Kershaw. She lives at 23 Cambridge Rd, goes to St Bede's School and is taught by Mrs Campbell. Her friend Julie lives at 121 Cambridge Rd. Her father works at a glue factory	The area called Little London in Leeds was part of a massive slum clearance which began in 1954, three years after Janice died. I had to visit the borough surveyor and persuade him to search archives for a map of the area before clearance. Having obtained this I found that Cambridge Road is between Little London and Woodhouse Carr (though it is now part redeveloped and part green space) There was a glue works about 250 yards east.
At age 12 (in 1933) she lives at 4 Cooper Street with Freda (14), Stuart (11), Allan (9) and Susan (7)	There was only one Cooper Street in Leeds, and it was in Little London.
At age 14 she lives at 5 Cooper Street. Carlisle Street is around the corner. She has just left St Bede's school. She has taken a CSE at school Sister Freda is 15 and works at Crowthers Mill, near home	There was a Carlisle Terrace School leaving age at that time was 14. There was a St Bede's church and school but they are a couple of miles west of where she lived so unlikely to be her school. Several Churches on the map are just marked 'Church' and there are several 'School's. She would have had a School Leaving Certificate (a simple statement of attendance really) Perseverance Mills was a large woollen mill near Crowther St and Crowther Place just a few hundred yards from Cooper St. Recent searches reveal that the Crowther family were very successful mill owners in

	Yorkshire and it seems very likely that locals would call this 'Crowthers'.
At 15 she says the Nelson Pub is just round the corner.	There were four Lord Nelson pubs in Leeds, one of which was about a mile away, but there was a Trafalgar at the end of their street.
There is a box makers called Fairbrothers in Fenton Street	There was a Fenton Street but it is almost off the map so unclear about the box makers There is a paper bag mill shown on the map near her home but I was unable to confirm that it was Fairbrothers.
Freda (17) still at Crowthers on winding, Stuart (14), Allan (12) and Susan (10)	This session was 2.5 years earlier than the one where she was 12 so the ages being consistent is significant.
At age 17 (in 1937) she mentions a shop called Castles, the number 43 Tram. Carr Mills is off Meanwood Road, there are gas tanks on the same road and a shoe works.	On Meanwood Road there was a Carr Mills and some Gas tanks with a shoe works nearby.
At age 18 she has travelled by bicycle to a small Zoo that has Monkeys and Birds and a Tea Room. She says it is a 'good bit away' from home. She says Freda is 20 and works at Crowthers.	There was a small Zoo in Canal Gardens which was part of Roundhay Park. This is three miles north of Cooper Street (12 minutes by bicycle) and it was quite popular in the 1920's and 30's as it was free to enter. It had Monkeys and Cockatoos in the collection and of course a Tea Room. In later years it became less popular but was redeveloped in the 1980's and renamed Tropical Gardens.
She has met Peter who lives on Kingston Street.	There was a Kingston Street very near Cooper Street
Her birth date is July 14th 1920. There is a St Mary's church in Leeds centre.	Mount St Mary's Church was a major church just east of Leeds Centre. It was only ever part built but it was functioning until the late 1950's and had a school and an orphanage close by. It became redundant as the parish population dwindled.
Her maths teacher was Mr Benson and the	There was a Benson Street

headmaster was Mr Forsyth	
At age 19 she is working at Crowthers, doing something with guns and earning about £4 per week.	
At 20 she lives at 4 Cooper St. Is pregnant. Her doctor is Dr Mathews. Home is in St Matthews parish.	St Matthews Church was about 100 yards from Cooper St
There are army bases near Leeds.	A few streets from Cooper Street the map shows Carlton Hill Barracks and Gibraltar Barracks. There was a Harewood Barracks off Fenton St.
There is a Cinema on Carlton St.	There was a Cinema in Carlton Street though there were several Cinemas around
At 21 she says St Marks is on Woodhouse.	St Marks Church was 250 yards west of Cambridge Road near Woodhouse St. The church is now called a Gateway Church called St Mark's Woodhouse and is a sort of evangelical church with conferencing and entertainment facilities available.
Now lives with Peter at 6 Carlisle St. Has an Uncle Bob living in Samuel St.	There was a Samuel St near Cooper St
She has worked at Lovell St leather works.	Lovell St was 200 yards south of Carlisle Terrace
Her mother's maiden name was Edna Williams.	
At 23 she has been married two years, wed Peter in St Marks. Has a daughter, Janice, who is nearly two and was christened in St Marks by a different vicar than the one that married them.	The Vicar listed in 1942 was not the one listed in 1940.
It is a tram ride to Crowthers	The No 6 tram from Leeds centre would have stopped near Carlisle Terrace and a further half a mile up Meanwood Rd there would be a stop near the Mill.
She doesn't have an ID Card	Everyone had ID Cards from 1939 to 1952 so she is not correct on this.
At 25 she is 4 months pregnant and has children aged 2 and 3.Her married name is Tomlinson.	There was a Tomlinson St near Cooper St
At 27 (in 1947) Tommy is her youngest child.	

Crowthers was on munitions in the war but is now back on wool	
At 29 she is back with her mother at 4 Cooper St. Her husband is 'on the run' for stealing. She remembers living in Carlisle St. Mr Jackson is their landlord.	A search for rent collectors revealed two Jacksons. There was also a Jackson Road
At 31 she says her children are Peter (aged 10), Janice (8) and Tommy (5). She dies	Ages are still consistent

Having obtained the map from 1933 (now available on Google but not when the investigation was conducted) it became apparent that virtually every name mentioned (streets or people) was on the map in the area where Janice lived.

This is the top part of a map of Leeds showing matching items. This was a fashionable area in the 1850's but by the 1950's it had deteriorated to the extent that a slum clearance programme was implemented.

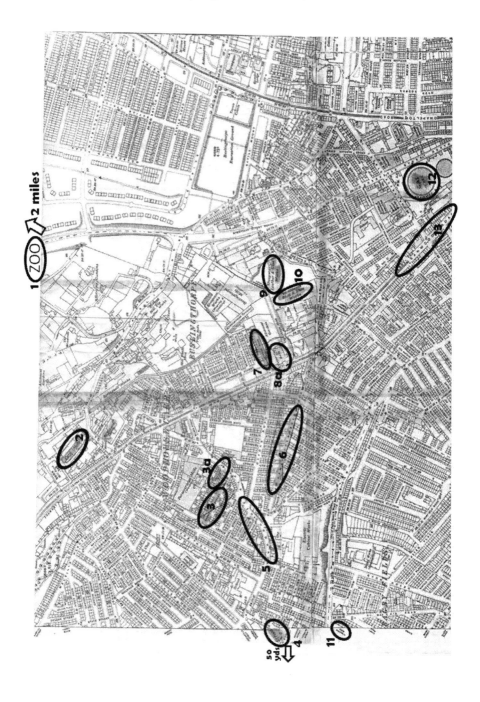

This is how the area looks in 2020. Some parts are recognisable but a lot of change from the 1950's is clearly seen.

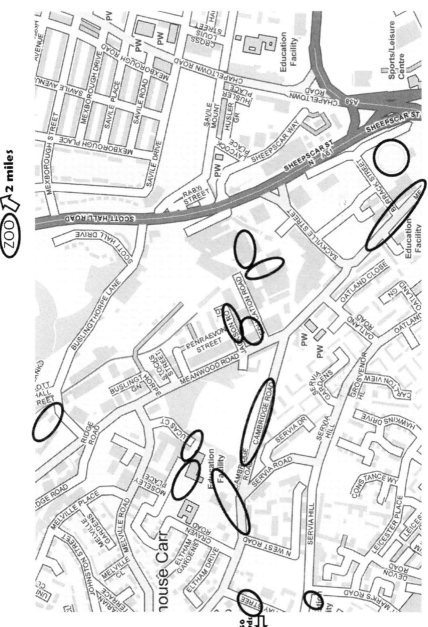

This is the lower part of the area showing more matching items.

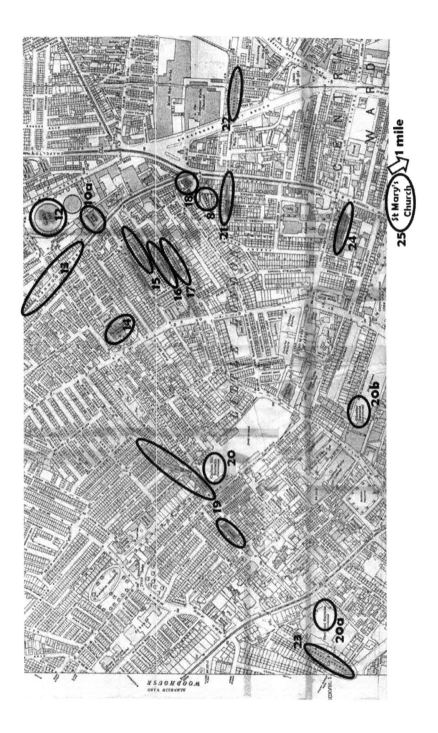

Here is the 2020 version.

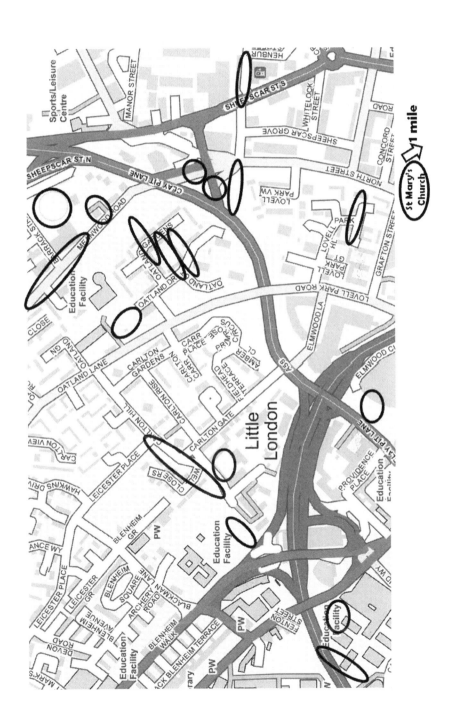

Since it is not easy to see details on the maps here is a referenced list of the 25 items recalled that are specific enough to be viewed as evidence. There are a number of other items on the maps that are not specific but which could be places she referred to such as schools, places of work etc. Numbers 7, 17 and 22 were names of people but turn out to be street names.

I have included the session during which the place was mentioned.

		Session	
1	The Zoo	4	
2	Carr Mills	5	Gone
3	Crowther Street (3a Place)	2	Gone
4	St Mark's Church	6	
5	Woodhouse	6	
6	Cambridge Road	6	
7	Jackson Road	3	Gone
8	Baths (and 8a Municipal Baths)	5	Gone
9	Glue Factory	6	Gone
10	Shoe Factory (also 10a)	5	Gone
11	Kingston Road	4	Gone
12	Gas Tanks	5	
13	Meanwood Road	5	
14	St Matthew's Church	5	Gone
15	Cooper Street	2	Gone
16	Samuel Street	6	Gone
17	Tomlinson Street	3	Gone
18	'Nelson' Public House	3	Gone
19	Carlton Street Cinema	5	Gone
20	Barracks (also 20a and 20b)	5	Gone
21	Carlisle Terrace	2	Gone
22	Benson Street	4	
23	Fenton Street	3	
24	Lovell St (Road/Grove/Terrace)	6	
25	St Mary's Church (Leeds Centre)	4	

Most of the places were either removed in the early 1950's or have been significantly redeveloped.

Thoughts and conclusions

This is one of the strongest cases in the search for proof of reincarnation.

Most of the checkable information from these sessions proved to be correct or very nearly correct, although three names given match to streets rather than people. Census records are not yet available for the period so I made a search of electoral and parish registers, where they were available, but have not yet found a record of a Janice Kershaw or Tomlinson. It seemed as though everything Janice talked about fitted except her name.

If this was imagination surely at least some of the names mentioned would not exist on the map. There is a hugely better chance of winning the Lottery Jackpot than making all correct guesses for this many pieces of information.

Whilst it was not possible to prove that Sylvia really had the memory of Janice in her own mind, it is very hard to understand how she could have known so much about an area of Leeds that largely ceased to exist shortly after she was born. She had never been to Leeds or had any reason to study it, and none of her relatives was connected with Leeds. Also, if she had wished to invent a lifetime, would she really have chosen one so ordinary, when imagination is such a powerful faculty?

This, and other cases where the final piece of evidence has been impossible to check (for example destroyed by recent fire), might lead us to think that some force is at work which wants us to consider the meaning of life, but never actually reach a conclusion - perhaps that would remove the whole point?

Although it is unusual to find a case as strong as this, it does indicate that there is more to this than fantasy, and the search for meaning in life is worthwhile.

20. Reflections

In this book you have learned about hypnosis and I hope I have improved your understanding of it. You have learned about regression and I hope you have a clearer understanding of that, both in terms of research into reincarnation and in terms of how it can and should be used to provide very effective and efficient help for anyone suffering with anxiety related problems.

Where do these regression memories of past lives come from? That is the important question and there are some very regular explanations offered to me so here are my thoughts.

Telepathy, inter-dimensional travel, spirit channeling, stone tape theory (events recorded in nearby physical material) are often proposed.

I am not going to claim that these things do not exist but even though I have experienced some of them myself to my knowledge none of them have actually been scientifically proven. I would love it if they were but generally I think they are more difficult to believe than reincarnation.

These explanations would mean that the experiences or memories should be accessible by any regressee and it should be possible for multiple people to produce the same material for investigation. In my experience and that of others that I am aware of the memories are uniquely available to one individual.

I would be interested to investigate with identical twins to see if each has a different set of memories or whether at the moment of conception one life-force takes up both of the new bodies.

Genetic memory (passed down from parents etc) is very often cited as a possible explanation.

Nobody to my knowledge has recalled their descendents lives. It would not be possible to recall the end of a life you had received genetic material from as they were not dead at the moment of your conception. Many regressions involve those who died young or never had children so the genetic line does not exist.

Cryptomnesia, or drawing on the enormous amount of information stored in the physical brain to concoct life stories to please a hypnotist.

If this were the source then where would information that is really not available (town plans from the 1940's e.g.) come from (spontaneous remote viewing perhaps? Another incredible but unproven talent!). Also it would surely be more likely that interesting characters from history would be dreamt up much more often.

Imagination is the obvious explanation for many cases but certainly not for all. Even if less than 5% of cases cannot be explained away then further research is worthwhile. Most telepathy is coincidence or anticipation of the thought patterns of those we closely know, most ghosts are not there, but in a small number of cases something real has happened and we will learn nothing if we keep a closed mind.

Many people have experienced déjà vu – recognising places not visited before in this life. Some people have recurring dreams about other lives. Some people have displayed talents for art, music, language, maths and other things that they never had any training in.

Perhaps these are rare cases of the subconscious making connections with the "unknown" area for a moment or even longer and perhaps this could explain where moments of inspiration or genius come from. Is it possible that as we evolve further we will have greater access to this "unknown" area if it will serve a worthwhile purpose?

Whatever the explanation there is enough to make us wonder, and to think about life and that is no bad thing. Perhaps if we could explain everything we would not need to experience a fragile physical existence?

Wisdom is not physical but physical experience seems essential for us to learn from. The transient elements of personal wealth and power die with the body but perhaps our souls are fed by selflessness, community, compassion and love.

Some researchers believe that each life holds a lesson for us and they ask their volunteers to think what it might be. Looking back over these cases I can't identify the learning points but I can accept that my thinking is limited by physical existence and the lessons are for a higher realm.

Perhaps the safest thing to assume is that until we do have enough wisdom we will be coming to 'school' a lot more and it would be sensible to keep it secure and reasonably comfortable, not just for our children but also for our future selves.

We are here to learn something. If we knew what it was then we would not be here.

So trying to discover a short cut to the answer is pointless because if you could learn it without experiencing it in this life you would not be here.

The fragility of life is what makes it possible to learn from mistakes. If life was not fragile mistakes would not matter.

The spirit inside us is not affected by time and space so cannot be harmed by physical things. We cannot understand what it understands or know what it knows so all we can do is accept that somehow what we do here is in some way helping our higher self or perhaps someone else's higher self.

Some of our visits here could be designed to help others learn something; from a human perspective I imagine that a brief life, or one spent in a miserable situation (abused, starved etc) might serve to help someone else learn something.

Of course, we all think about things from our human perspective; we can't avoid that (if we could we would not be here) and though we might try to consider what a spirit might want we will not succeed.

Our spirit can see what our body sees but our body cannot see what our spirit sees. It is like looking down the wrong end of a telescope. Or perhaps trying to understand what life is like for a mouse and ask if they also wonder why they exist.

I believe we should do our best to learn from this life and not worry about what will happen to us when we die.

Don't just let time go by but see every day as a chance to learn something new, just as though you were training to become a doctor or learning to drive a car and this universe offers all the books and all the roads you need to become completely expert.

Maybe some of us are meant to go through life as patients or passengers and others are meant to be the surgeons and the drivers but we all have the chance and the responsibility to make the most of our existence.

In the end it is up to you to decide whether to believe that life is an accidental result of nothing and that it is generally pointless, or to believe that it is a miracle that we are privileged to be part of multiple times to gather enough wisdom that leads to something.

I hope I have made you think. I choose the second option and that choice has consequences.

The life that you and I are currently living is important but what is more important is that we understand that this life is not all there is. We will live other lives in the future as part of our journey to an even bigger future so as we live this life we need to also focus on what we are adding to our soul.

What is most important is that we develop our soul. We may have many lives but we only have one soul. Make yours as pure and loving as it can be.

Thank you for spending time with this book. If you can spare just a little more to put a review on the selling site it would be much appreciated.

To make giving a review easy if you are in the USA or the UK you can simply copy the URL address and paste it in your browser bar or scan the QR code to go to the review page.

USA - use these.
https://www.amazon.com/review/create-review?asin=B08XZWG95K

UK - use these.
https://www.amazon.co.uk/review/create-review?asin=B08XZWG95K

Printed in Great Britain
by Amazon